LACOCK

From Old Photographs

CHRIS BREACH

AMBERLEY

Acknowledgements

I thank and am indebted to the diligent work of local, regional and national postcard photographers/publishers. Also, to those other photographers and social historians who have contributed. They have provided an opportunity to look back at the past, seldom with a motor vehicle in view. Every attempt has been made to seek permission for copyright material used in this book. If, however, we have inadvertently used copyright material without permission or acknowledgement, or if any facts in the book are incorrect, I apologise and will make the necessary corrections at the first opportunity.

To make my initial idea of a book become a reality, I am appreciative to all those at Amberley Publishing who have worked on its production. I would like to offer my special thanks to Nick Grant and Jenny Stephens for much-needed and helpful advice given to a first-time author. I am particularly grateful for the images, many by Harold White for a Second World War propaganda booklet, provided by Wiltshire and Swindon History Centre. I would like to offer my special thanks to Claire Skinner, Tom Plant and the team at Chippenham for their invaluable assistance. I would also like to express my gratitude to the National Trust and Science and Society Picture Library, who have also provided photographs. Thanks to Brooks Smith Maps for the rather special map of the village.

Finally, I acknowledge the support and encouragement of my wife, Rosemary, and thank her for typing the manuscript. Any proceeds that I personally receive from the sale of this book will be donated to a well-known cancer charity.

Front cover: George Inn, Hay Cart and Milk Churns. (WSA2664/3/4J/21BW)

First published 2019

Amberley Publishing
The Hill, Stroud
Gloucestershire, GL5 4EP

www.amberley-books.com

British Library Cataloguing in Publication Data.

A catalogue record for this book is available from the British Library.

ISBN 978 1 4456 8668 4 (print)
ISBN 978 1 4456 8669 1 (ebook)

Origination by Amberley Publishing.
Printed in the UK.

Contents

Introduction

Lacock village and surrounding locality is steeped in history, with its origins dating back to the time of the Iron Age. The River Avon, fertile land and extensive forest would have made it an appealing place to settle. Lacock or Laycock is derived from 'lacuc' meaning small stream. This was the Saxon word for Bide Brook, around which some of the earliest inhabitants came to live. Relics of a Roman presence have also been found in the area. The Domesday survey completed in 1086 describes Lacock with Edward of Salisbury as the Lord, having thirty-nine households, plough lands, meadow, woodland and two mills. Ela, daughter of the Earl of Salisbury, whilst still a child, was chosen by King Richard I to be the wife of William Longespée, the illegitimate son of King Henry II. He was a powerful baron and a witness of Magna Carta when it was signed by King John in 1215. This may explain how Lacock came to have one of the three copies. Ela, on the death of her husband William, founded Lacock Abbey in his memory. It was a religious house for women and she laid the foundation stone in 1232. The abbey prospered throughout the Middle Ages until the late 1530s when King Henry VIII disbanded the monasteries. Following this, the abbey with its lands was granted to William Sharington for £783. It remained with his family and descendants until it was gifted to the National Trust in 1944 by Matilda Talbot. In the Victorian period Lacock Abbey was to become famous as the home of William Henry Fox Talbot, a pioneer of British photography. It is ironic that Britain's birthplace of photography is in one of the most photogenic villages in England. Without this revolutionary discovery of the negative photographic process, whereby an image could be fixed on paper and reproduced, a book such as this using images would not have been possible.

The village and parish of Lacock is situated between Chippenham and Melksham in the county of Wiltshire. It includes Bowden Hill, Notton, Reybridge and Bewley Common. Nearby, the historic Lackham House, which is now part of Wiltshire College, offers land-based courses and has a Lacock address. Medieval Lacock remains unspoilt, well preserved and has changed little in appearance over many centuries. This is due to the stewardship of its first private owner William Sharington, his descendants, the villagers through the ages and, more recently, the National Trust. Other than maintenance, repair and modernisation, the houses remain much as they were when originally built. They are in a variety of styles, sizes and have different elevation details reflecting their age. Some of the larger jettied houses had woollen looms. Stone and timber-frame construction was popular as those materials were available locally. Virtually all properties are listed buildings, being of special architectural or historic interest. They are mainly terraced, occupied and arranged around four principal streets in a roughly rectangular pattern.

The village prospered from the woollen industry and it is remarkable that it is still virtually intact from its origins. Its character has changed considerably since the time of these photographs. At the beginning of the twentieth century, Lacock would have been self-sufficient with a wide variety of shops and tradespeople. In more recent years it has become well known not only for its abbey, photographic pioneer and historic buildings, but as an ideal setting for film and television productions. These have included *Downton Abbey*, the BBC's period dramas *Cranford* and *Pride and Prejudice*, and also *Harry Potter and the Philosopher's Stone* and *Harry Potter and the Chamber of Secrets*. Whilst the book was nearing completion in September 2018, a shoot for the movie of *Downton Abbey* was taking place in a transformed High Street. It was a triumphant celebration scene with a flag-waving crowd in 1920s costume, to welcome a procession of soldiers and horses from the Royal Artillery.

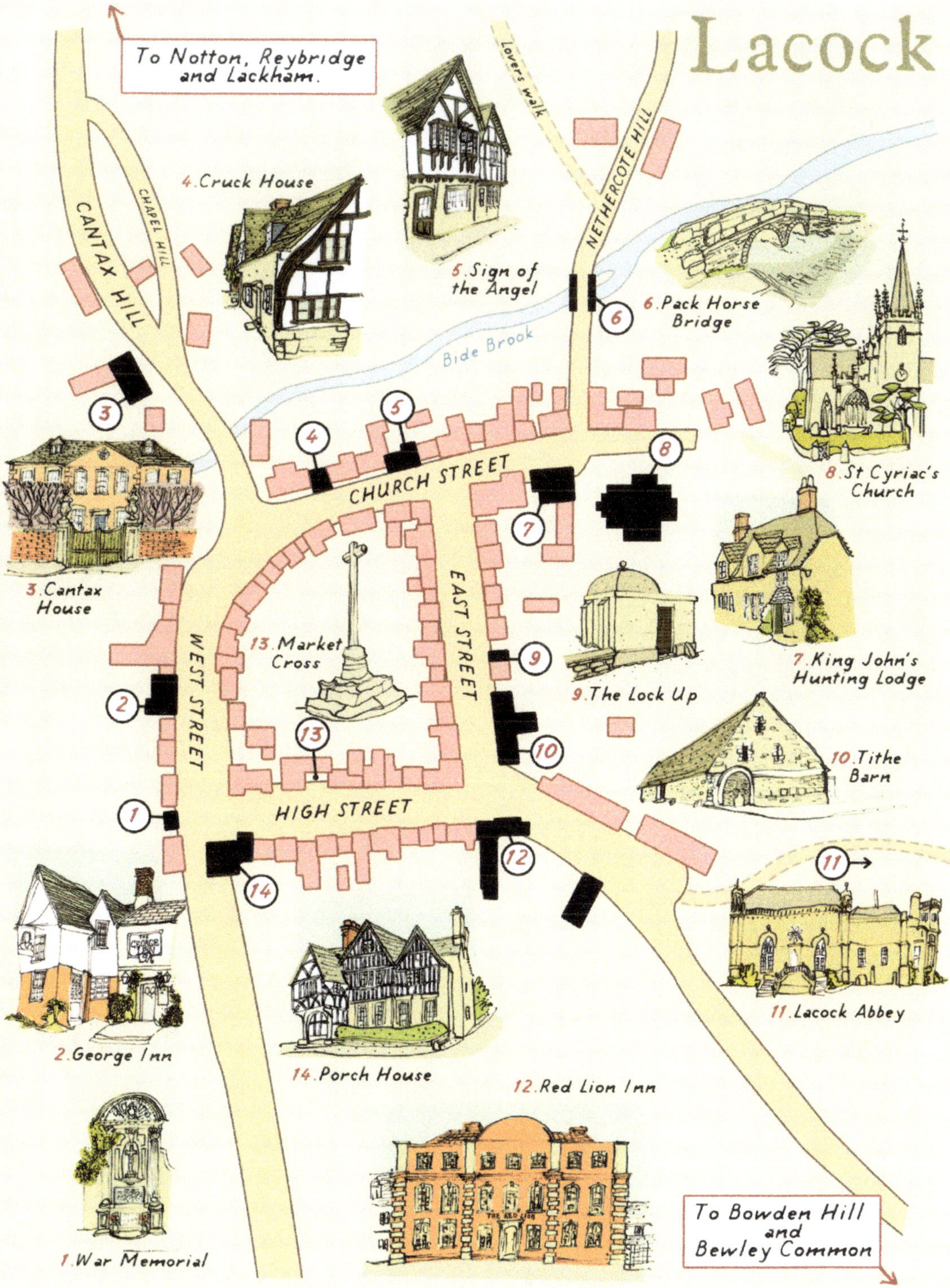

Lacock
To Notton, Reybridge and Lackham.
Lovers Walk
Nethercote Hill
Cantax Hill
Chapel Hill
4. Cruck House
5. Sign of the Angel
6. Pack Horse Bridge
Bide Brook
3. Cantax House
Church Street
8. St Cyriac's Church
7. King John's Hunting Lodge
East Street
West Street
13. Market Cross
9. The Lock Up
10. Tithe Barn
High Street
11. Lacock Abbey
2. George Inn
14. Porch House
12. Red Lion Inn
1. War Memorial
To Bowden Hill and Bewley Common

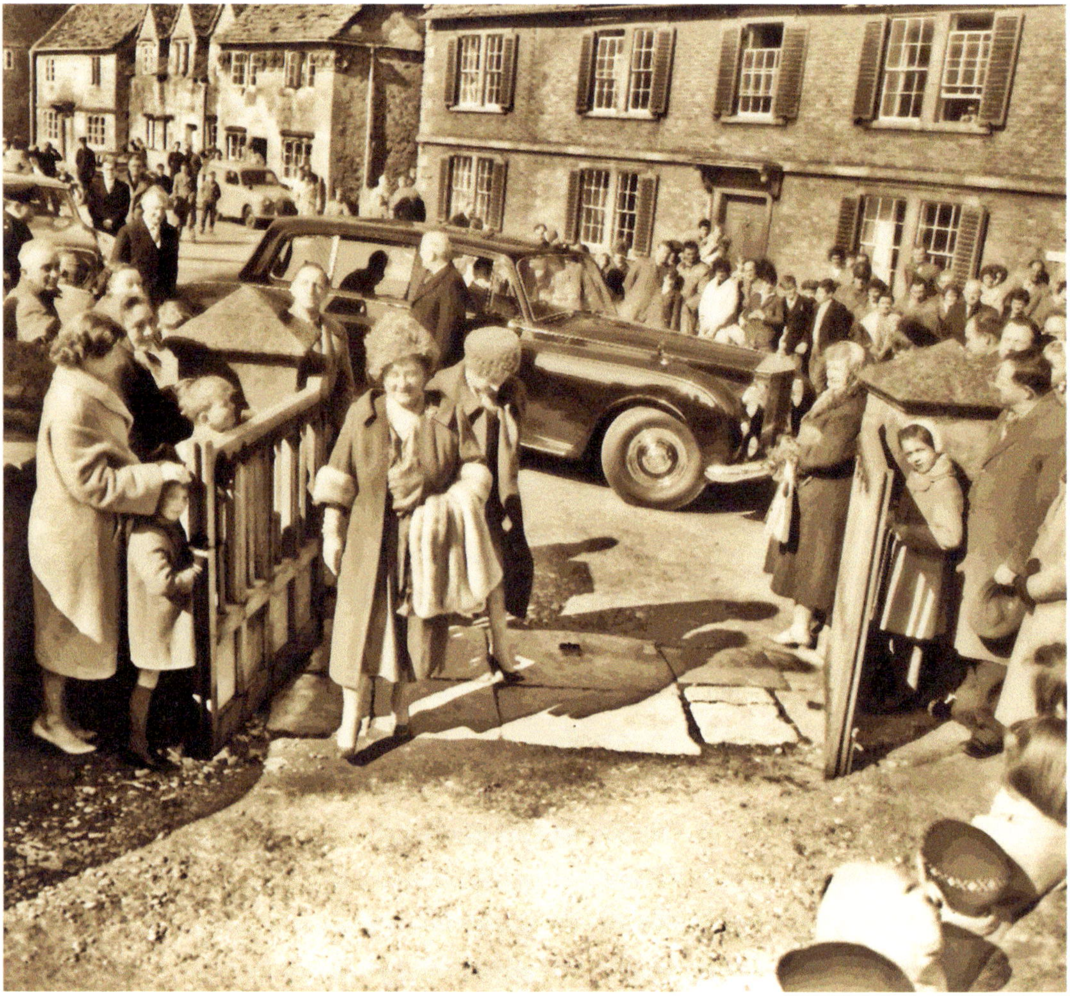

Royal Visit
Her Majesty Queen Elizabeth the Queen Mother at Lacock Church. (WSA1772/1/2764)

I

Lacock Abbey and Britain's Birthplace of Photography

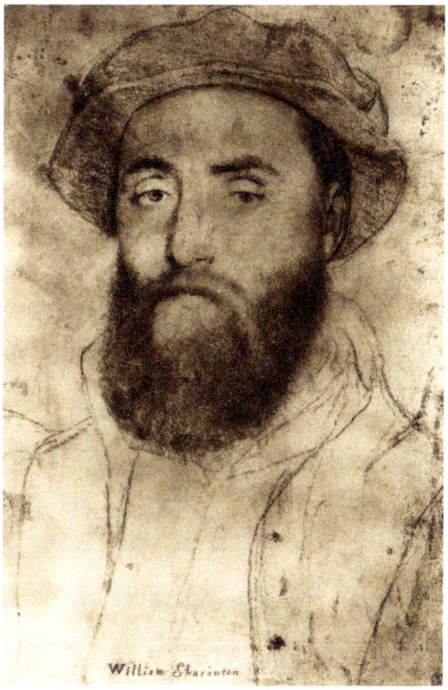

William Sharington, *c.* 1495–1553
William Sharington was the first person outside of a religious order to own Lacock Abbey, originally a nunnery. It was purchased while Henry VIII was on the throne in 1540 for £783, following the Dissolution of the Monasteries. Conversion work into a private residence retained much of the monastic building which may otherwise have been lost, and a three-storey octagonal tower, Renaissance chimneys and a stable courtyard were added. Sir William Sharington narrowly escaped execution on embezzlement charges and was a Member of Parliament and High Sheriff of Wiltshire. (WSA2664/3/4J/30BW)

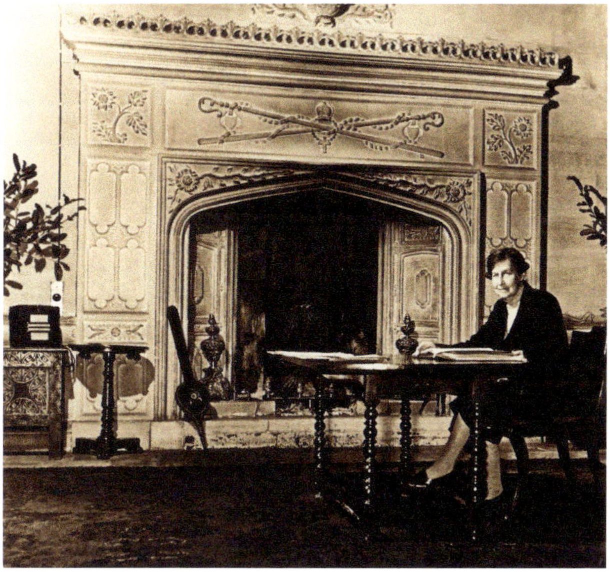

Matilda Theresa Talbot MBE, 1871–1958
Matilda changed her original surname of Gilcrest-Clark to Talbot in honour of her uncle, Charles Henry Fox Talbot, who had left her the Lacock Estate following his death in 1916. This included the abbey, majority of properties in the village and a large parcel of land. She was the last private owner before gifting the estate to the National Trust in 1944 for future generations to explore and enjoy. She also presented the Lacock Abbey Magna Carta to the British Museum in 1946. This photograph of Matilda was taken in front of the grand fireplace in the abbey's Gothic Revival hall. (WSA2664/2/3F/10/29BW)

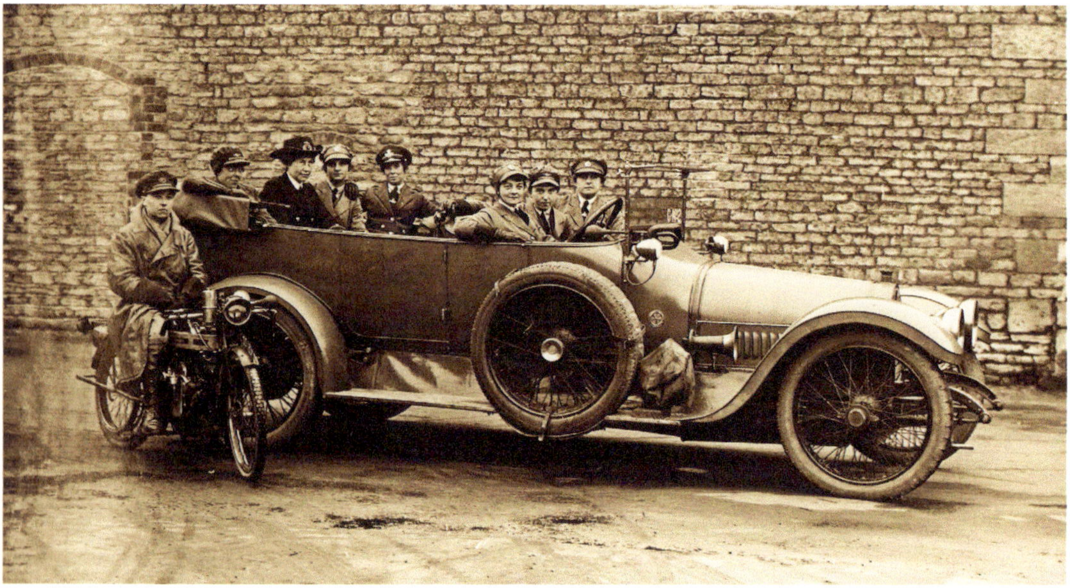

Matilda Talbot, Wartime Service

The much-admired and respected Matilda joined the Wrens, eventually becoming a Principal. She was stationed at Cranwell in Lincolnshire. In this photograph, taken around 1918, she is in a dark uniform seated in a convertible motor vehicle with her officers and ratings. She was decorated for her services and good works in both the 1919 and 1947 King's New Year Honours. (WSA/2664/3/1F/15)

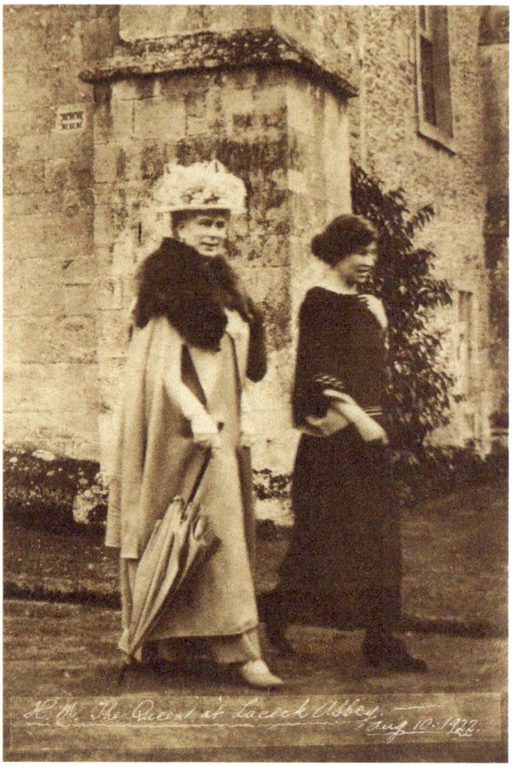

Queen Mary at Lacock Abbey

Queen Mary is seen here with Matilda Talbot on 10 August 1922. Two days later whilst in the West Country, Queen Mary of Teck was also to visit Dyrham Park in Gloucestershire. Her husband, George V, was king from 1910 until his death in 1936. Both of these important and historic properties are now in the ownership of the National Trust. (WSA2664/2/2F/4BW)

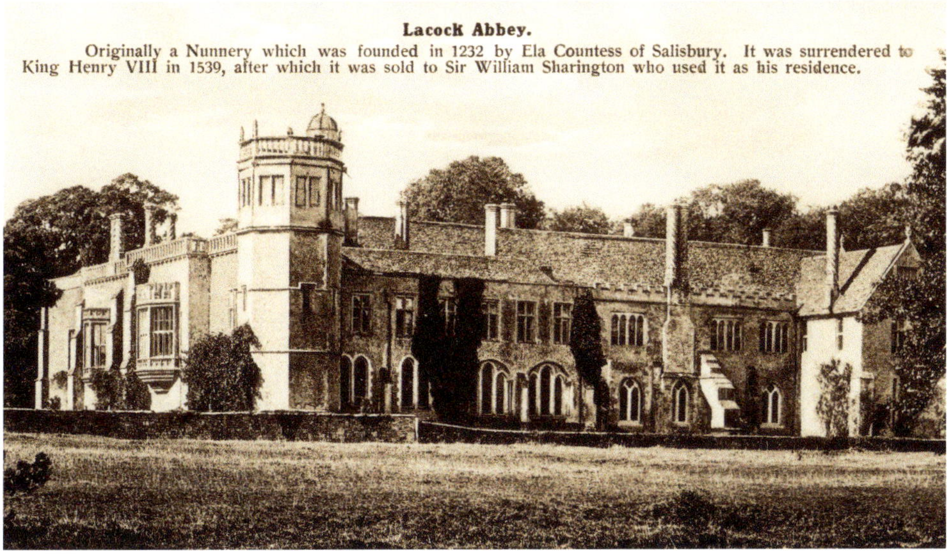

Lacock Abbey

Lacock Abbey was originally a nunnery founded in 1232 by Ela Countess of Salisbury in memory of her husband. It was surrendered to King Henry VIII in 1539 after which time it was sold to Sir William Sharington who used it as his residence. It was altered and converted into a substantial private mansion incorporating accommodation on the first floor. He demolished the abbey church and added an octagonal, three-storey tower, used as a strongroom, on the south-east corner.

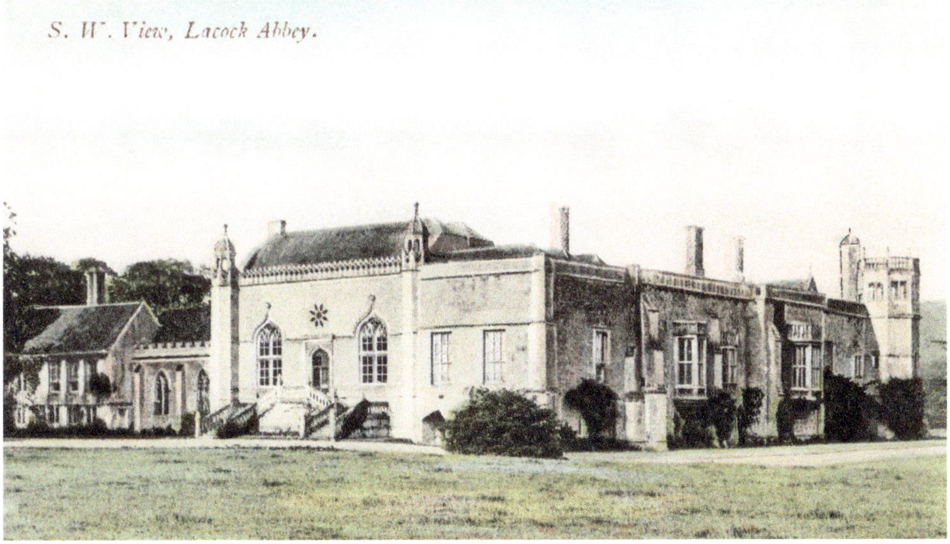

South-west View

Postally used in 1905, this postcard has the message: 'went all over this today'. Before the abbey was opened regularly to the public visitors were still given an opportunity to tour the property. Elevations are in local stone with several styles of architecture prominent including medieval, Renaissance and Gothic. Two flights of entrance steps are in view, as are the three oriel windows on the south side. The smaller one in the centre was made famous by William Henry Fox Talbot as the subject (latticed window) of his earliest existing photographic negative in August 1835.

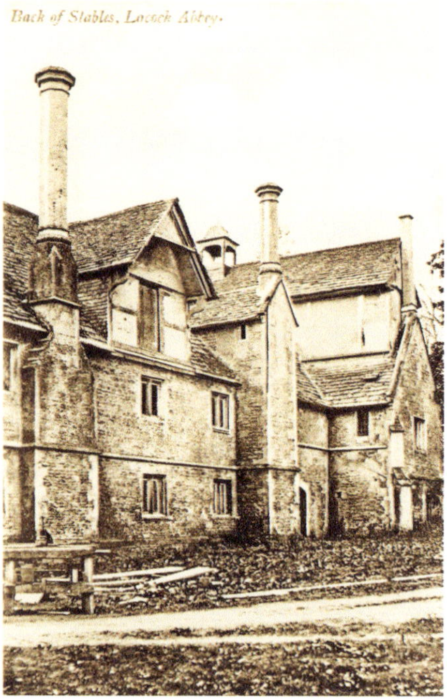

Back of Stables

This image is an early Edwardian postcard illustrating part of William Sharington's extension to the north end of the Augustinian nunnery. Horses and carriages were an essential part of daily life, so stabling was an integral part of larger properties. Lacock was on an important stagecoach route from London to Bath. This card shows the bell tower, stone tiled dormer with deep eaves, impressive tall chimney stacks and differing rooflines, all clad in stone roof tiles.

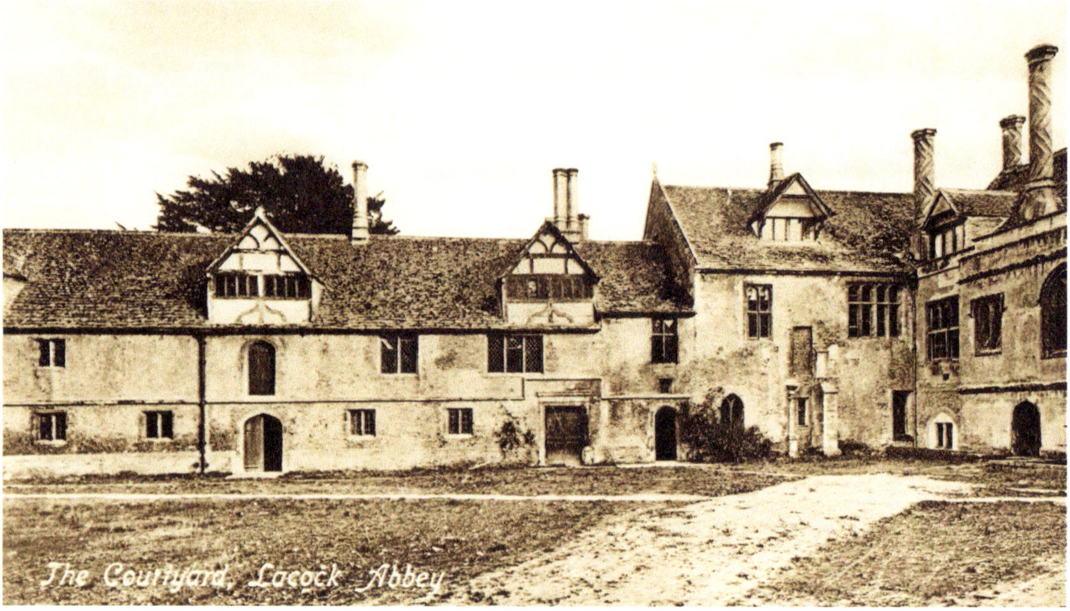

The Courtyard

Although there was a range of outbuildings to support his home, Sharington incorporated elegant features within the original structure. This building was extended and altered at later dates and included stables, dairy, bakehouse and brewery with haylofts over. Sharington built a brewery when he acquired the abbey in 1539 and this one is probably a replacement, in use until the eighteenth century or, perhaps, somewhat later. The courtyard, together with the outer yard on north side, was used as the setting for the Lacock Medieval Pageant in 1932.

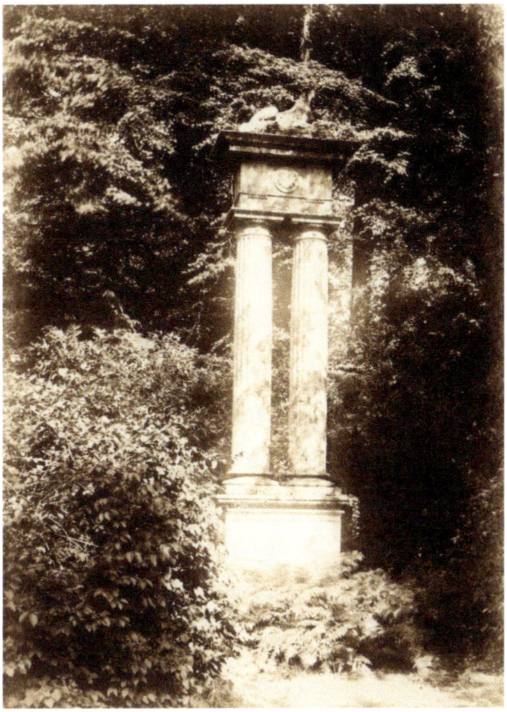

Sphinx Folley

This photograph, taken around 1900 in an overgrown setting, has a handwritten note at the rear: 'Lacock Abbey, columnar chimneys in garden'. It is an imposing ornament on the north side of the entrance drive, standing around 25 feet in height. It was created from two redundant fluted sixteenth-century chimneys from the abbey and utilised around the eighteenth century to stand on a large panelled stone base. John Ivory Talbot is reputed to have engaged mason Benjamin Carter to carve the sphinx for the top. It is rumoured that at midnight, when there is a full moon, it jumps to the ground and drinks in the nearby River Avon.

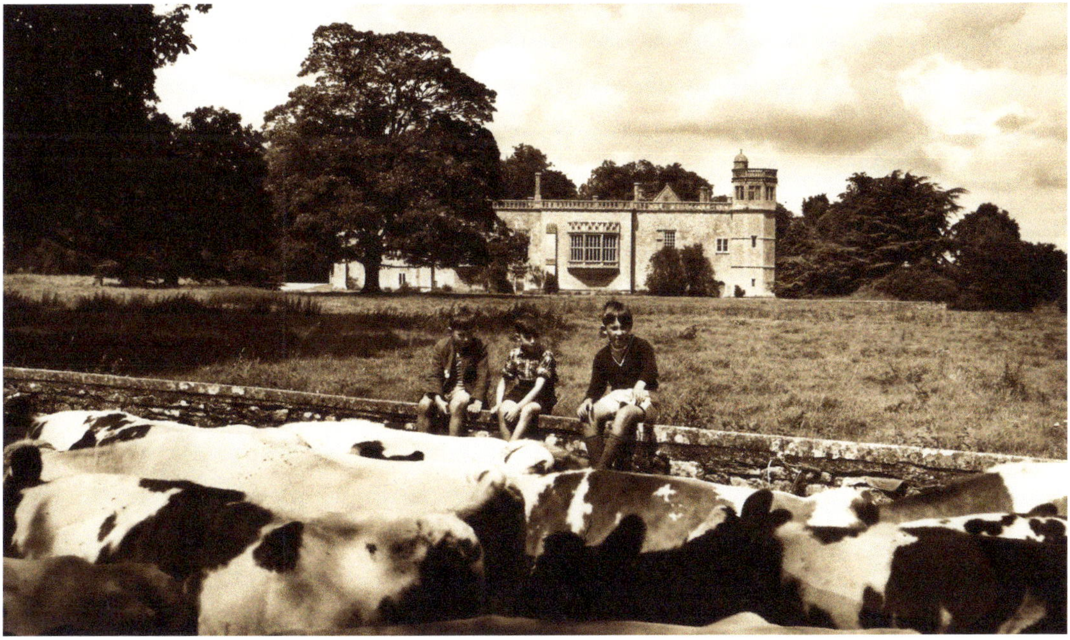

Cows in the Road

At one time this would have been a familiar sight as milking cows walked down the High Street and the road to Bowden Hill. They would be returning from their grazing to the local farm at milking time. In this photograph, three young boys sit on the abbey grounds boundary wall to let them pass. During the Second World War part of the abbey was used as a school for evacuees. (P45588HPPC c/o WSHC)

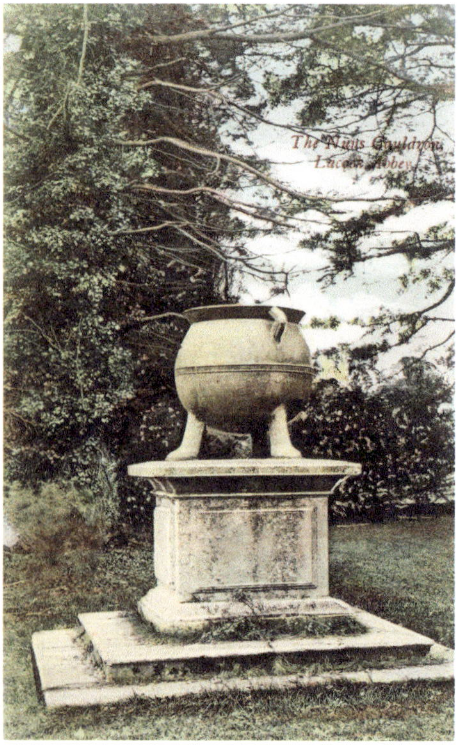

The Cauldron, Lacock Abbey

Before it became famous, this early Edwardian postcard shows the large cauldron supported on three legs and standing on a stone pedestal in a wooded area of the grounds – probably removed from the kitchen, where it is likely to have been used as the nuns' cooking vessel. Standing around 3 feet high it was moved again, inside the abbey to the Warming Room. The handles are ornamented with 'long beards', likely to have had rings which are now lost. Local village children used the cauldron for play.
It is now known throughout the world by Harry Potter enthusiasts, having featured in a classroom scene filmed at the abbey in 2001.

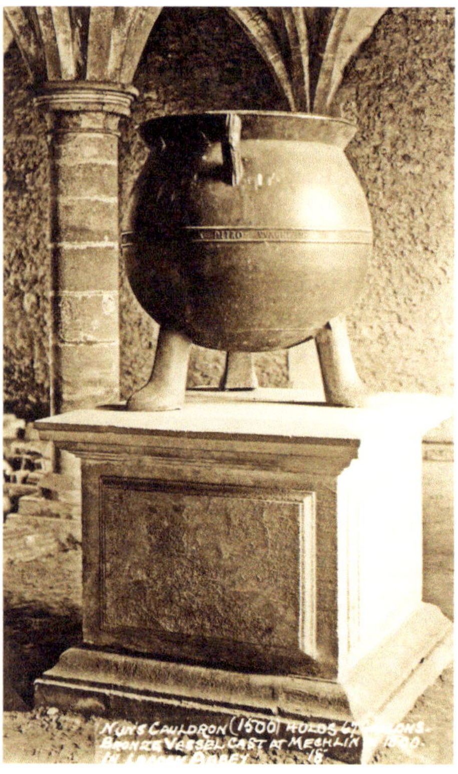

Nuns' Cauldron

Close-up view of the vast bell-metal pot with caption 'NUNS CAULDRON (1500), HOLDS SIXTY-SEVEN GALLONS, BRONZE VESSEL, CAST AT MECHLIN IN 1500, IN LACOCK ABBEY'.
The Latin inscription around the widest part of the bowl records that it was made by Peter Wagheuens and 'Praise be to God and Glory to Christ'. There are a few surface dents on the outside, believed to be the result of thieves trying to break it up and destroy centuries of history.

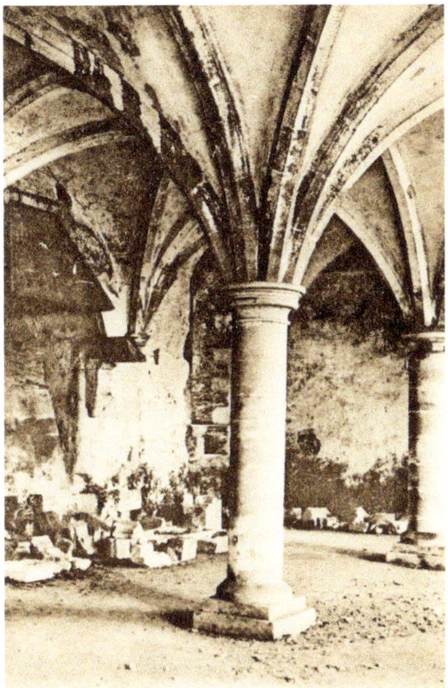

The Warming or Common House. Lacock Abbey

The Warming or Common House

Several piles of ancient stone masonry are in view. In this area a fireplace would have provided the nuns with their only source of heat. To the side are other stored pieces recovered from the grounds and parts of the cloisters. Within the room is the nuns' cauldron and a large stone tank, both believed to have been moved from the grounds before a wall was rebuilt in *c.* 1903. The Warming Room at Lacock Abbey is now very well known, having been used as a classroom in the *Harry Potter and the Philosopher's Stone* film.

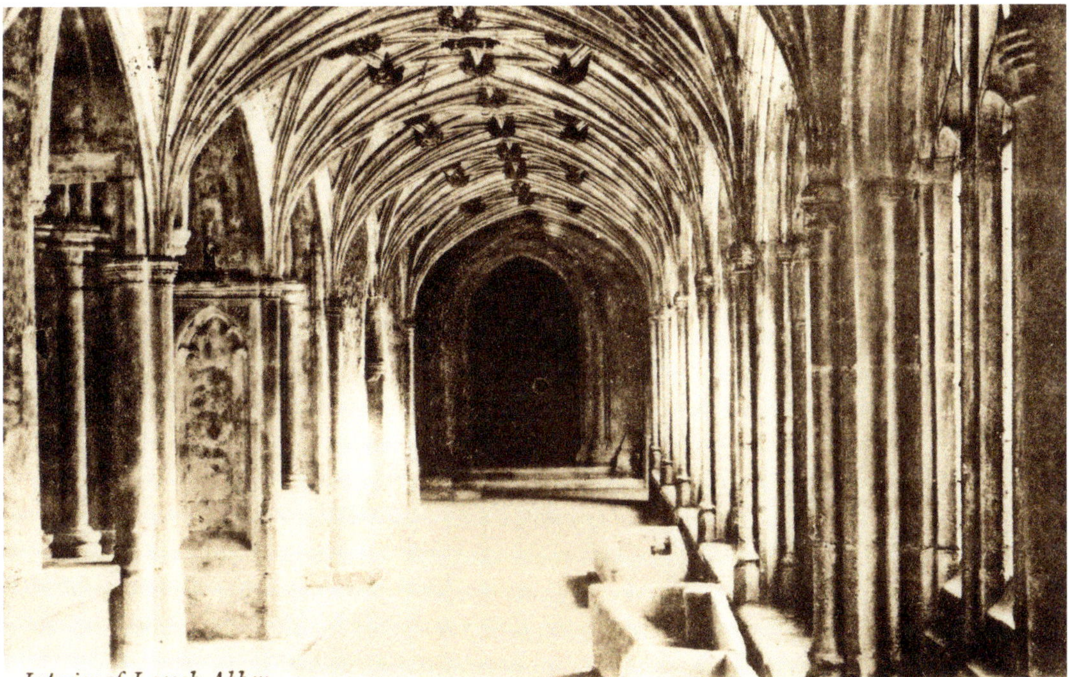

Interior of Lacock Abbey. Publ. by R. Wilkinson & C°. Trowbridge.

Interior of Lacock Abbey

This card, by a local photographer, was postally used in 1904. It shows a cloister view with empty stone coffins along the wall and fifteenth-century stone bosses displayed in the vaulting. There were originally cloisters around the four sides of the court, but these were replaced in the fourteenth and fifteenth centuries by a cloister walk on the north, south and east sides. From these, access was gained to some of the abbey's most important rooms.

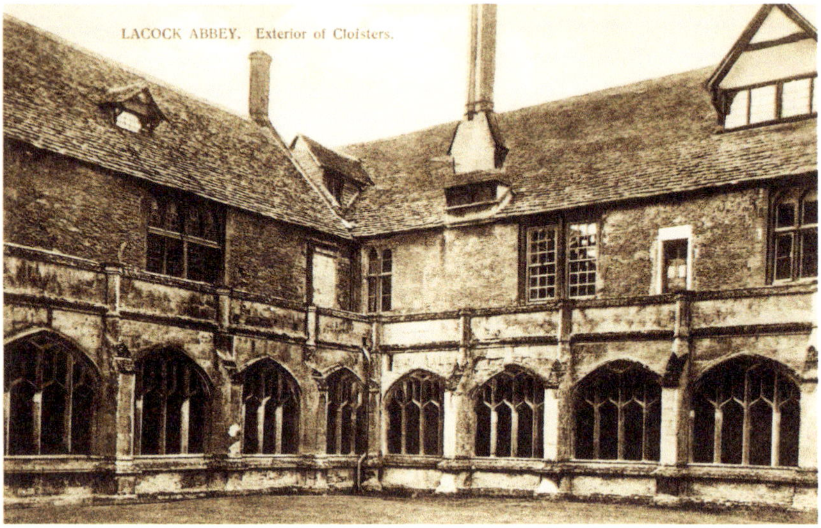

Exterior of Cloisters

This part of the abbey was adapted by Sharington to provide a family home. He retained the monastic element and adapted upper-storey accommodation. The work included impressive carved chimneys and dormer windows seen on this early postcard. It is rumoured that during the Second World War, Matilda Talbot arranged for the Lacock Magna Carta to be secretly buried in the Cloister Court grassed garden, for safe keeping. When the war ended it was recovered and Matilda Talbot took it on a lecture tour of the United States, later to present it to the nation.

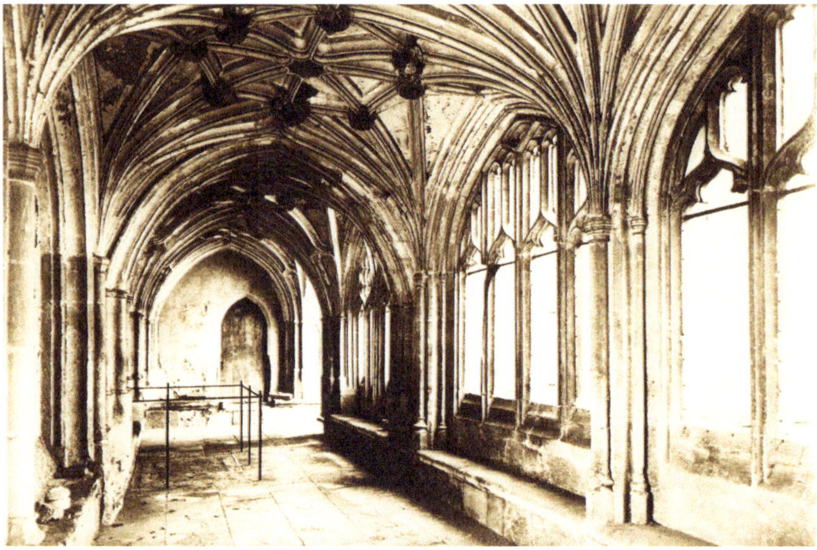

The Cloisters, South Walk

This photograph, taken around 1900, has a handwritten note at rear: 'Lacock Abbey, bay of S walk of Cloisters'. Originally built in the thirteenth century with some later alterations, it is still largely intact. As a fine example of its type, it provided an ideal location for scenes in the Harry Potter productions filmed at Lacock Abbey. Towards the north end of the cloisters is a railed tombstone to Ela, who founded the abbey in 1232 and became its first abbess. She was regarded as one of the important women of the Middle Ages.

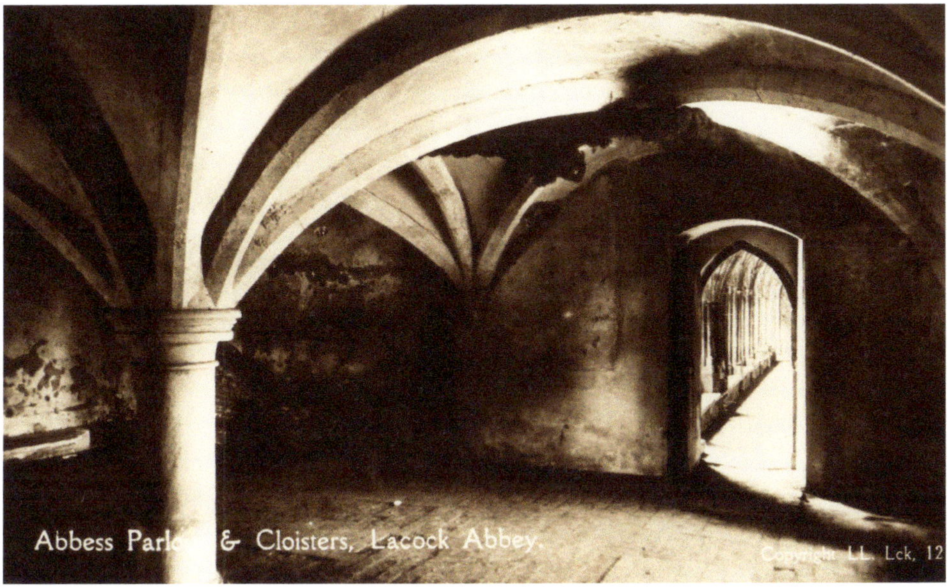

Abbess Parlour and Cloisters

A private space for the female head of the convent of nuns, with access from the cloisters. Originally this convent began its work under the leadership of a prioress with a group of nuns. Ela, Countess of Salisbury, who founded the abbey, became its first abbess in 1241. She held the position until five years before her death in 1261 at the age of seventy-five.

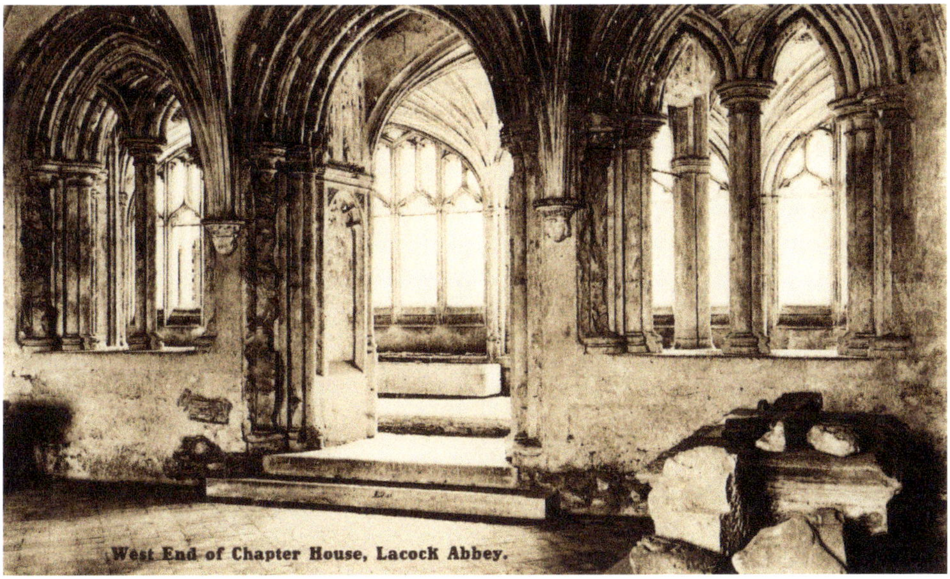

West End of Chapter House

Postally used in 1918, this card shows pieces of ancient medieval stone masonry, now removed, in a corner of the room. Access from the cloister is through a fine archway. The room was probably used for business and other meetings. A fireplace was located in the northern wall and was made for Sharington, who may have wished to use the Chapter House as a living room, but it was later destroyed.

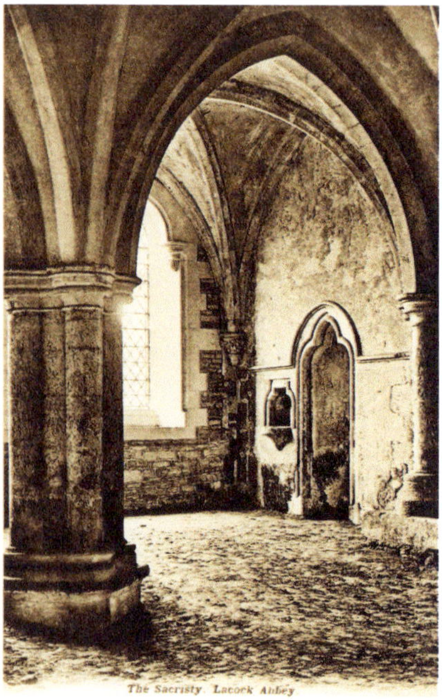

The Sacristy
An interesting view on this early Edwardian postcard of the recessed wall piscina and the arched doorway, which originally gave access to the abbey church, now demolished. The stone basin was used for washing holy vessels and the room itself for keeping sacred items, vestments and articles of worship. Harry Potter enthusiasts will know the atmospheric thirteenth-century sacristy as the scene of Professor Snape's potions classroom where he teaches his students 'how to bottle fame', amongst other things.

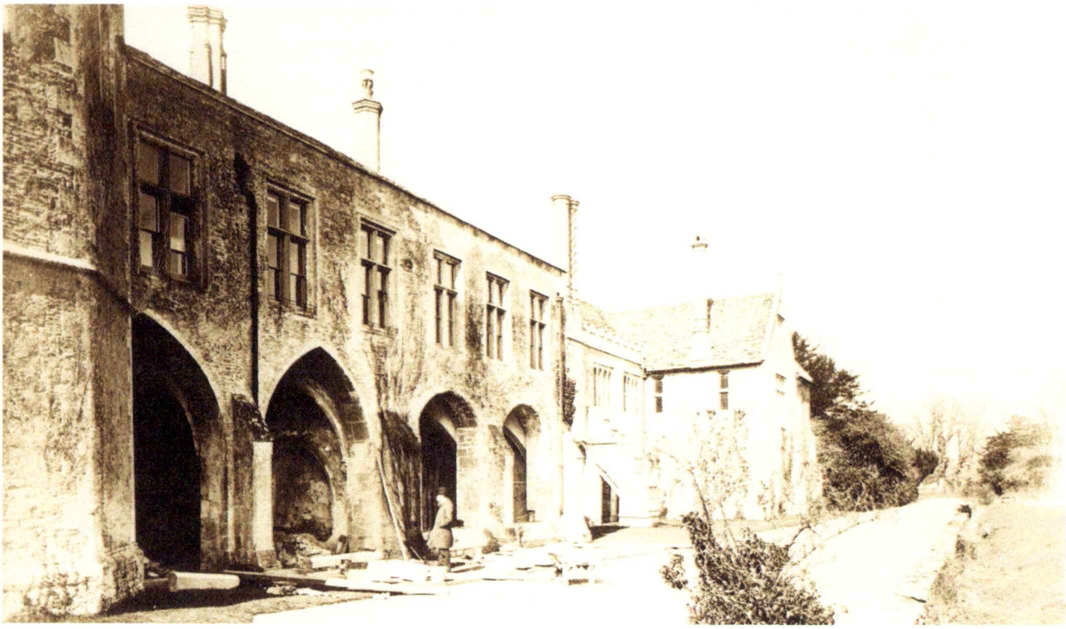

Building Work East Front, *c.* 1890s
A rare sepia photograph with contemporary note at rear – 'Lacock Abbey. The East Front' – showing building work in progress. Following the inheritance of the Lacock estate in 1714 by John Ivory Talbot, he decided to make alterations to the abbey. These included the removal of external walls to the Warming Room, Chapter House and Sacristy. This would create a ruin-type feature, albeit open to the elements to be appreciated with the grounds. These walls with windows were subsequently reinstated sometime after 1877 when Charles Henry Talbot had inherited Lacock. The large heavy stone tank was probably moved inside to the Warming Room before the arches were enclosed again.

William Henry Fox Talbot, Father of British Photography

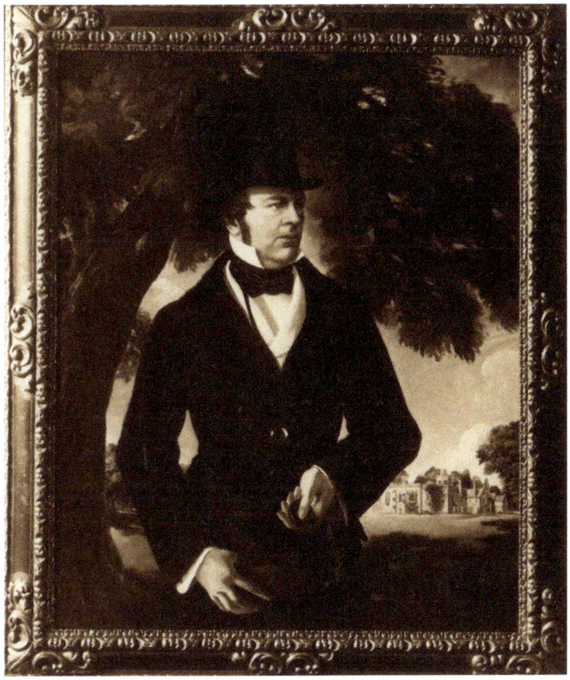

William Henry Fox Talbot was born in Melbury, Dorset, in 1800 and educated at Harrow and Cambridge. In 1826 he moved into his ancestral home, Lacock Abbey, was married and had four children. He became a Member of Parliament for Chippenham for a brief period in 1832 but his interests were in science, nature and the natural phenomena. The title of 'Father of Photography' was given to him because of his invention of the negative-positive process. Photography – being able to permanently record – is one of the greatest inventions and it has impacted on us all. (P48324HPPC c/o WSHC)

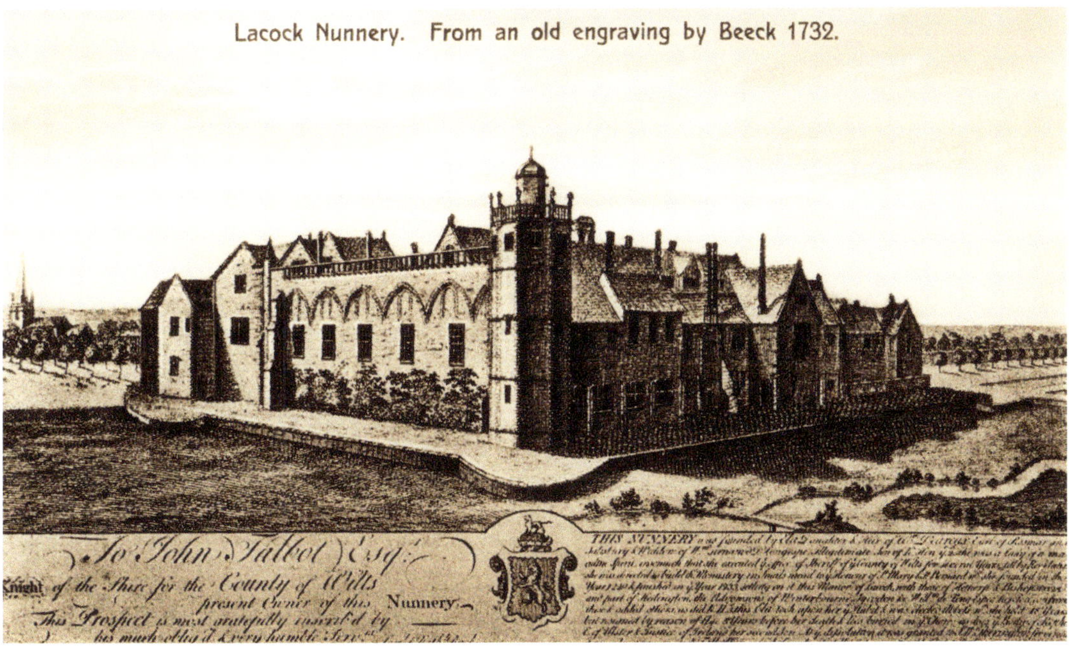

Lacock Nunnery

Before photography was invented and photographs introduced, images were recorded by various means including paintings, drawings, sculptures and engravings. The Edwardian postcard illustrates a copy of an engraving by Beeck in 1732. Part of the inscription on the bottom reads: 'To John Talbot Esq, Knight of the Shire for the County of Wilts, present owner of this Nunnery'. Without the revolutionary invention of photography, books such as this would not be possible.

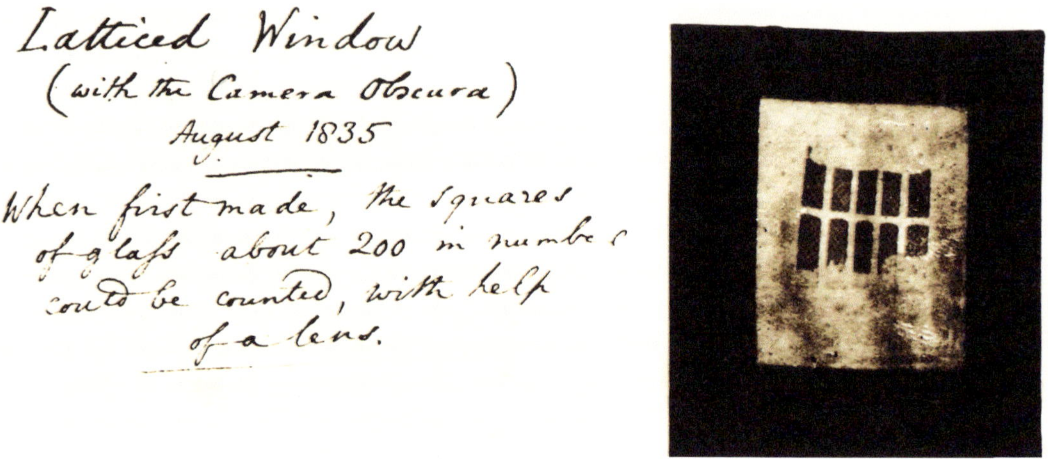

Earliest Camera Negative in Existence

Latticed window in the South Gallery of Lacock Abbey, August 1835. Photogenic drawing negative by Fox Talbot (1800–77) with comments in his handwriting, taken with the small wooden camera obscura. This is believed to have been made for him by a village tradesman. In 1834 Fox Talbot developed the process which enabled a negative image to be produced on sensitised paper using a small camera. It was not until 1839 that Fox Talbot publicly introduced his new paper-based system from which was developed the calotype process and patented by him in 1841. (Science and Society Picture Library)

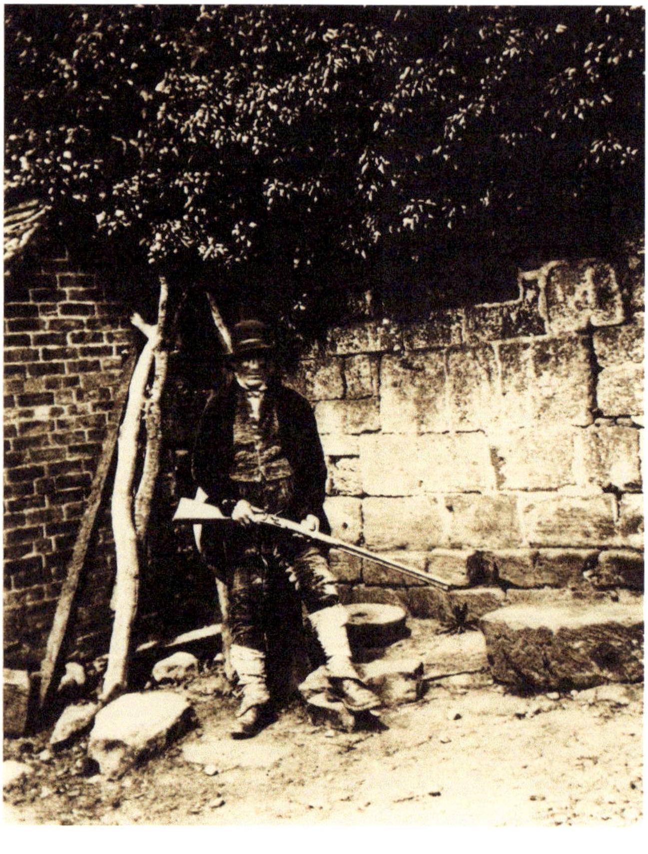

Gamekeeper at Lacock Abbey, *c.* 1830s

Calotype taken by Fox Talbot. It was in the grounds of Lacock Abbey between 1830 and 1840 that Fox Talbot, a photography pioneer, scientist and inventor with an interest in light, carried out his revolutionary experiments. He investigated the light sensitivity of different chemicals. Following many trials he found that a series of coatings of weak silver chloride solution on paper were promising, and, in 1834, was able to obtain distinct images of leaves. (Science and Society Picture Library)

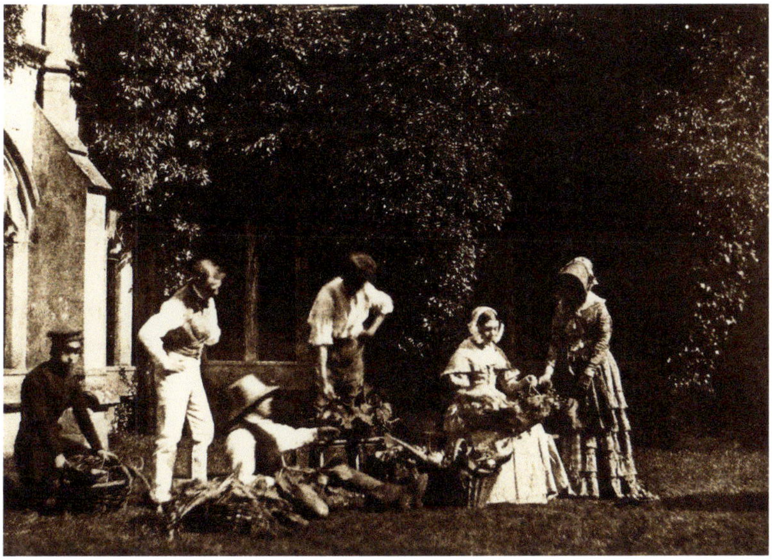

Group outside Lacock Abbey, *c.* 1845

A salted paper print, this photograph is attributed to Fox Talbot and fellow photographer Revd Calvert Jones. The participants in this calotype, selling fruit and flowers, are probably domestic staff from the abbey. Trained to keep still for a few seconds, a picture of the group could easily be obtained. Any number of prints could be provided from the same shot by transferring the negative image onto special paper to make a positive print. Those prints were called calotypes. (Science and Society Picture Library)

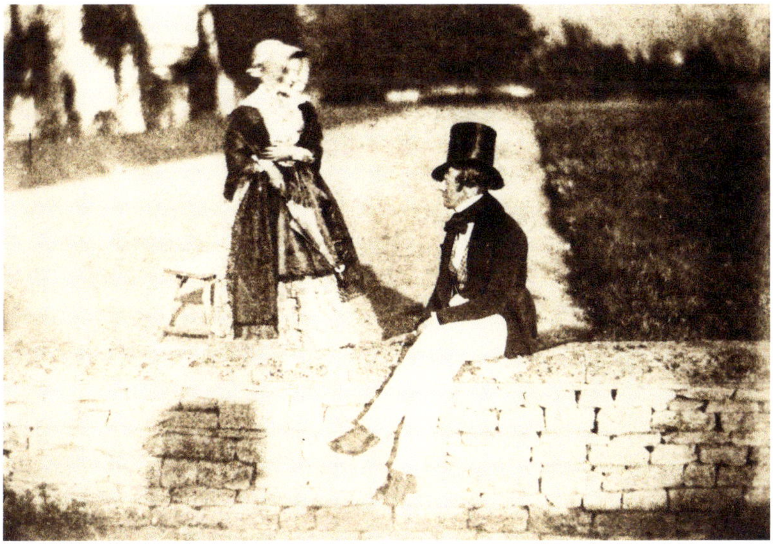

Kit Talbot and Lady Charlotte Talbot, *c.* 1845

A salt paper print from a calotype negative taken at Lacock Abbey by Revd Calvert Jones. Elegantly dressed, and posing for the photograph, Kit (1803–90), with Victorian top hat, is seated with a standing Lady Charlotte (1809–46) wearing a Victorian bonnet. They were relatives of Fox Talbot and as such, ready subjects for photographs taken in the grounds of Lacock Abbey. (Science and Society Picture Library)

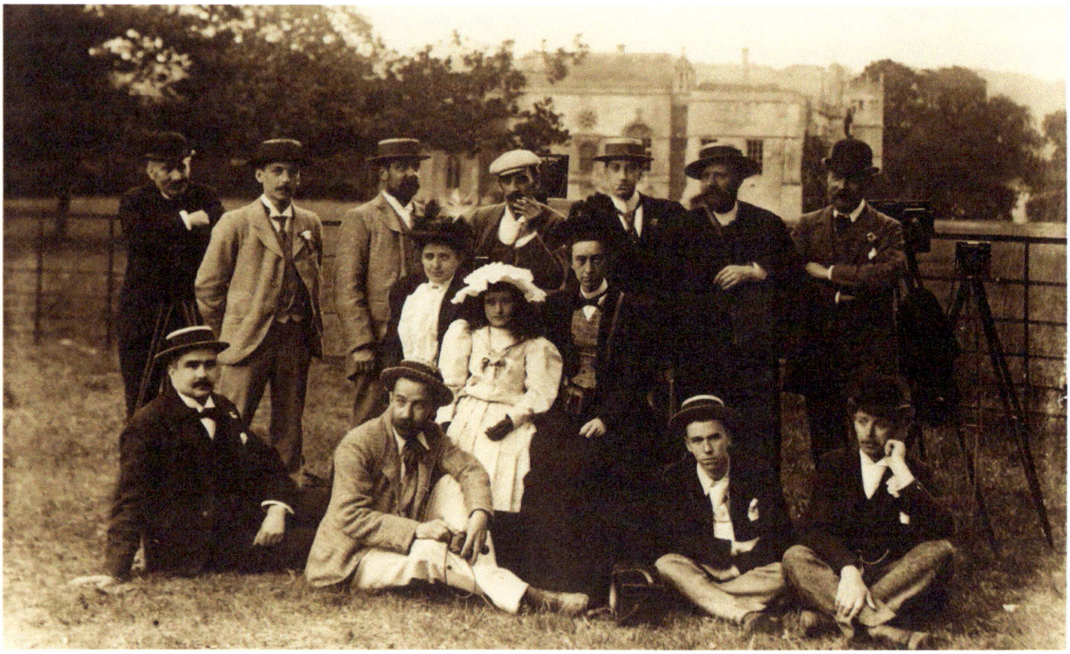

Trowbridge Camera Club, Visit to Lacock Abbey

Taken in 1895 this photograph records a visit of the Trowbridge District Photographic Society to Lacock Abbey, the home of the founder of photography, Mr Fox Talbot. The excursion was arranged by Mr R. H. Foley, the agent for the estate. The abbey was revisited once more by the club in 1945 and, at that time, all but one of the members appearing in the photograph could be identified. (WSA2664/2/2F/4BW)

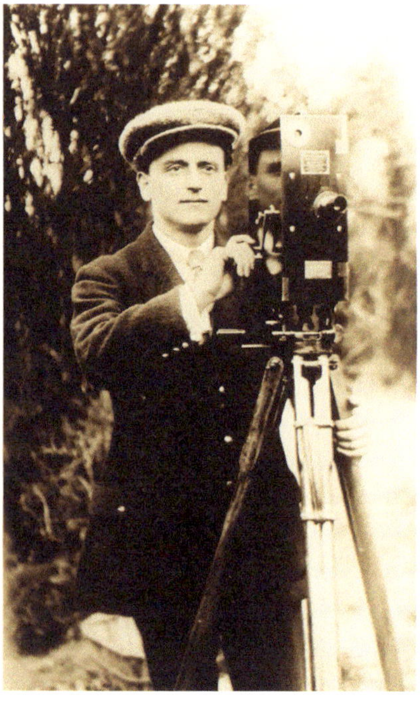

Hand Crank Movie Camera *c.* 1900

Following the invention of photography, and during the Victorian era, the movie camera was developed. This is a rare and unusual postcard with smartly dressed photographer operating a hand crank silent movie camera on tripod base. He has one hand on the camera handle and the other to steady the tripod support. Early cameras were only provided with a basic levelling device at the head of the tripod. The camera was fixed during the course of the shot. The earliest films were without sound, less than a minute in length and in black and white. The first film studio was built in 1897.

The Magic Box – Film with Photographic Theme

William Friese-Greene, born in 1855, is played by Robert Donat with a cast of over sixty British stars. It is a romantic biography in Technicolour made for the 1951 Festival of Britain. Friese-Greene was a British photographer and inventor, covering both the Victorian and Edwardian periods. He is particularly known for designing a motion picture camera which he subsequently patented. Lacock Abbey, the home of British photography, was used in scenes, as was St Cyriac's Church for his wedding. He died in London in 1921 whilst at a cinema and film meeting. (WSA1772/1/592/1)

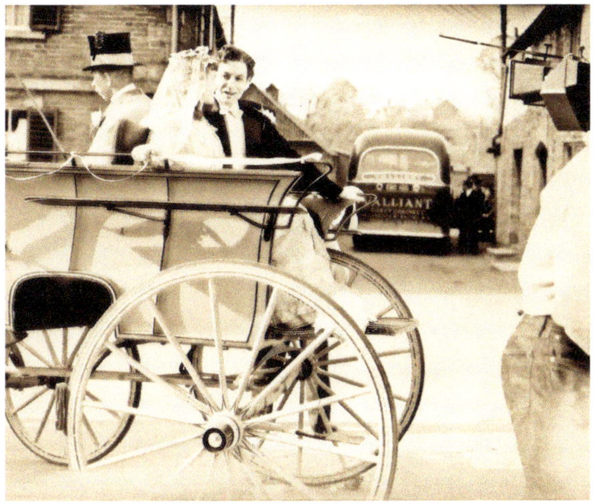

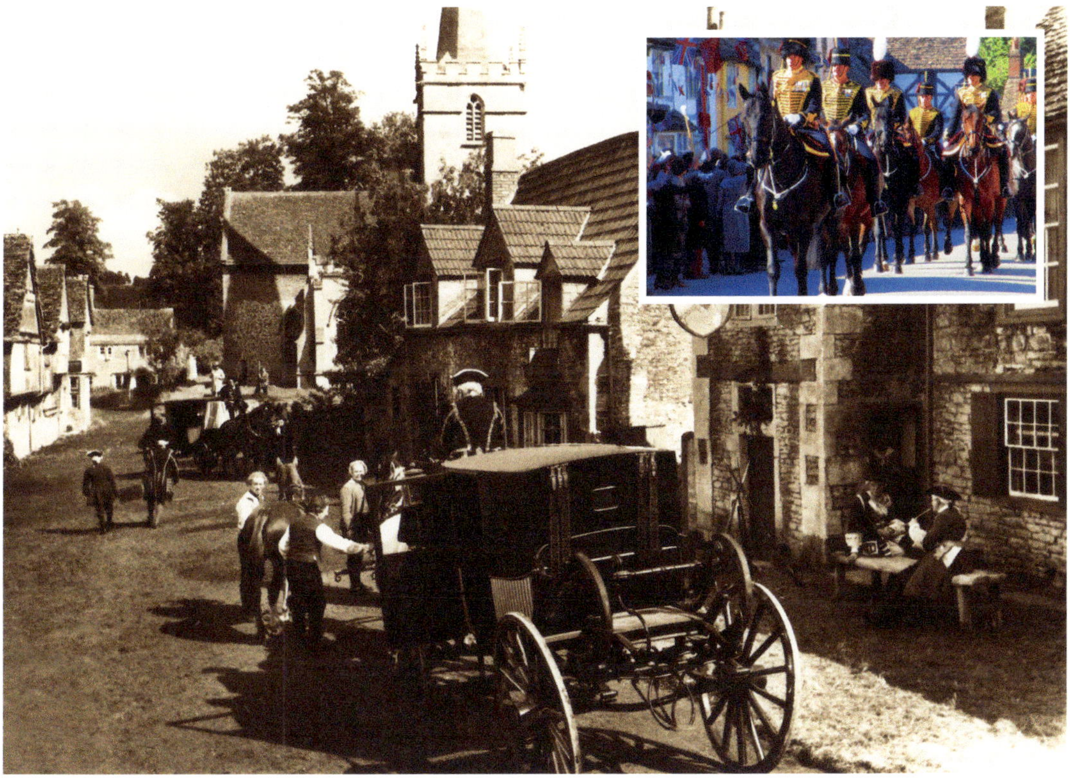

Filming – Past and Present

The village has provided the ideal backdrop for many film and television productions. The wide High Street with historic buildings either side has often been featured. There are no television aerials or satellite dishes to be removed. A horse-drawn coach film scene outside a renamed Carpenters' Arms and probably the oldest house in the village, King John's Hunting Lodge, is in progress. The church and a house in a Harry Potter film are also in view. (WSA4140/1/NON/16) *Inset*: September 2018. Filming for the new *Downton Abbey* movie. Royal Artillery being greeted by flag-waving crowd in 1920s costume, each side of the High Street.

2

High Street

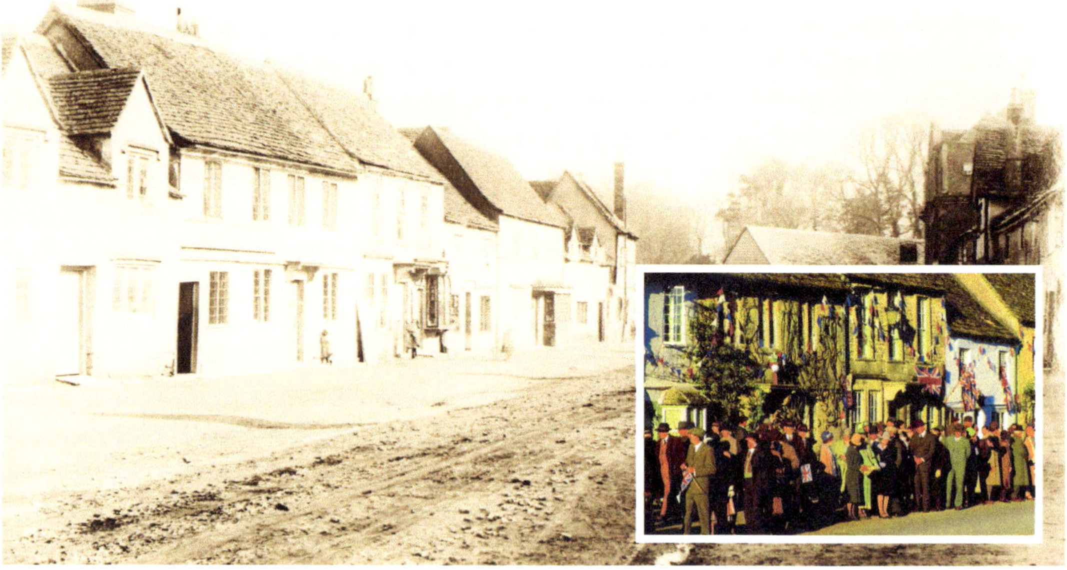

Lacock High Street, *c*. 1900

There is a pencil-written note on rear of photograph: 'Lacock view looking East'. The Saxon word for Lacock is 'Lacuc', meaning little stream, and this refers to Bide Brook on the north side around which the village became established. This view reveals the wide muddy road, cart tracks, rut, extensive pavement area and small children close to the shop. The village would have been self-supporting at this time with all the shops and trades people it needed. *Inset*: September 2018. Filming for the *Downton Abbey* movie. Crowd in 1920s, costume in High Street.

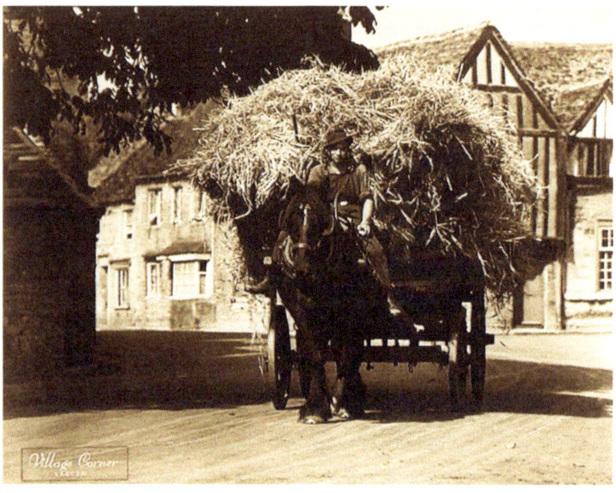

Village Corner, *c*. 1940s

The corner of High Street with East Street and a fully loaded horse-drawn farm waggon. The road has been much improved and is now surfaced. A bay-front property, now the National Trust Shop, is in view, as is part-timbered Chamberlain's House. Lacock was first mentioned in the Doomsday Book in 1086, with a population of below 200 people. (WSA/X3/164/25)

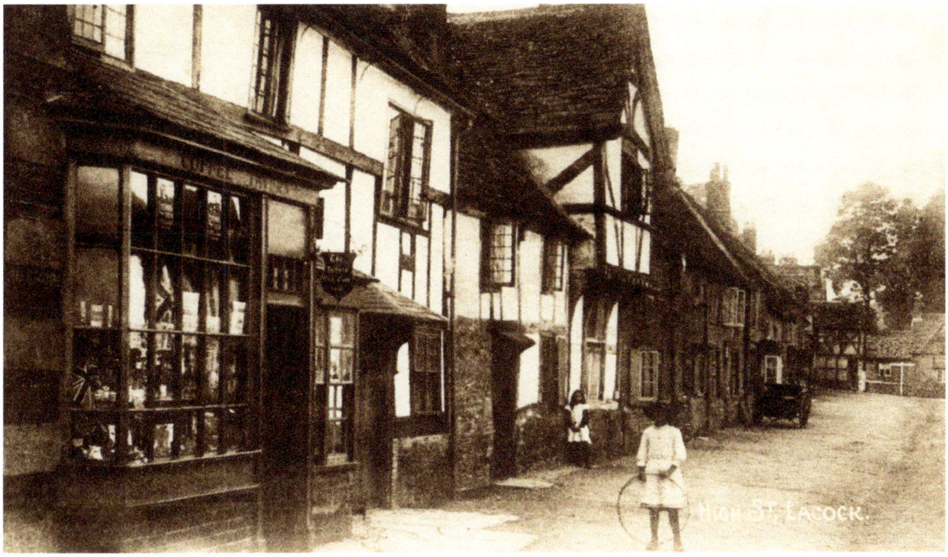

High Street, 1916
In the foreground is the Coffee Tavern with hanging shield-shape sign 'The Picture Postcard Shop'. It is thanks to our local photographers and publishers that village history has been recorded. A small girl posing for the photographer is standing by the shop with a play hoop. This involved rolling it along the ground and keeping it upright. The road was once called New Market Place and livestock were sold in front of the school.

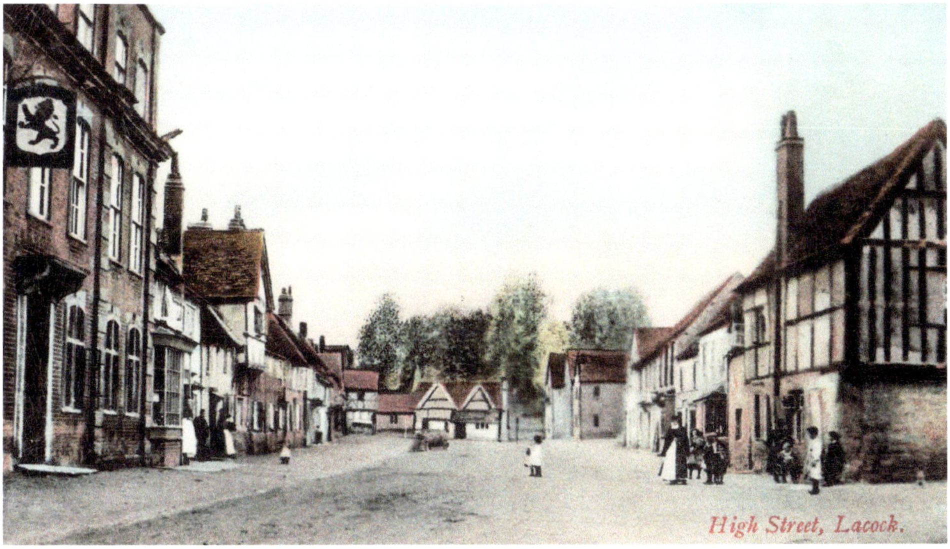

High Street, 1907
Some animation on this card, which also provides us with an idea of the considerable width of the road and mixed periods of architecture. These historic properties are virtually all owned now by the National Trust and so carefully preserved by them. The village comprises principally of four streets arranged around a rectangle. Its main part was probably established to provide accommodation for workers of the abbey in the thirteenth century. Houses and buildings date from this time and also the next six centuries.

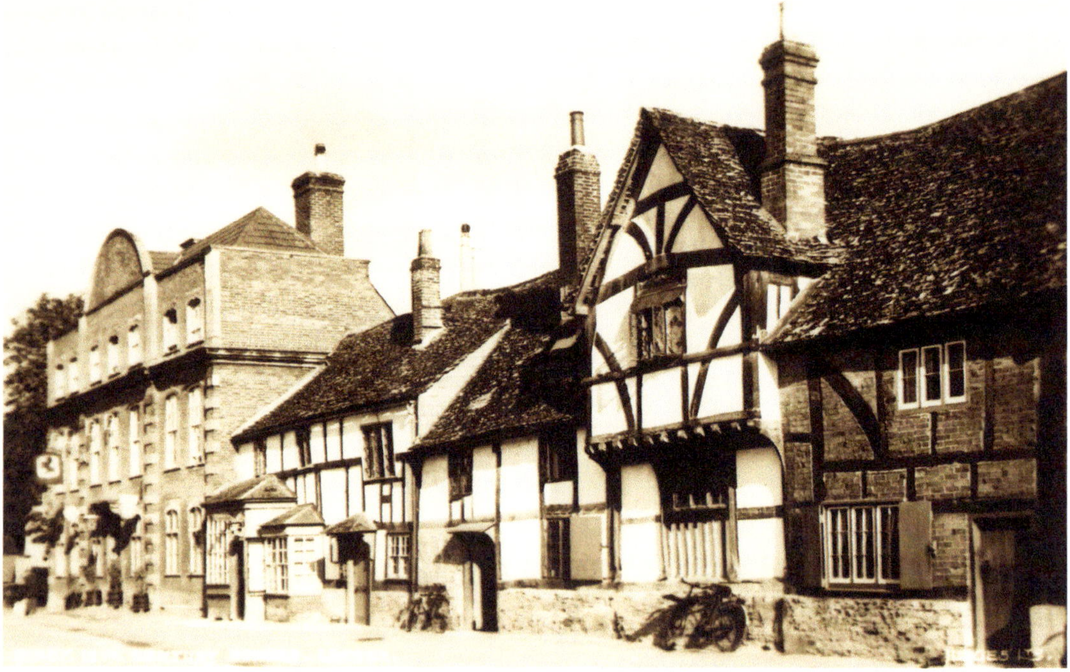

Fifteenth-century Houses

This image shows commercial and residential properties in this part of the High Street. The variety of building materials can be seen including stone from the Corsham area, timbers cut from the nearby forest (long gone) and in-fill wall panels. These are in brick and those rendered, probably traditional wattle and daub. The different roof levels add interest to the street scene.

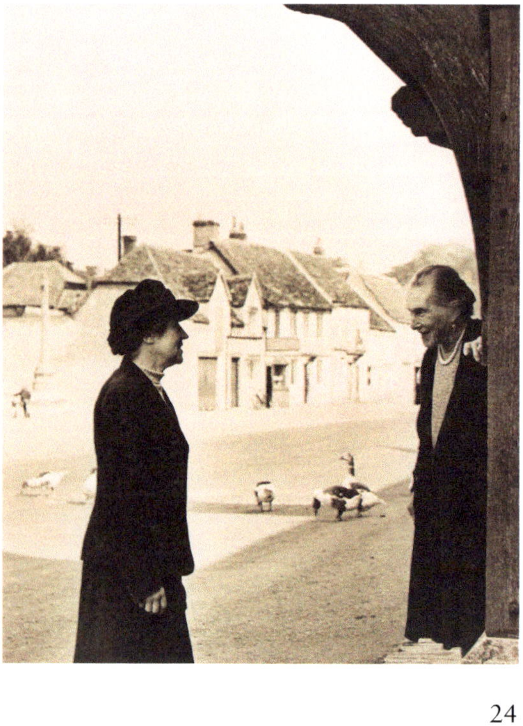

Miss Matilda Talbot outside Porch House, *c.* 1940s

The April 1958 issue of *The Lacock with Bowden Hill Bulletin*, edited and published at Lacock Vicarage, reports the sad death and grievous loss of Miss Matilda Talbot. She was much loved here and by friends from all over the world. The magazine included affectionate tributes from the Parish Church, Bowden Hill, News of Friends, Lacock Womens' Auxiliary and Lacock Choral Society. Local people remembered kindnesses of this great lady who had been an inspiration to others. Taking an active part in village life, she died at the age of eighty-five years, having been the last private owner of Lacock Abbey before gifting it to the National Trust. (WSA2664/2/3F/10/48BW)

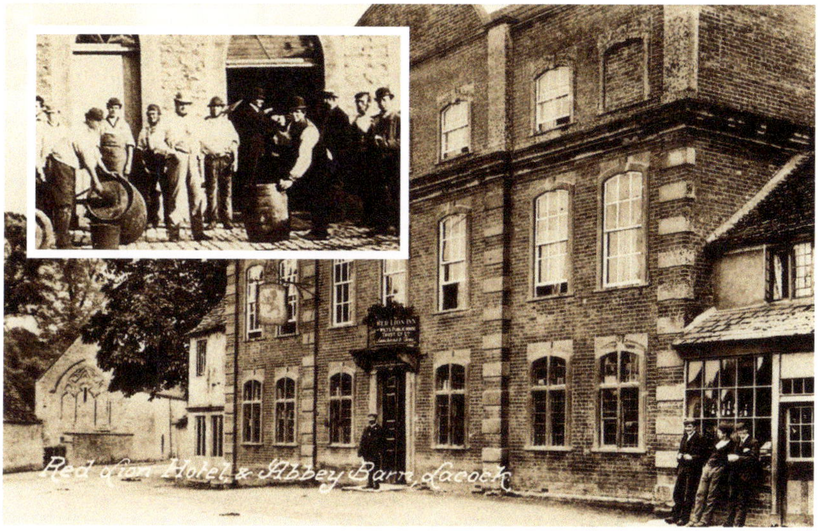

Red Lion Inn

On this early Edwardian postcard, the Red Lion Inn is described as the Red Lion Hotel. It had several letting bedrooms, two bars and stabling at rear for travellers' horses. It has been in continuous use as an inn since being constructed in the Georgian era. It is likely that there were originally older properties on the site. With its brick three-storey elevation to High Street with stone side extension, it will be recognised for its appearance in television and film productions. It is one of the largest buildings in the village. In the past, the Lacock Abbey Estate rented a room for rent collection from its many tenants. *Inset*: Lacock Brewery sold beer to the inn. (© National Trust/Rachel Topham)

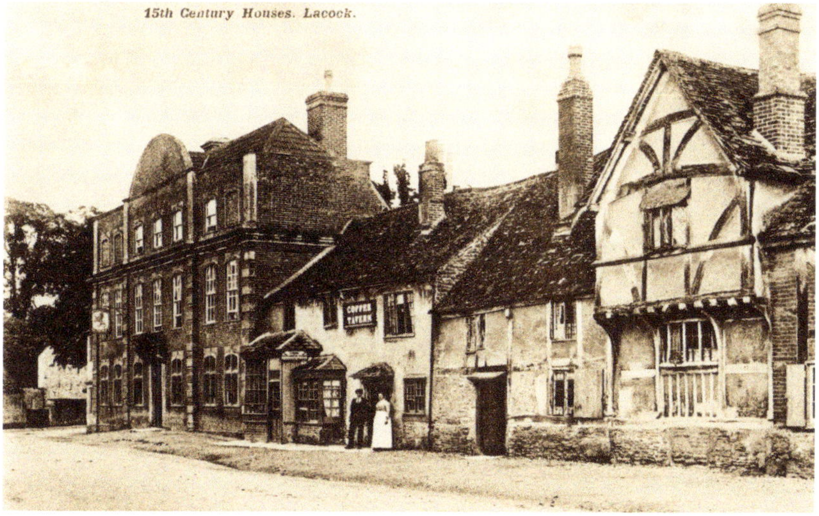

Red Lion and Fifteenth-century Houses

Over the years there have been many tenants and managers of this large historic Grade II listed building which occupies one of the most prominent positions in the High Street. In the late 1700s it was also a meeting place of the 'Lacock Friendly Society' who held an annual event in the field behind the Red Lion. This land was at one time part of the public house tenancy. Around 1900, photographs of the time show external signs indicating it sold Kingsford's beer and ales from Lacock Brewery and was operated by Wilts Public House Trust Co. Ltd.

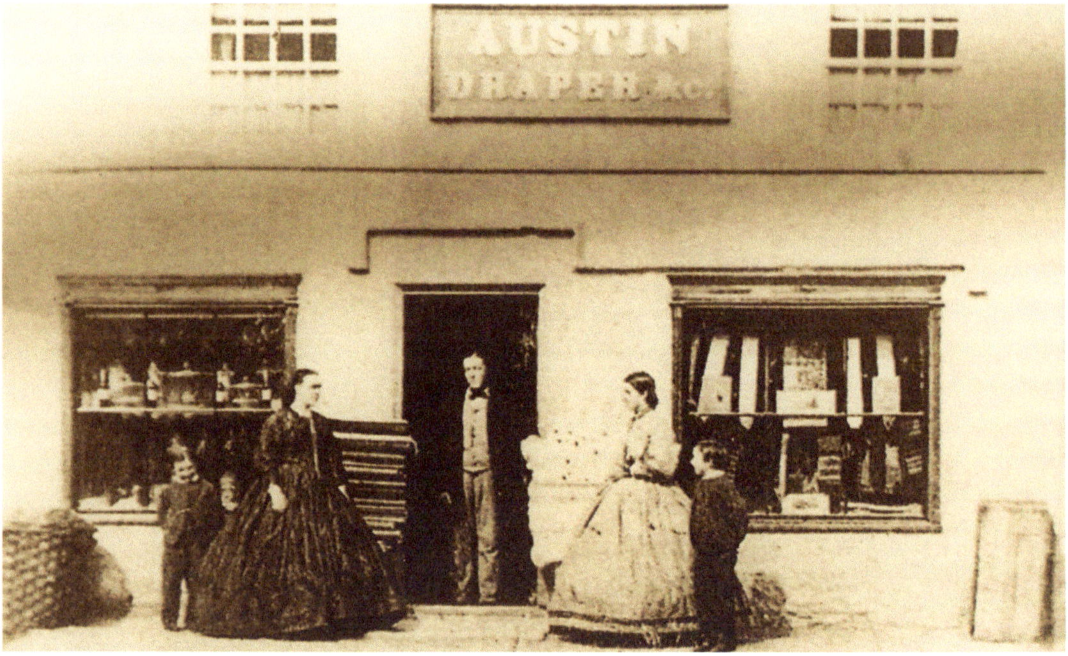

Austin Draper's Shop, High Street, *c.* 1866

The two ladies in elaborate costumes pose for the camera outside the shop for this early photograph. Over many years Lacock, like other villages, has ceased to be self-sufficient. It is interesting to note from the Kelly's Directory of 1899 the variety of shops, trades and businesses that were active. The list included four grocers, a butcher, two drapers, a brewer, two bakers, three boot and shoemakers, a toy and fancy dealer, a tailor, a dressmaker, an ironmonger and assessor of taxes, and a shopkeeper. (WSA3476/1/191)

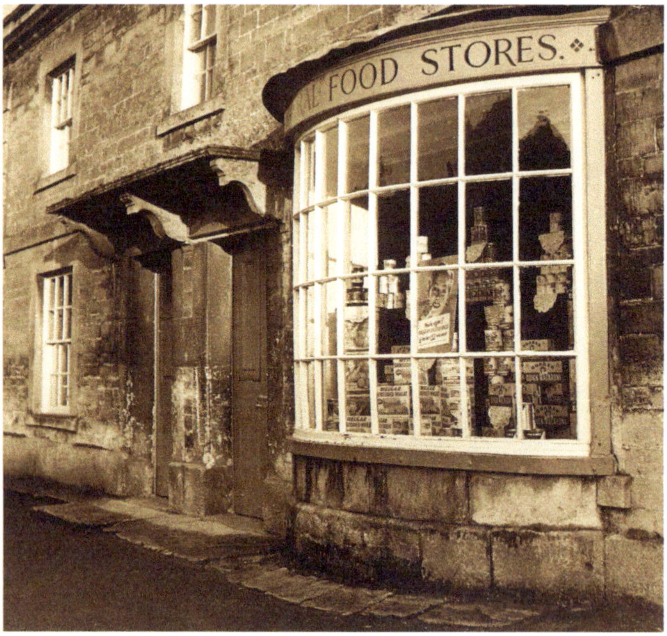

Food Stores

In 1899 the village also included a timber merchant, hurdle maker, two plumbers, two smiths (one a farrier), slater and plasterer, chair maker, coal merchant, carpenter and builder, miller, four innkeepers and a coffee tavern. There was also a nurses' home, surgeon, medical officer and public vaccinator. The Post Office had the assistant overseer, collector of poor rates, assessor and collector of taxes. This working village served a population that was recorded in 1891 as being 1,179 persons in the civil and 909 in the ecclesiastical parish. Fortunately, the store is still open today and incorporates the Post Office. (WSA2752/32)

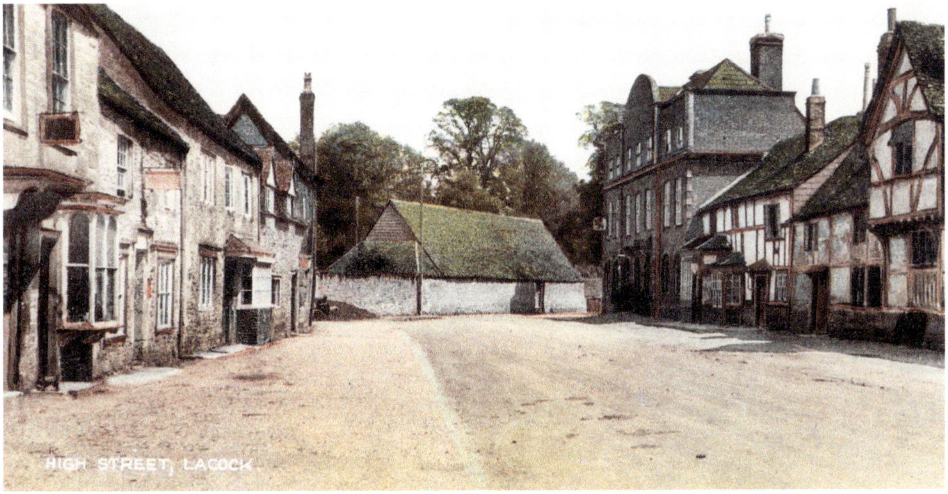

No Motor Vehicles

This image shows an early Edwardian postcard from an unknown photographer providing an empty street view. Several hanging signs are visible on the front of properties indicating commercial usage. Due to their age and type of construction, it was costly and ongoing for the abbey estate to maintain the many houses and buildings. This work would have provided employment for local trades people. The Red Lion, with domed façade, is clearly visible. The area in front of it has been a traditional Boxing Day meeting place for the Avon Vale hunt.

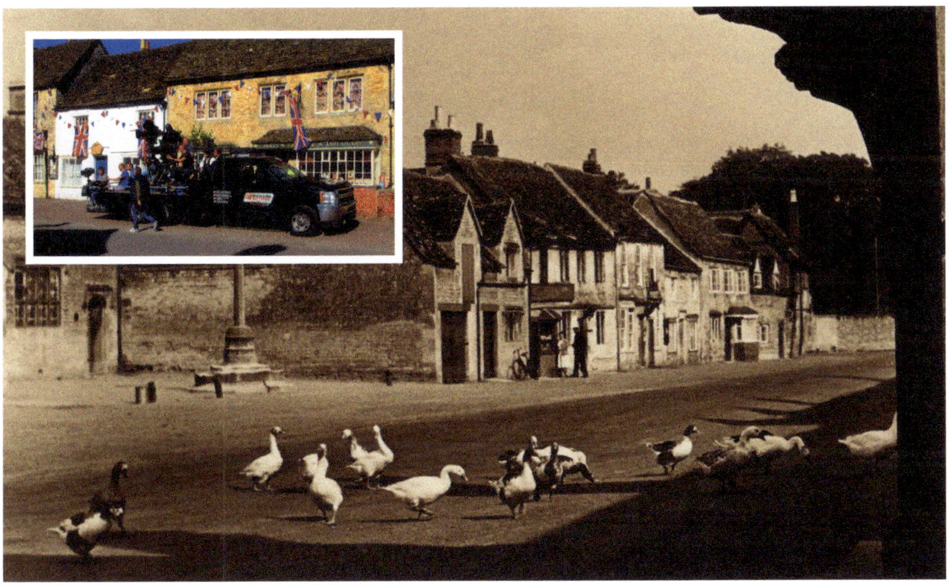

Not Unusual, *c.* 1940s

At one time it was a very common sight to see geese from a nearby holding wandering freely in the street. They appear in many photographs and postcards until the arrival of the motor vehicle in some numbers, to the village. In the front of the picture is part of Porch House and opposite, the school and market cross. (WSA2664/2/3F/10/22BW) *Inset*: September 2018. Filming for the new *Downton Abbey* movie. Camera crew outside the National Trust shop, renamed Hatts Chemists and Druggists.

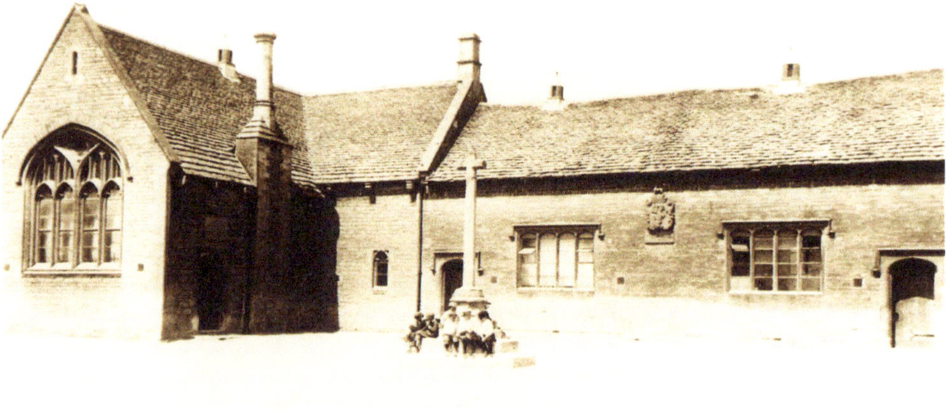

Village School, *c.* 1910

To enable a school to be built in a central position in the village, cottages had to be demolished to provide the site. The mixed elementary school for all ages was founded by William Henry Fox Talbot. The reason for this was to record his twenty-first birthday in 1821. It was not, however, until 1824 that it was first opened to accommodate 100 pupils. The school has always been connected to the church and was known at one time as Lacock National School. It was maintained by fees paid by parents and voluntary subscriptions. (WSA3476/1/191)

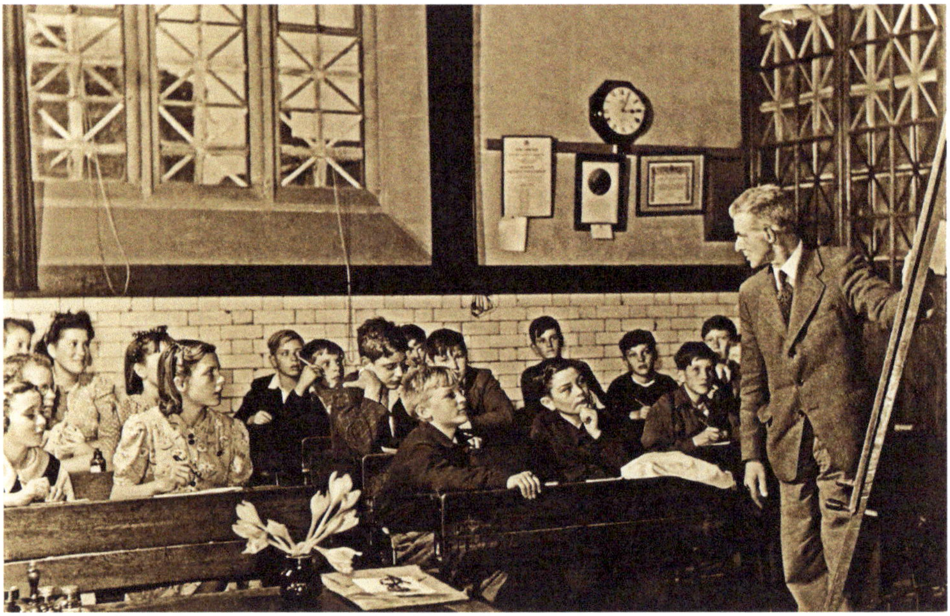

Lessons at School, *c.* 1945

This image shows an attentive class of smartly dressed pupils. As their numbers grew, in the early days of the school, another classroom was added in 1852. Later, in 1859, a grant enabled a new school to be built on the site of the old to provide 300 pupil spaces. Around 1900, all the children were in a single room, sat on forms and wrote on slates. By 1907 the school was controlled by Wiltshire County Council, at which time pupil numbers were declining. In the 1960s, the older children were placed in nearby senior schools. It then became Lacock Church of England Primary School. (WSA2664/2/3F/10/40BW)

Children at the Market Cross, *c.* 1945

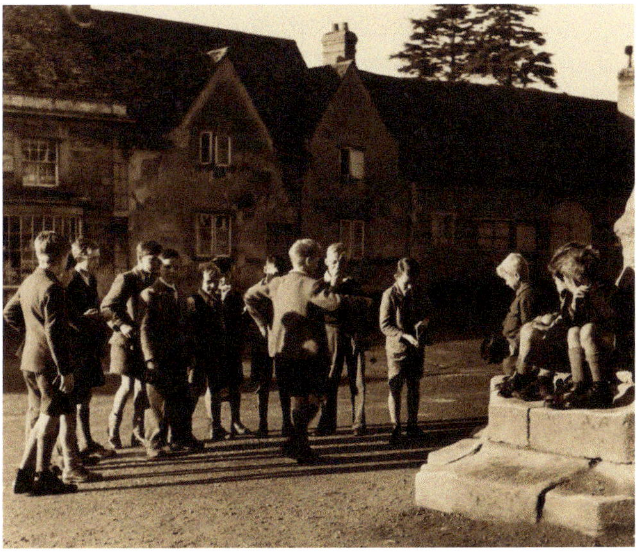

This image shows a group of schoolboys in both long and short trousers outside the school watching and playing a game of 'conkers'. The small brown fruit of a horse chestnut tree was removed from its prickly outer skin. It was threaded on a string and used to hit and demolish the 'conker' of the opponent, with strikes taken in turn. A trick was to soak the fruit in vinegar to harden it. The school is just one of a few nineteenth-century buildings in the village, but it blends remarkably well into its surroundings. (WSA2664/2/3F/10/58BW)

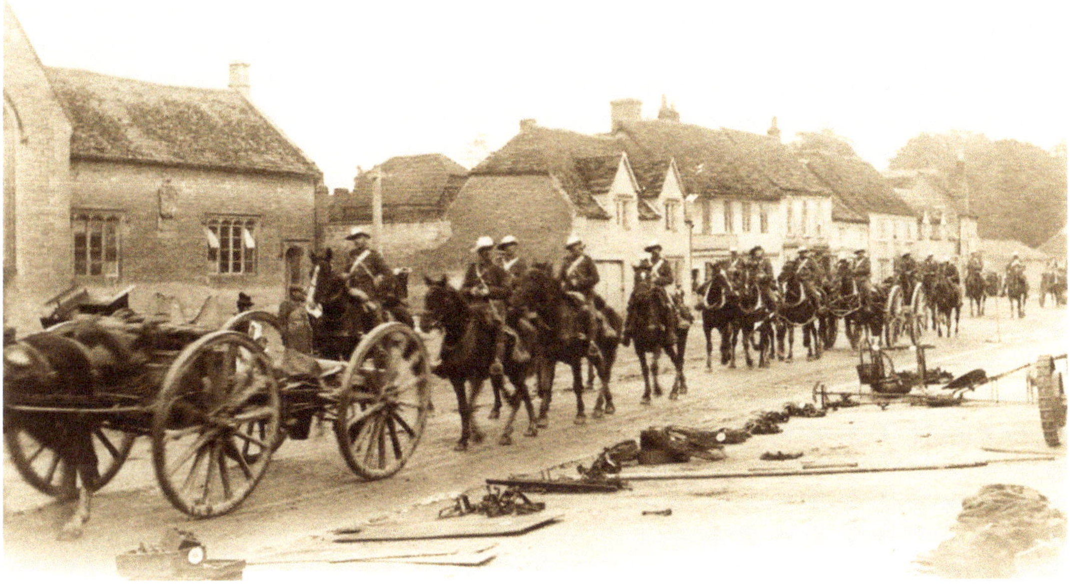

Mounted Troops

Mounted troops are seen here riding down the High Street in a westerly direction, passing the school and market cross. The photograph was taken in the First World War period. It is likely they were some distance from their barracks or camp, which may have either been Trowbridge (some 10 miles), or Salisbury Plain area (around 25 miles). They are wearing slouch caps, which were worn after the South African War. As British forces from the plain were moved to fighting fronts in the First World War, they were replaced. This involved bringing troops over from Australia, Canada, New Zealand, South Africa and later America. (© National Trust/Rachel Nordstrom)

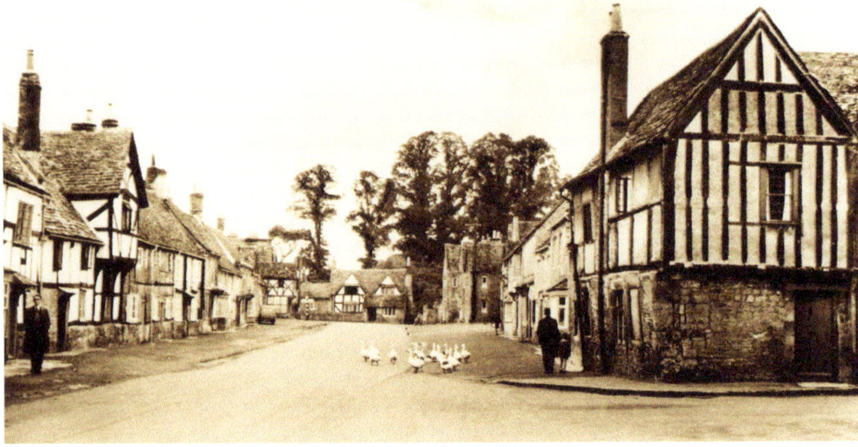

Peaceful Scene

It is easy to see how these fine historic buildings from different centuries combine together to provide one of the most attractive street scenes to be found anywhere in England. Many of the High Street houses would have originally been small shops. Since built, only a few external alterations have been made, but internal improvements and modernisation have been undertaken. Although the properties have no front gardens or forecourts, they have gardens at the rear. In the past, these would have been essential for growing produce and keeping any livestock, but these plots are not easily visible from the street.

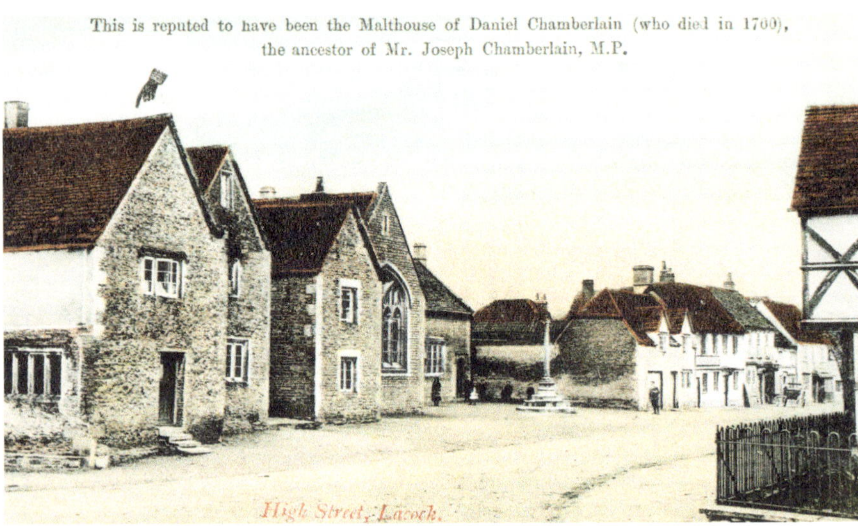

Probably the Malthouse of Daniel Chamberlain

All the streets in Lacock, with their appealing properties dating from the medieval period, have been popular with film makers and television production companies. The village provides an almost ready-made set for historical features. There are no television aerials, satellite dishes, overhead cables or front gardens and only limited street lighting. Removal of the motor vehicles, modern signage, contemporary features, the provision of soil on the streets and people in period costume brings Lacock back to life, as it was in the past. The property in the front corner of the card is reputed to have been the malthouse of Daniel Chamberlain, who died in 1760. He was an ancestor of Joseph Chamberlain MP.

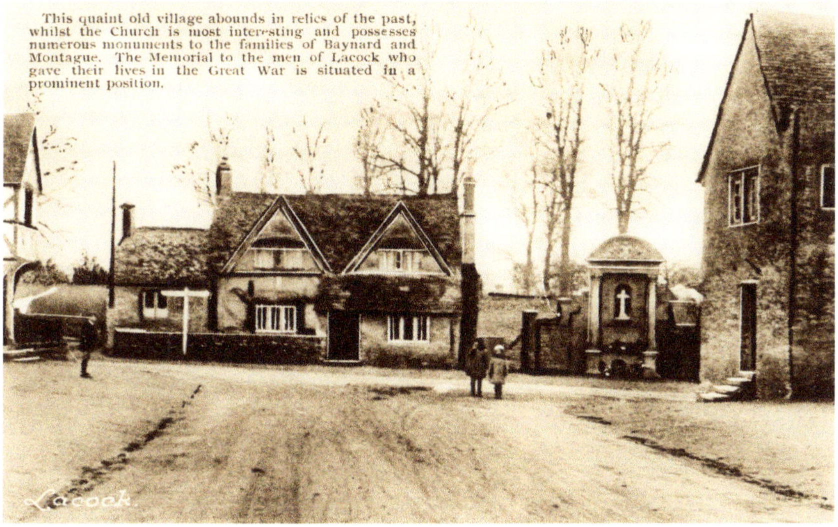

War Memorial

A winter scene with no leaves on the trees and children in warm coats. The caption of this early Edwardian card reads: 'This quaint old village abounds in relics of the past, whilst the church is most interesting and possesses numerous monuments to the families of Baynard and Montague. The memorial to men of Lacock who gave their lives in the Great War is situated in a prominent position'. Those who also gave their lives in the Second World War are remembered. The ladies of Lacock look after the memorial and provide fresh flowers throughout the year. It was unveiled in 1920 by Miss Talbot from Lacock Abbey.

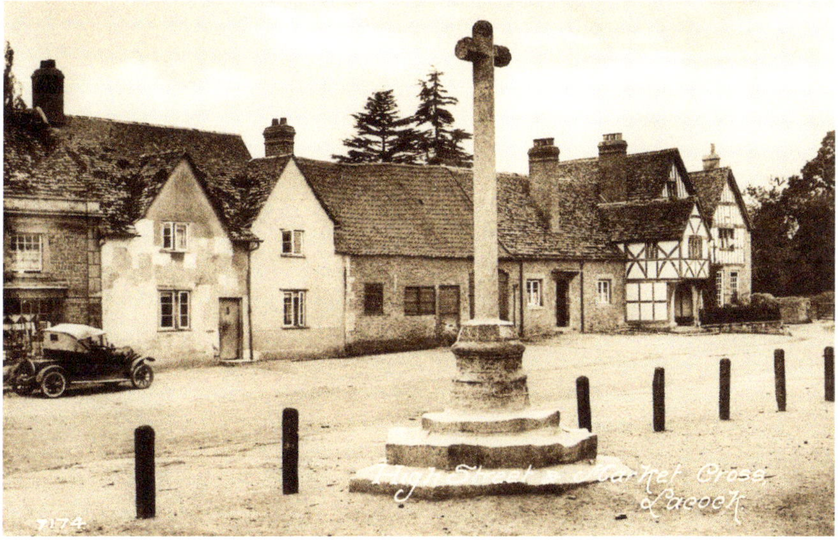

Market Cross

One of the first motor vehicles to appear on a postcard or photograph in the High Street is a convertible with hood parked outside the village stores. This business is still open today from the same premises and incorporates the Post Office. Porch House is clearly visible on the corner of the High Street and road to Melksham. The market cross is the prominent feature here and the posts to the schoolyard have now been replaced by a wall.

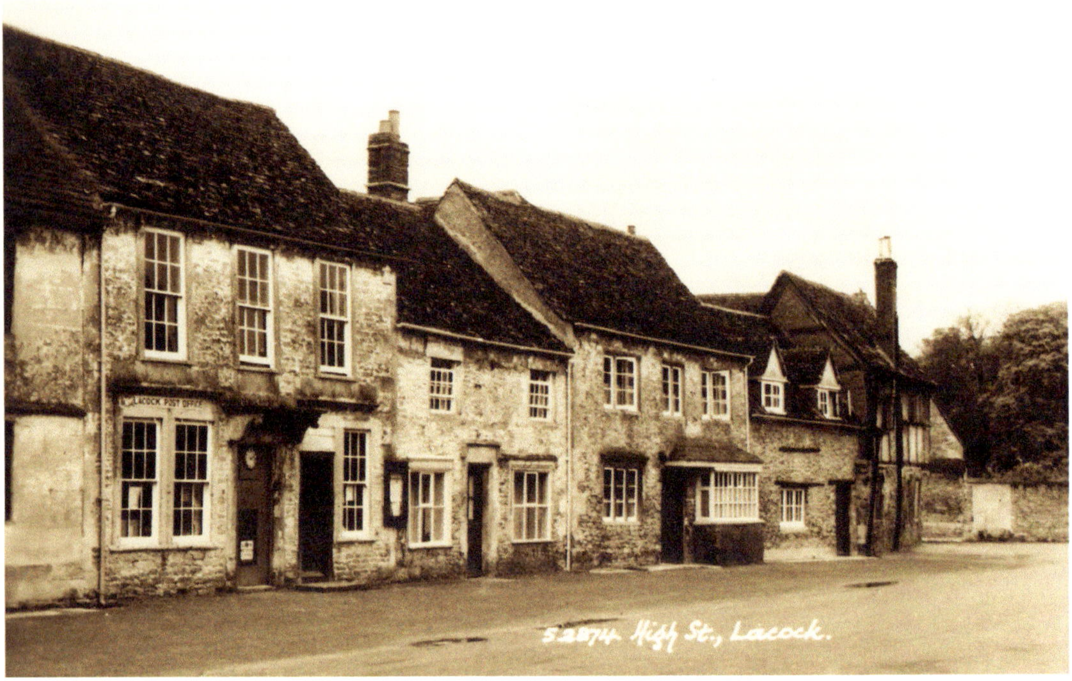

Post Office, Harry Potter in Lacock

Over the years, the Post Office has moved to several different High Street locations. As reported in Kelly's Directory of 1875, it was part of John Austin's drapery store. It is no longer situated in the premises shown on this card with a clock in the door but in the village stores, which is still in business. A gentleman by the name of Harry Potter ran the Post Office from 1927 for around forty years. A directory of 1899 indicates that there were two postal deliveries and three collections a day, with limited Sunday service at that time.

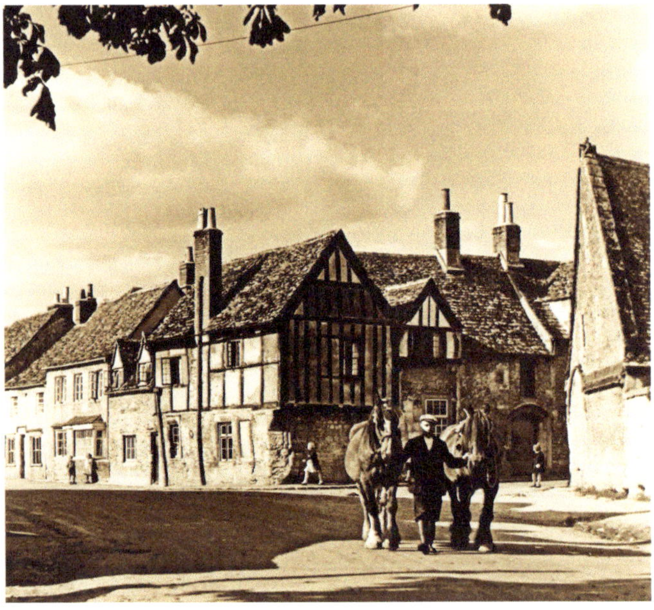

Pair of Working Farm Horses, *c.* 1940s

Often described at the beginning of the twentieth century as a bustling, vibrant working village, then later as quiet, tranquil, unspoilt and peaceful one. The photograph with working horses being led to the nearby farmstead illustrates this. Once again, Lacock is bustling with the many visitors to the abbey, Museum of Photography, church and village. It is also well known for its appearance in many films and on television productions. Virtually all of the houses and buildings are occupied by tenants of the National Trust, although a few remain in private ownership. (WSA2664/2/3F/10/16BW)

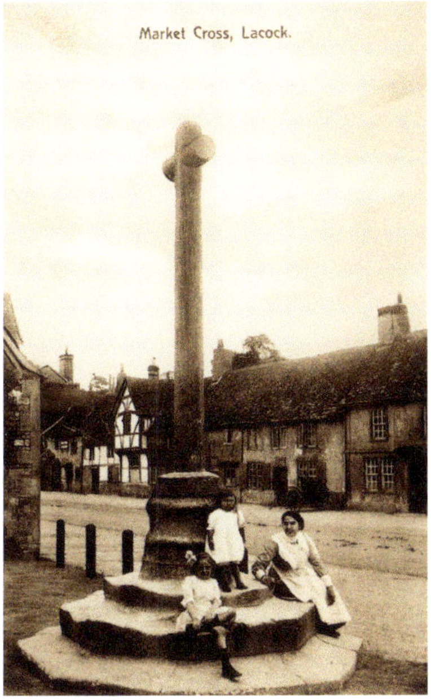

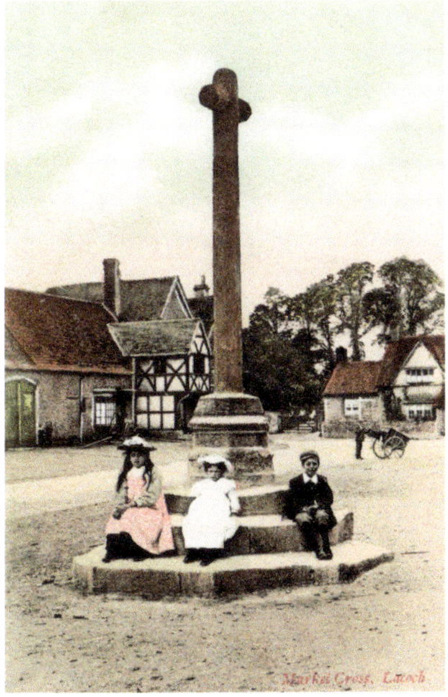

Above left and right: Market Cross

These early Edwardian postcards show the important and prominent medieval stone cross. It is listed for its architectural and historic interest. Originally, it was located in the Market Place in front of St Cyriac's Church in Church Street. Later, in the early 1700s, it was moved to another position outside the Red Lion in the new Market Place, close to the Manor Barn in the High Street. The end of the nineteenth century saw it relocated again, in front of the village school, where it proved popular with the children for playing, climbing and sitting.

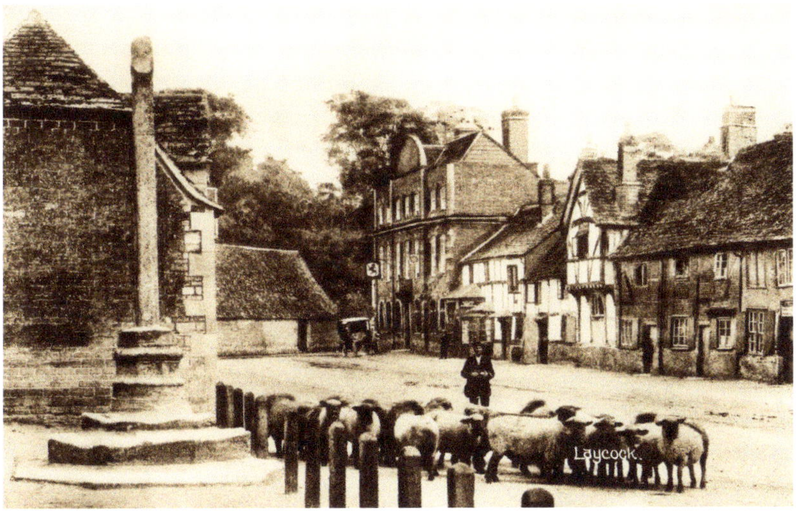

Lacock Spelt with a 'Y'

It was not uncommon for the High Street to be used for the movement of livestock such as sheep, as shown on this Edwardian postcard. The Cross on an octagonal shaft, continues to have considerable significance for the village. It was originally used to make a Market Square where historically rights had been granted to hold regular fairs and markets. In the medieval period, Lacock held both of these.

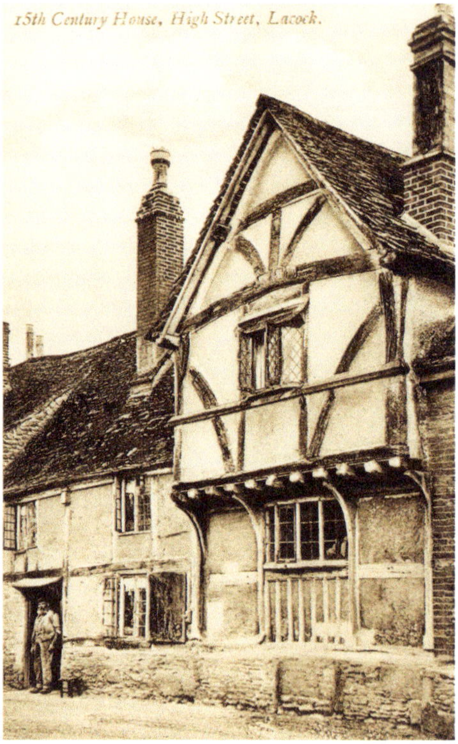

Fifteenth-century Weavers' House

Following the introduction of broad looms in the fifteenth century, weavers' cottages needed more floor area to accommodate them. An enlarged first-floor space was created as a result of cantilevered construction, as shown on this postcard. As early as the thirteenth century Lacock became known for its spinning, weaving and cloth industry. It generally prospered through the years until the time of the 1851 census. This recorded the final decline with just a few hand knitters and weavers remaining.

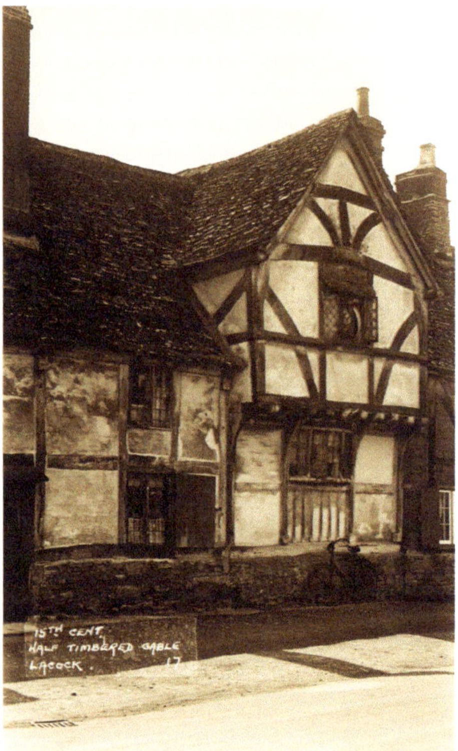

Fifteenth-century, Half-timbered Gable

Another view of this timber-framed weavers' cottage built on a stone base. The geography and geology helped to transform and develop a thriving woollen industry. The village was on the important cloth route from London to Bath, crossing the River Avon at Reybridge. The fertile pastures, flocks of sheep, clear water and availability of 'Fuller's earth' were the ingredients for the trade and all available here. The Avon and its tributaries provided water for scouring and fulling, procedures in woollen cloth making. Reybridge Mill, or an area close to it, was probably used for this purpose.

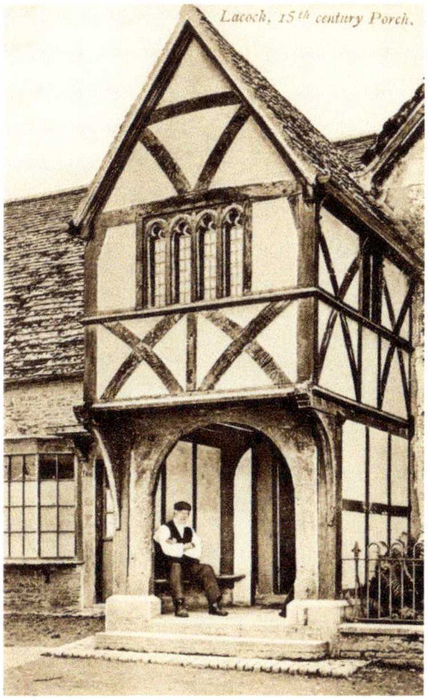

Fifteenth-century Porch

A particularly impressive and highly characterful feature of Porch House. It steps forward in a unique way to break the straight line of the High Street cottages. The distinctive jettied porch is part of an important landmark building on the corner, at the end of the street. On this early Edwardian postcard, by a local Lacock photographer, the occupier, probably the blacksmith, is seated in the porch. In the 1980s, the eastern end was partitioned off to provide a separate cottage.

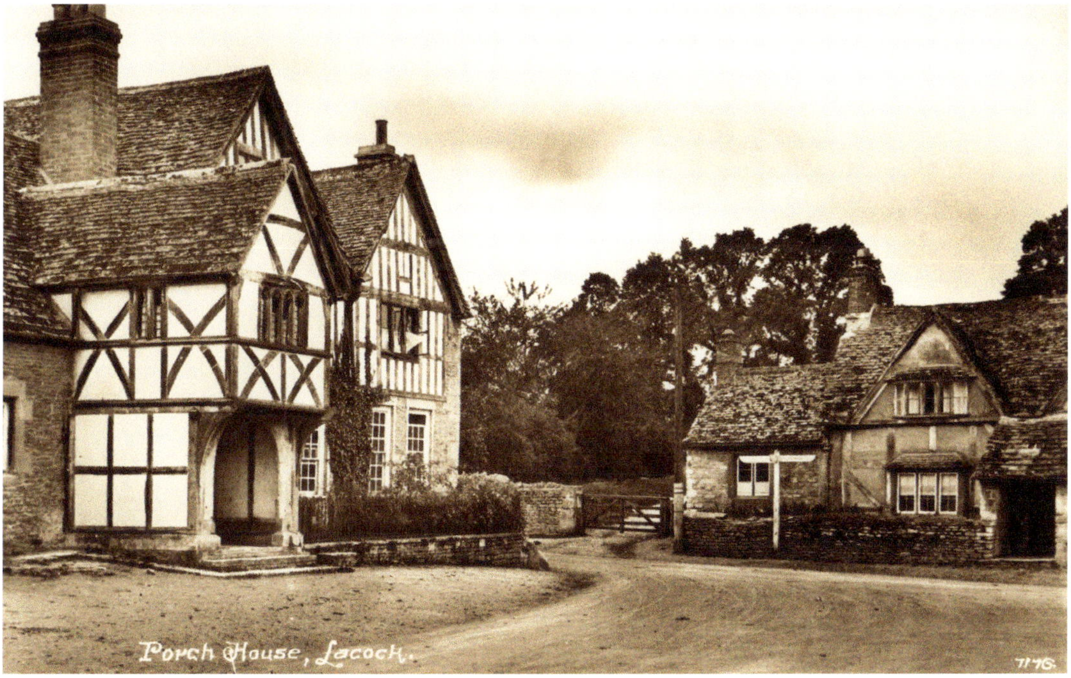

Porch House

Porch House is one of the largest and most important houses. Originally, reputed to date from the fourteenth century with alterations in subsequent centuries, it is Grade II listed. The construction is of timber framework and rubble stone under a stone slate roof. It is one of the finest structures in the village. Old pictures have shown that some of the external timbers were originally plastered over. The house stood on the once-busy corner of the Chippenham to Melksham road until the Lacock bypass was built in 1964. This took the increasing through traffic away from the village.

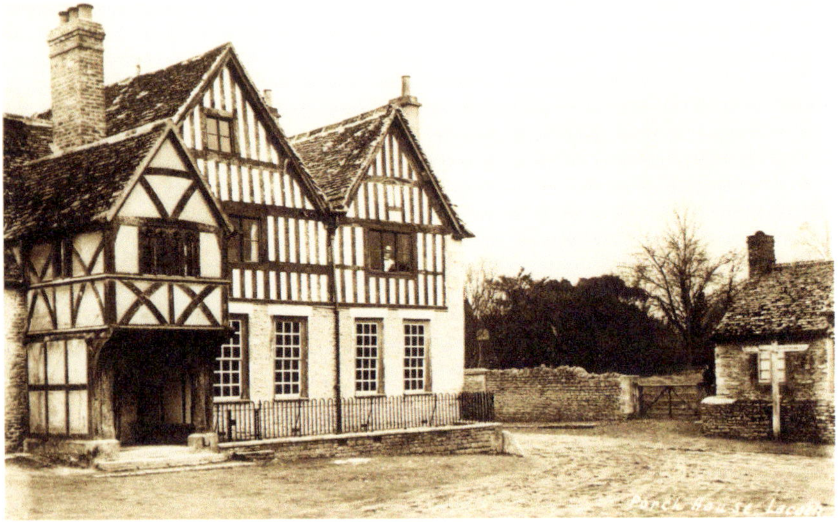

Porch House
Another view of this historic building with a domestic servant clearly visible in a first-floor window. It has belonged to a number of prosperous inhabitants, one being a clothier early in its history. This is suggested by the wide proportions of the rooms to accommodate broadlooms. In the nineteenth century, Porch House was home to a smithy, wheelwrights and nail shop. The long run of railings were ideal to tether customers' horses. Weavers in the village also enjoyed some prosperity and often had the resources to improve their own cottages.

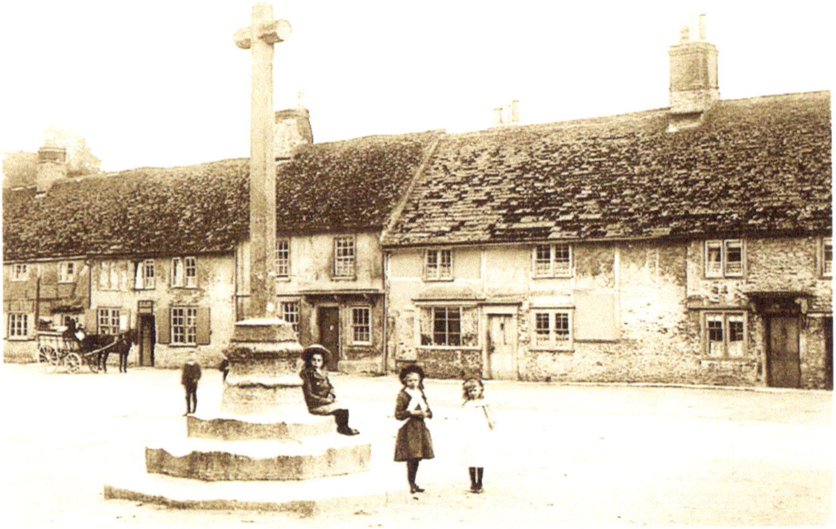

Landscape View, *c.* 1905
Local children pose for the photographer's camera at this popular place. In the past, this row of historic cottages has provided homes for country people, those associated with the woollen industry and the abbey estate. Before travel became more convenient, villagers were restricted to occupations in or close to Lacock. Although steeped in history with ancient buildings of considerable interest, the village is not a museum. Today it is preserved and maintained by the National Trust, who own many of its properties. (Courtesy of Wiltshire and Swindon History Centre)

3
East Street

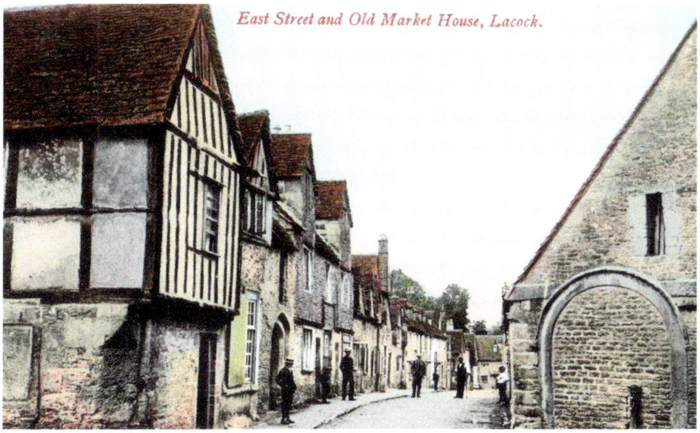

Old Market House

Following construction of the abbey and its various buildings, local inhabitants occupied the cottages. The large medieval barn on the corner of the street has an original arched entrance, now enclosed. It would have played an important part in feudal life. The Market House was the place villagers took produce such as corn, for the benefit of the estate. They were also required to undertake all types of duties, as and when needed. The produce given and work provided was in return for occupancy of a cottage.

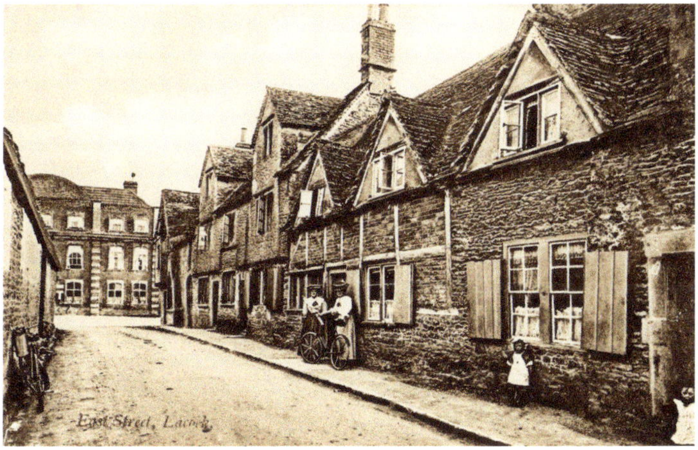

Gabled Cottages

A view taken from Church Street end and looking towards The Red Lion. An early Edwardian card by a local Lacock photographer captures two children in smocks posing for the camera. The two ladies, one with a bicycle, have long skirts and are wearing bonnets. They stand in front of the only cottage in the street with a timber frame and brick in-fill elevation. The wooden shutters have now been removed.

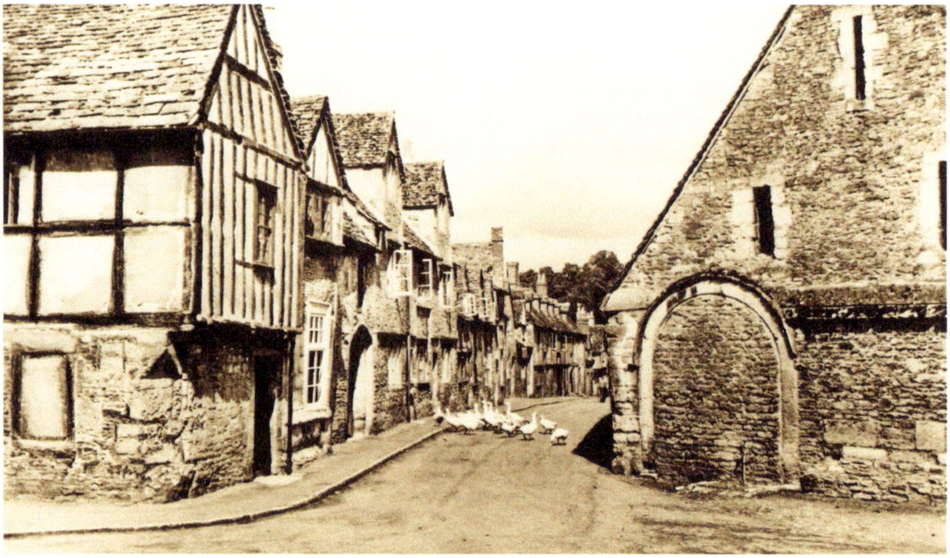

Flock of Geese

Several families have lived in Lacock for many generations and contribute to its unspoilt and continued survival, which helps to maintain its past heritage into the future. The village was not affected by the Victorian period of industrialisation. In consequence, the large stock of historic buildings, dating from the thirteenth to eighteenth centuries, remain virtually intact. This card provides a far-reaching view towards Church Street.

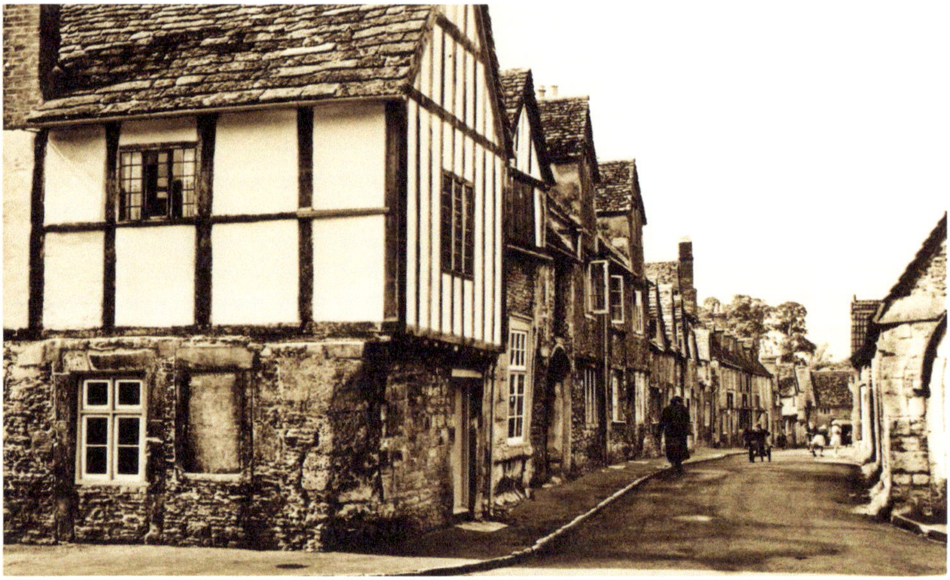

Chamberlain's House

A close-up view of the imposing, timbered building probably once occupied by the abbey chamberlain. In 1811, a nationwide census was conducted and it was recorded that there were 280 houses in Lacock occupied by 295 families. Namely, 130 families in agriculture whilst 154 were engaged in trade or manufacturing. This included leather workers, carpenters, wheelwrights, tailors and small tradesmen. Due to the widespread depression numerous people were without work.

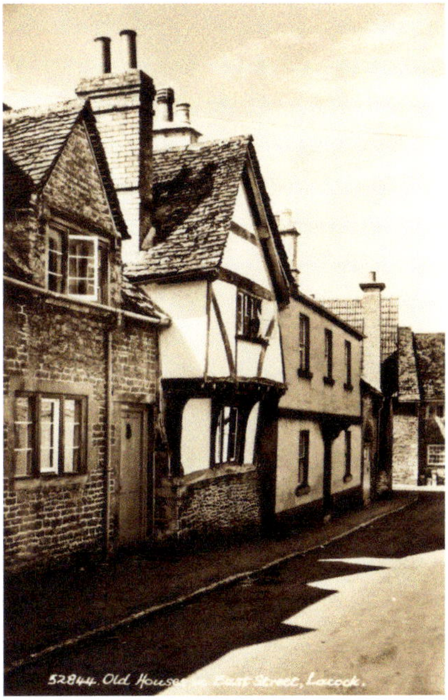

Jettied Weavers' Cottage

This property with splendid architectural features, like its neighbours, is Grade II listed for its special importance. However, by 1817, over 150 people in the village were receiving regular parish benefit and even more were obtaining occasional benefits. In 1810, an Act abolished the necessity for paupers to wear 'L. P.' badges (Lacock Paupers) but the local paymaster wanted this to continue. Conditions were harsh during this period and by 1831 the population had actually fallen. To reduce unemployment, twenty villagers were subsidised by several prosperous locals, to emigrate to Quebec.

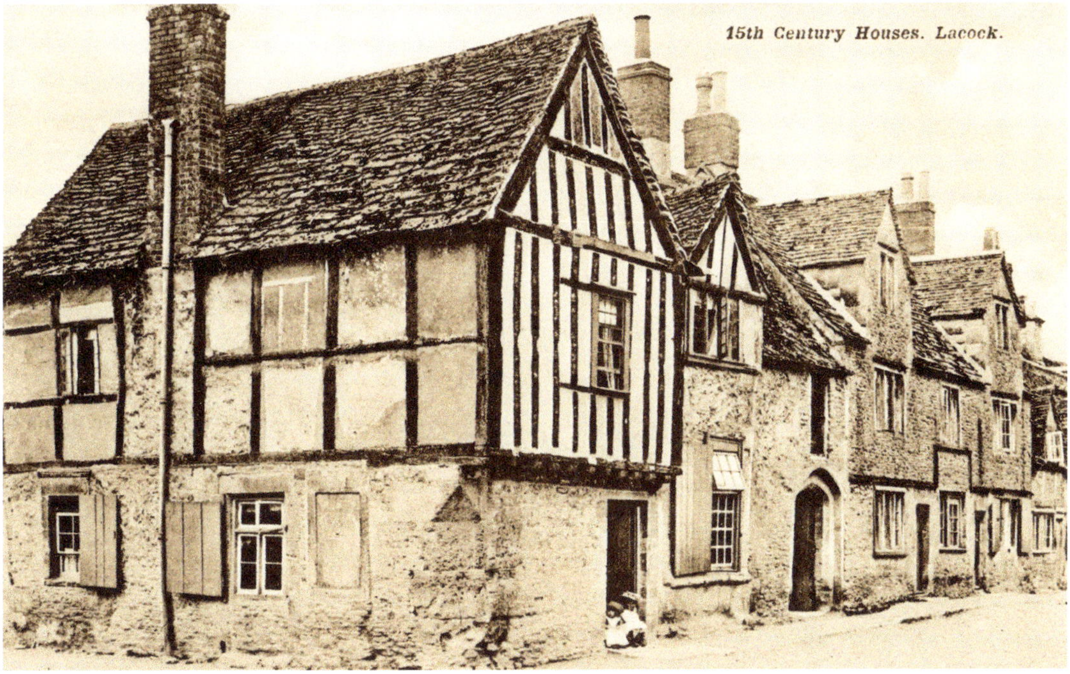

Different Styles

Local Lacock photographer captures two small children sitting in the doorway of Chamberlain's House on this early Edwardian card. The delightful street scene includes two- and three-storey listed cottages, virtually all with stone elevations. Some have attics, extensive cellars, dormers and unusual features. Those with different floor levels have steps for access to accommodate the incline. Between the 'lock-up' and Village Hall is a historic open space. It is now a lovingly maintained true cottage garden.

LOT 19

(Coloured Yellow on Plan).

The Substantial Stone-built Butcher's Shop, Dwelling House, Yard and Slaughter House

Situate in East (or Middle) Street, Lacock, and numbered Part 325 on Ordnance Plan.

THE SHOP

is very light with good window and l
board office.

THI

contains a Living Room, good Sitti
There is a well with pump in the Wasl

with gate to roadway containing Tw

S:

with drained stone floor. This build
Co.'s Mains connected thereto. At t

Let to Mrs. Austin on a yearly tenar

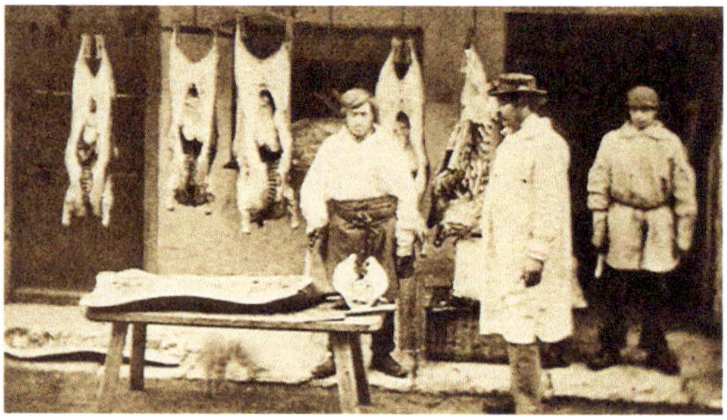

19

Former Butcher's Shop

The brief auction particulars for this property. It was last sold in the late 1970s and is now Watling Goldsmiths. When sold in 1927 it was advertised as 'substantially stone built butchers' shop, dwelling house, yard and slaughterhouse'. The description continued with 'the shop is very bright with good window and has been modernised. There is a stone floor and matchboard office. The dwelling house contains a living room, good sitting room, washhouse, refrigerator house and larder. There is a well pump in the washhouse. Above are four good bedrooms, yard with gate to roadway containing two stall stable, open cart shed with loft over. Slaughterhouse with drained stone floor and fully licensed.' (WSA1409/15/243) *Inset*: Lacock butchers, *c.* 1900. (© National Trust/Rachel Topham)

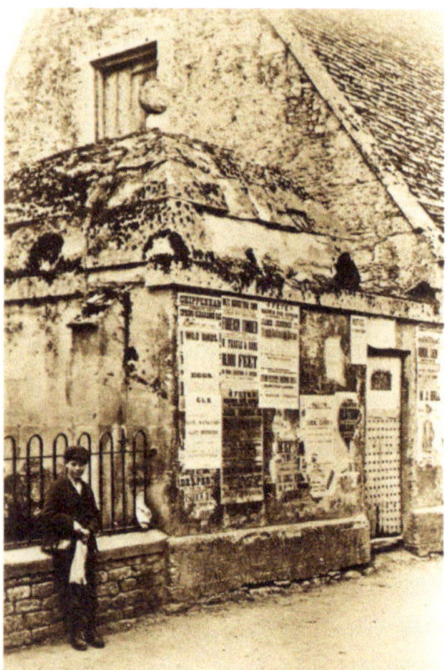

Eighteenth-century Lock-up

As can be seen here on this *c.* 1905 photograph, the lock-up has been in use for bill posting. One of these reads: 'Fete, Monkton Park, Chippenham, James Jennings steam galloping horses.' It was a small but sturdy stone building with domed roof used for the short-term detention of local rogues and drunks, usually overnight. They were either released or held to be put before the local magistrate. The listed building has a heavy nailed wooden door with light and ventilation provided by grilles. It was also called the blind-house for lack of any windows. It is rumoured that when dancing bears performed in the village and their handlers got drunk, both were incarcerated here overnight. (WSA3476/1/191BW)

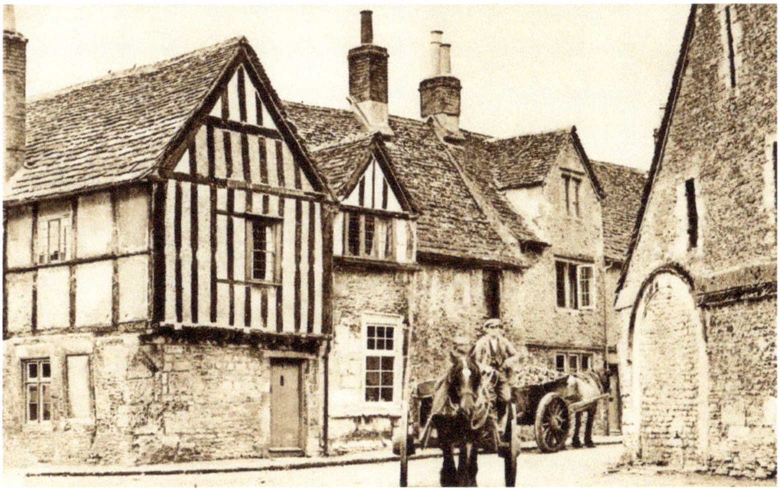

Village Corner

This image shows two farm carts, one loaded with fodder outside Manor Barn. Farming has always been an important part of the village life and scenes such as this were once common. Until fairly recently, the barn was let with the Manor Farm and used for storage. The early timbered Chamberlain's House would have been occupied by a prosperous or influential resident such as the abbey chamberlain.

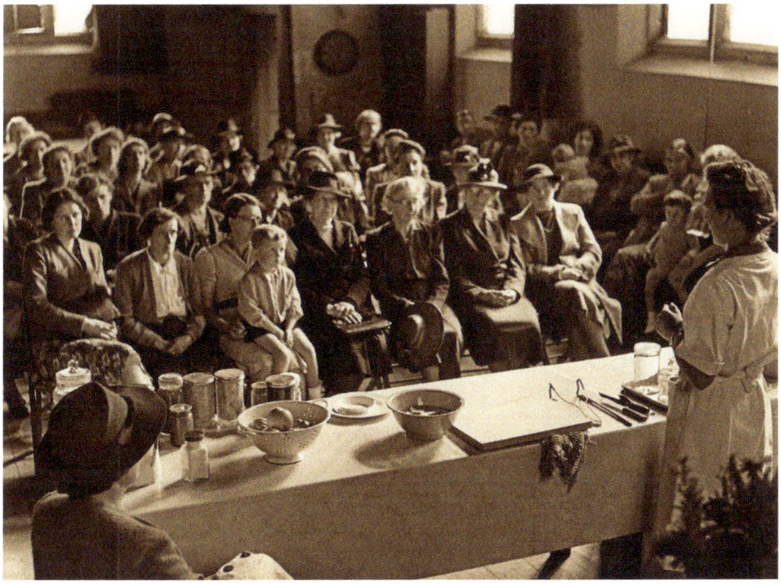

Cookery Demonstration, *c.* 1945

Women's Institute meeting in the village hall. The group was founded in 1919 by Matilda Talbot of Lacock Abbey, where originally the monthly meetings were held. These were well supported by local villagers and eventually the venue was moved to the village hall, where meetings are still conducted. Matilda Talbot remained president until around 1950 and cookery demonstrations were always popular, as this photograph illustrates. The organisation was initially started in 1915 to revitalise rural communities and encouraged food to be produced during the First World War. (WSA2664/2/3F/10/45BW)

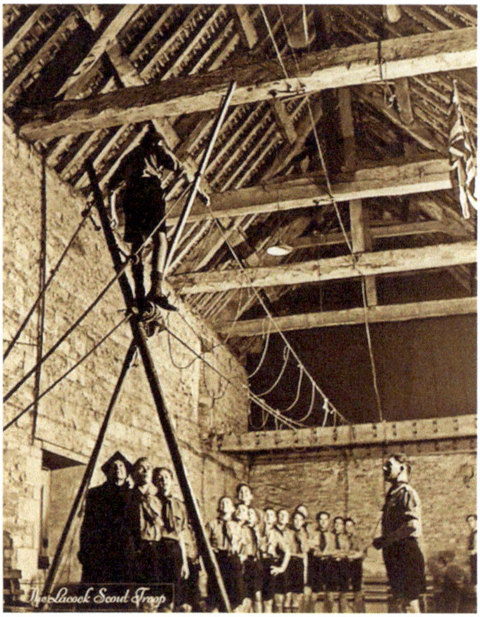

Lacock Scout Troop, *c.* 1940s

Manor Barn, a most important and remarkable building, was once the meeting place for the Scouts. This photograph shows that it provided an ideal venue for a challenging exercise. The troop, established over 100 years ago, now meet in the village hall, originally built in 1889 as the Oddfellows Hall. This remarkable, virtually intact, medieval barn dates from the fourteenth century and is Grade I listed. The substantial construction is of rubble limestone, cruck beams, earth floor and stone slate roof. In the 1970s an appeal was made for funds to assist with urgent repairs so that the building could be opened to the public. (WSA/X3/164/8)

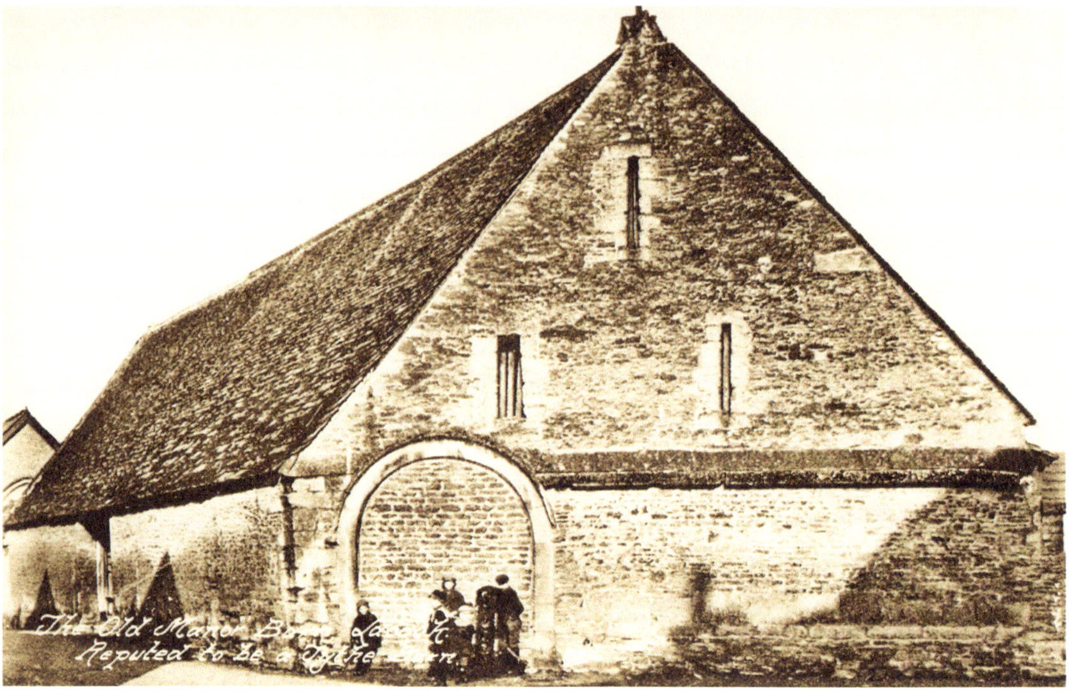

Manor Barn

A Lacock photographer capturing the size of the building includes in the caption on this early Edwardian postcard 'reputed to be a Tythe Barn'. Being part of Lacock Abbey Estate, it was probably used for the collection and storage of tythes. Since this time, it has been used for various agricultural and social purposes. It has also featured in television and film productions. The card shows a group of children around a water pump in front of a former entrance. There were several village pumps before each cottage had its own water supply.

4
Church Street

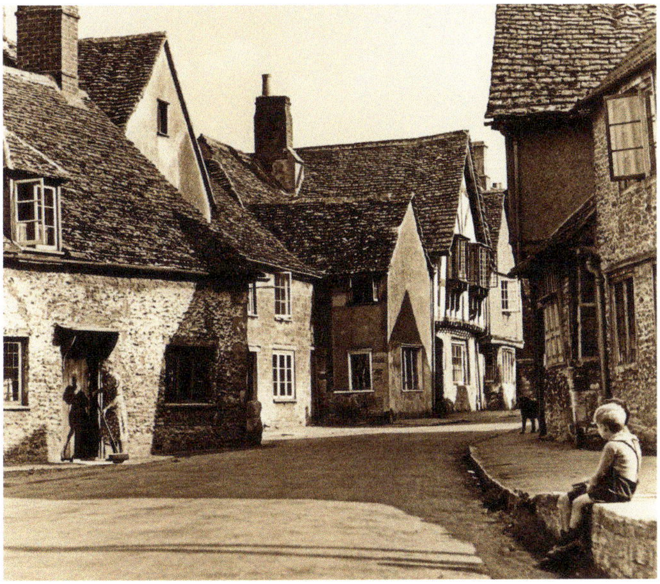

Peaceful Scene, *c.* 1940s
This photograph provides a tranquil view looking east. It is taken from the wide entrance on the corner, leading to St Cyriac's Church. A small boy sits on the edge of the raised pavement, known locally as 'the brash'. Opposite, a woman sweeps outside the cottage which is now well known for its large, exposed cruck beam on the east elevation. (WSA2664/2/3F/10/36BW)

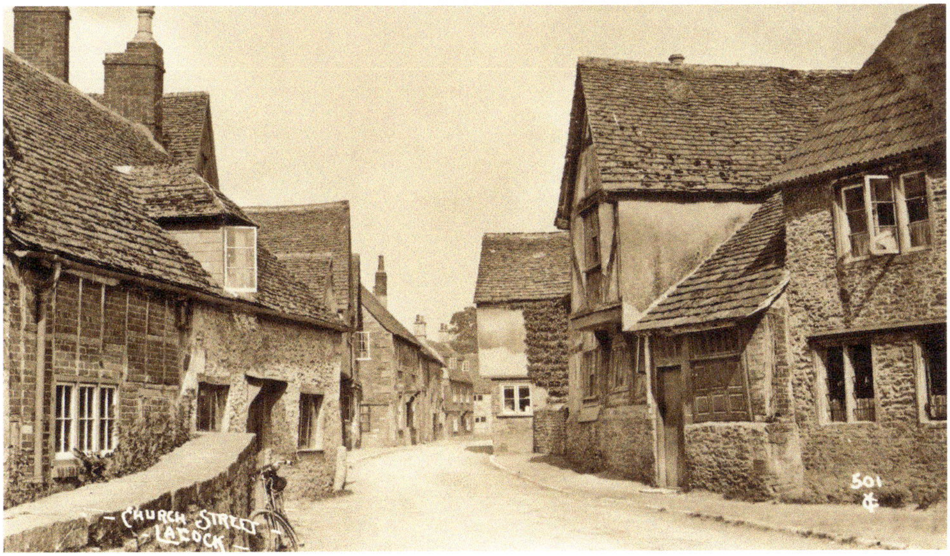

Empty Street
This street comprises historic listed buildings of many styles with dormers and gables. They are well represented on this early Edwardian photographic postcard. A bicycle leans against the stone wall. This picture was taken before the intrusion of numerous motor vehicles. It provides an uninterrupted view that can be fully appreciated along this quiet street.

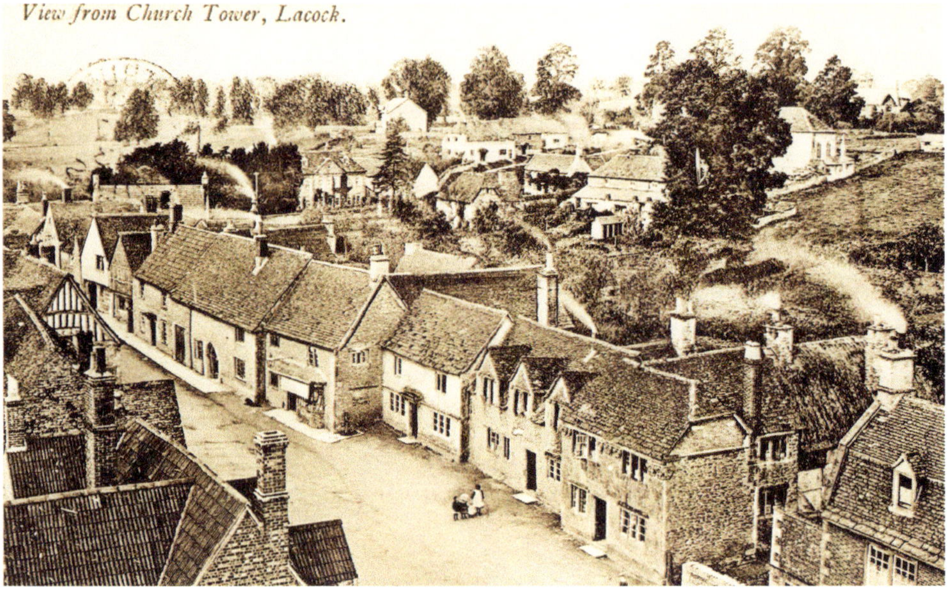

Aerial View

Taken from the church tower by a local photographer, a panoramic view of much interest is produced. Postally used in 1913, the postcard offers a rare sight of the village, looking towards the north-west. A close inspection reveals the stores, 'Sign of the Angel', Cantax House on the road out of the village and the rear of the chapel. The latter adjoins open land and is in the top right-hand corner. All of these properties are still here today, although the chapel is now a private house.

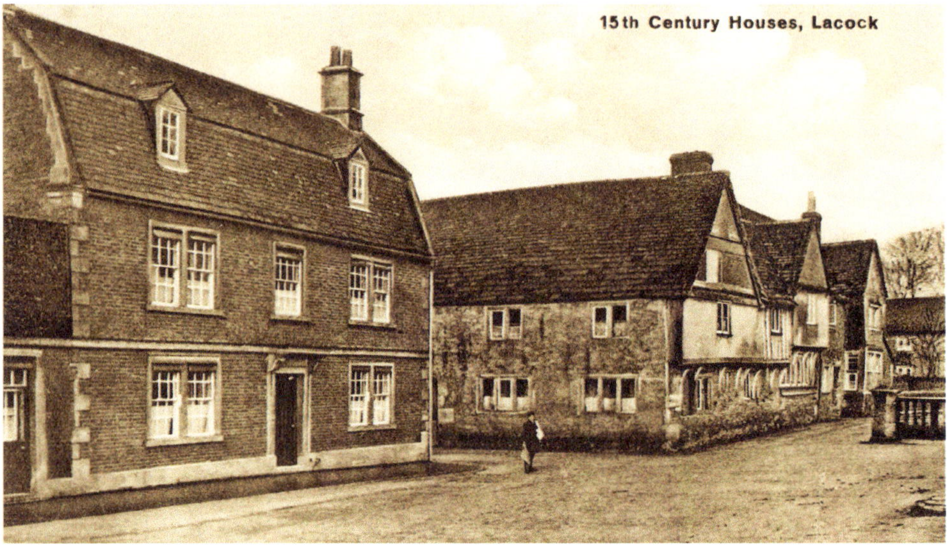

The Red House

Unusual for the village is this red-brick façade that provides part of the name for the property. It is located on a corner adjoining the lane leading to Pack Horse Bridge, Nethercote Hill and Lovers' Lane. The building is dated 1778, is Grade II listed and was extended in the 1920s. Unlike many of the houses in Lacock, which have stone slate roof coverings, this one has a plain tiled mansard roof with gabled dormers. The wide part of the street shown here was where the market was once held.

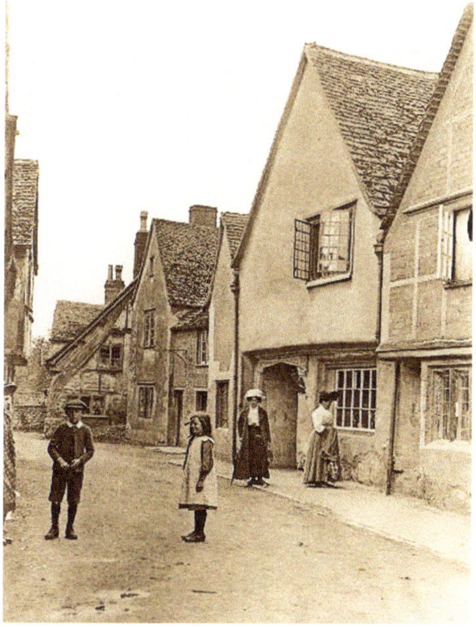

Renowned Property, *c.* 1905

The medieval property has an exceptionally fine frontage, shown here as being part rendered and with a single first-floor window to the entrance section. It was built *c.* 1480 with timber framing and jettied, with rubble stone beneath a stone slate roof. It was probably an inn originally and later converted into a wool merchant's house when the trade flourished. At some period, it was a public house and then went into private use for several decades. In 1911, it was recorded as being a shop and by 1939 was that of a guest house and tea gardens. It is now 'Sign of the Angel', once again providing food and accommodation. (Courtesy Wiltshire and Swindon History Centre)

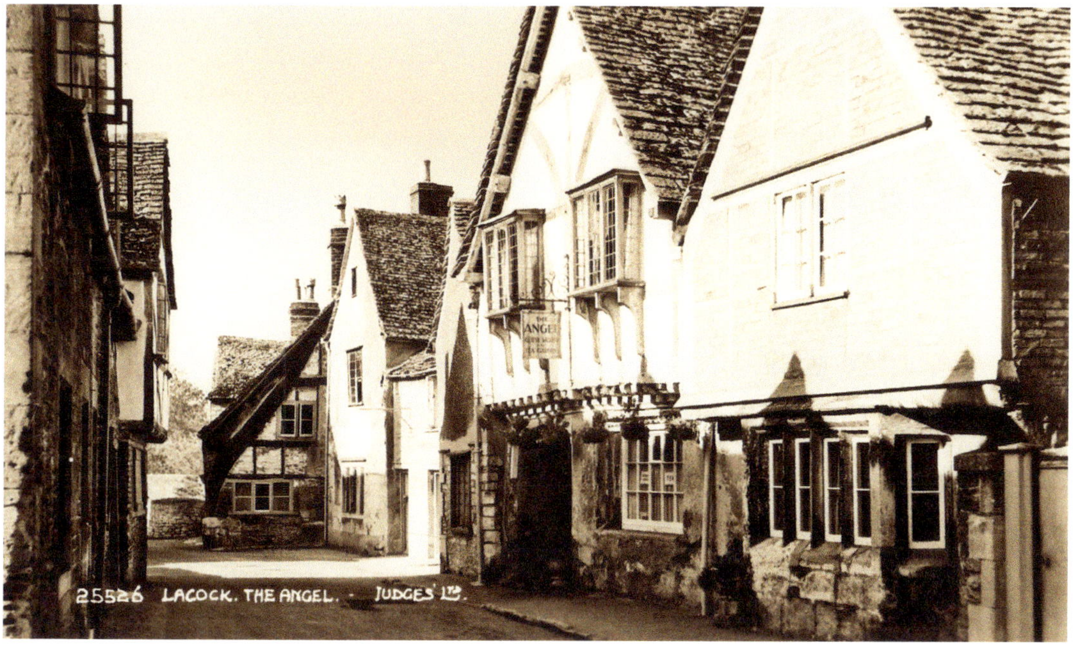

The Angel

It is interesting to note that there are now two first-floor windows over the entrance section; render has been removed and historic timbers revealed. In the early twentieth century the Poor Law was administered from here. This important listed building has many internal features including a Tudor arched fireplace, panelling and a wealth of historic timbers. The name comes from the English gold coin called 'an angel' introduced by Edward IV in 1465, which was in circulation at the time the property became an inn. The Babberton Arms sign was hung outside the Angel for the filming of a scene in *Harry Potter and the Half Blood Prince*.

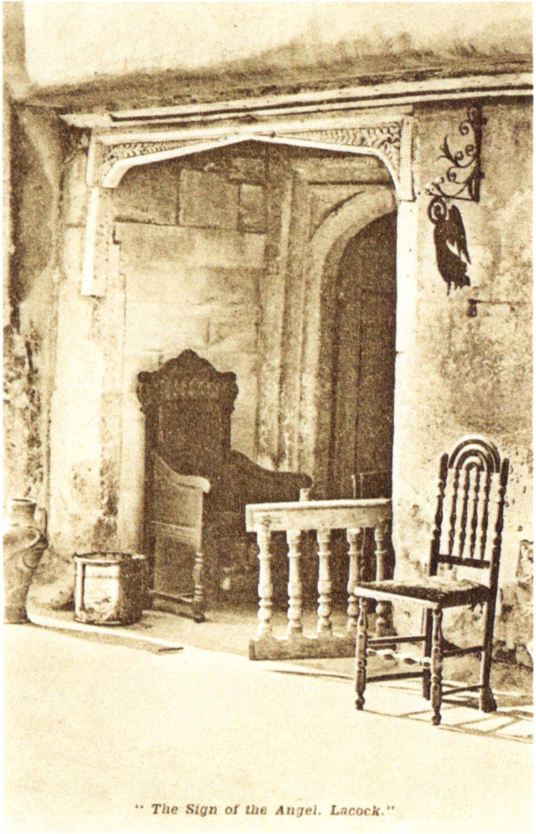

Tudor Entrance

In the early part of the twentieth century, a Lacock photographer produced this unusual view of the entrance to the 'Sign of the Angel', with various chattels displayed. The intricate carved Tudor stone frame is visible, as is an angel hanging from a wall bracket. There is a door from this recess leading to the front room on the right. The entrance and integral passage provides a reasonably wide access to the rear where no other existed. Horses were stabled at the back when the property was a coaching inn.

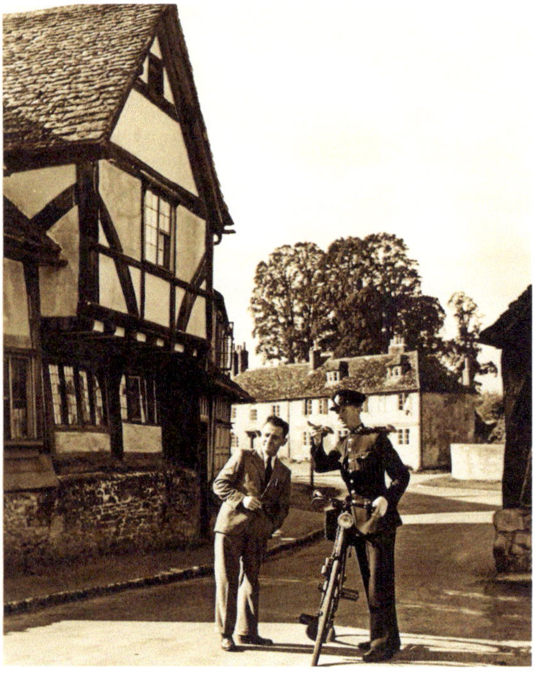

Policeman on the Corner, *c.* 1940s

At one time, like many villages, Lacock had its own resident police officer with a police house provided. He was well respected in the community and is seen here with his bicycle, giving directions. The photograph also provides a close-up view of a medieval jettied timber-framed weaver's cottage and the corner of the Cruck House. (WSA2664/2/3F/10/19BW)

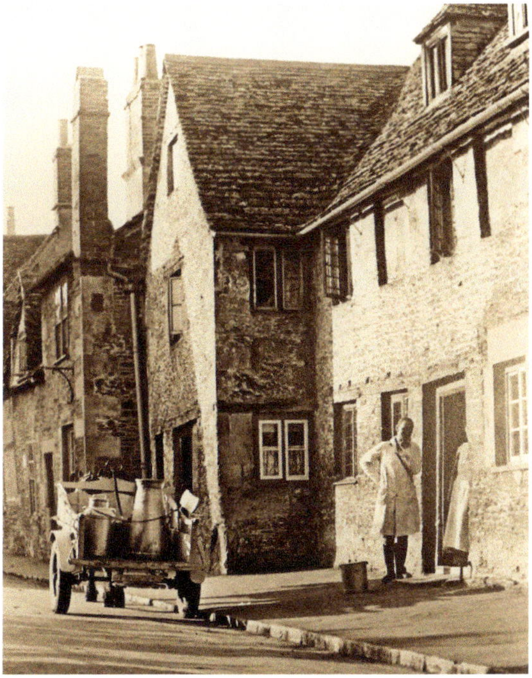

Delivering Milk, *c.* 1945

Before glass milk bottles were readily available the local milkman/farmer would take metal churns on the round, as seen in this photograph. In Church Street he stops to talk to a customer, in a more leisurely era. Customers' containers could be filled and charged for by dipping a measure into the churn. The horse-and-cart delivery system was later replaced by battery electric vehicles known as 'milk floats'. Lacock residents without transport relied on doorstop deliveries. (WSA2664/2/3F/10/4BW)

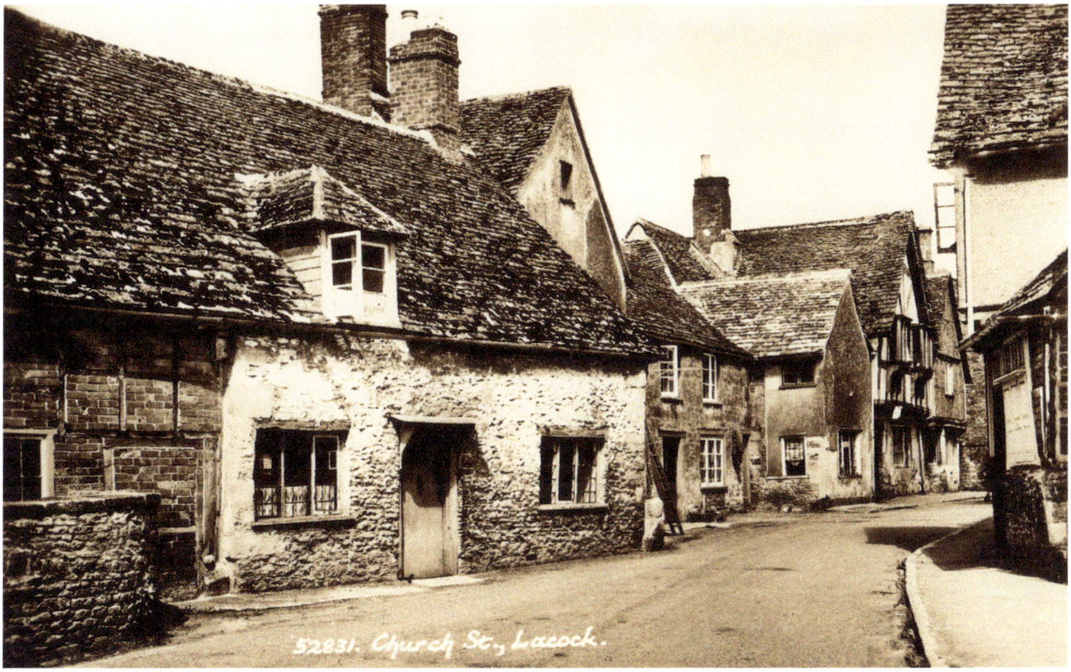

Cruck House

A close-up view of this small, well-known listed Grade II cottage, probably built in the fourteenth century and refronted in the eighteenth century, of rubble stone with stone slated roof. Part of the end cruck is clearly exposed on the east elevation. It provides a strong and important visual feature when looking down the street from the church end.

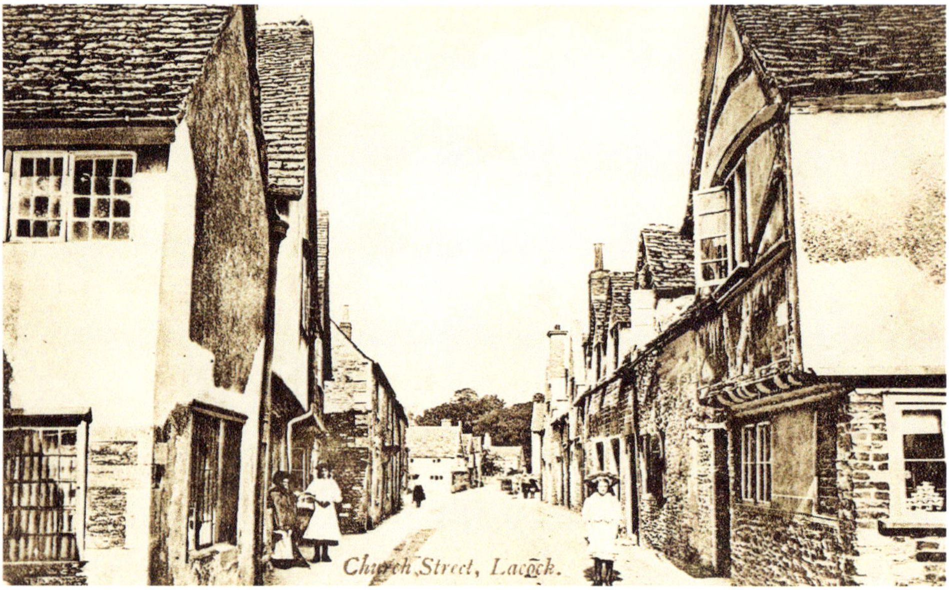

View looking East, *c.* 1904

The *Survey Gazetteer of the British Isles* dated 1904 describes Lacock as 'parish and village, Wilts, on River Avon, three miles South West of Chippenham, 3734 acres, population 1159, Post Office, Telegraph Office. The seat called Laycock Abbey was the residence of W. H. Fox Talbot (1880–1877), the inventor of the Talbotype process of photography, the Abbey was founded as an Augustinian Nunnery in 1232 and still retains many of its monastic features'.

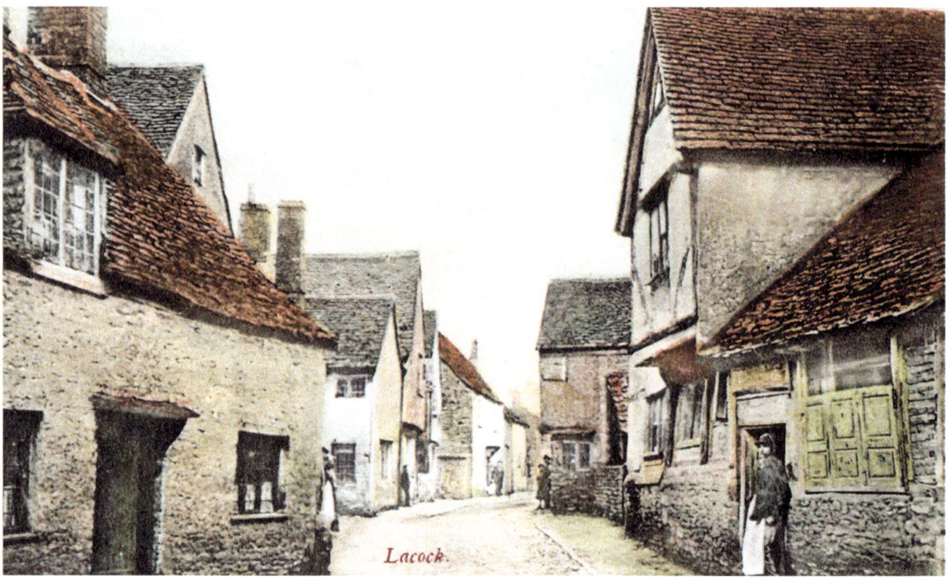

Village Shops

A postcard sent in 1906 looks east from Cruck House. Rumour has it that one of the occupiers of this property kept a fattening pig under the stairs. Before refuse collections, rubbish was often just thrown out into the street, ideal for a scavenging pig. Once fat, the animal was slaughtered, meat salted down and hung from the ceiling.

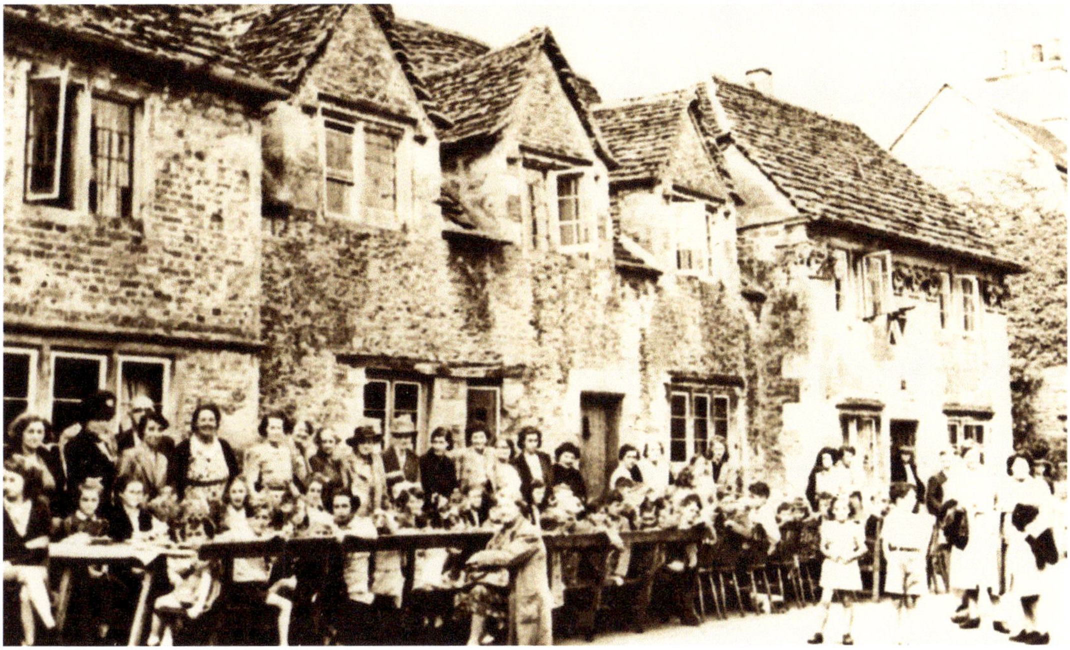

Peace Celebrations, 1945

Two street parties were held in Church Square in May and August. They were to celebrate the end of the Second World War and the war in Asia. Children from the village are seated at long tables and their mothers stand behind, all posing for the camera. Millennium and other celebrations have been held in the village since this time. (WSA3476/1/191)

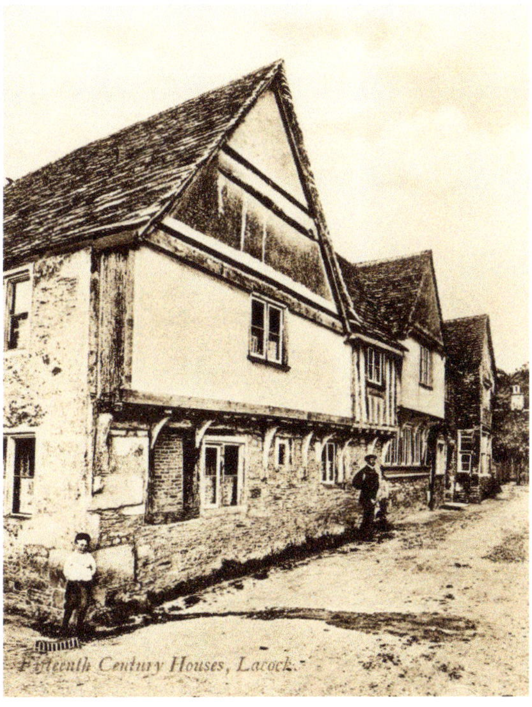

Poor House

An early Edwardian postcard provides a close-up view of this impressive corner-sited house, situated opposite St Cyriac's Church. It was built in the fifteenth century and altered in the seventeenth, when a stone fireplace and pigeon loft were added. The construction is of timber frame and rubble stone beneath a stone slate roof. It has a jettied first floor and is likely to have had non-domestic use during stages of its life. The former Poor House is listed Grade II. Since this photograph was taken render has been removed from the south elevation to expose a wealth of timbers.

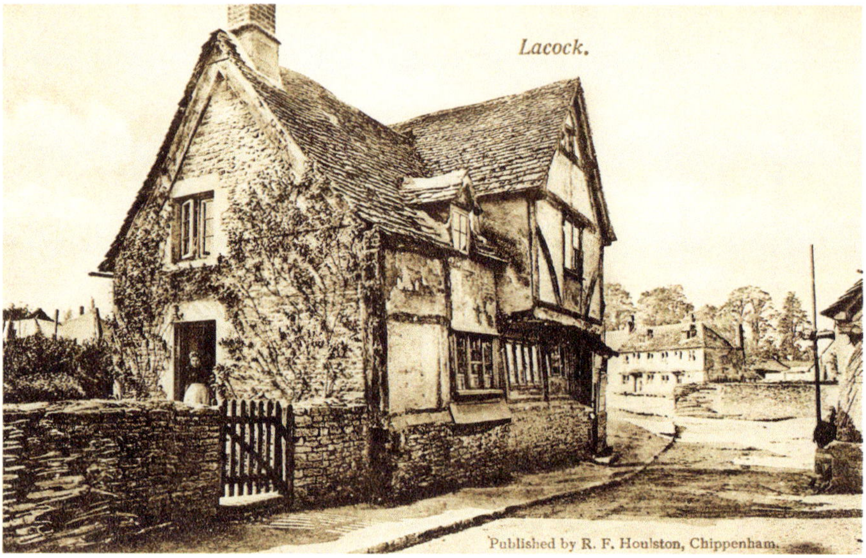

Decorative Detailing

A local photographer captures a lady standing in the doorway of the prominent late medieval Grade II listed property. This early Edwardian postcard illustrates well another Lacock jettied house. Built of timber frame on a limestone rubble plinth, the attractive elevations are beneath a stone slate roof. The house has a garden wall and gate on east side, a rare feature. In the village, virtually all the other gardens are to the rear of the cottages.

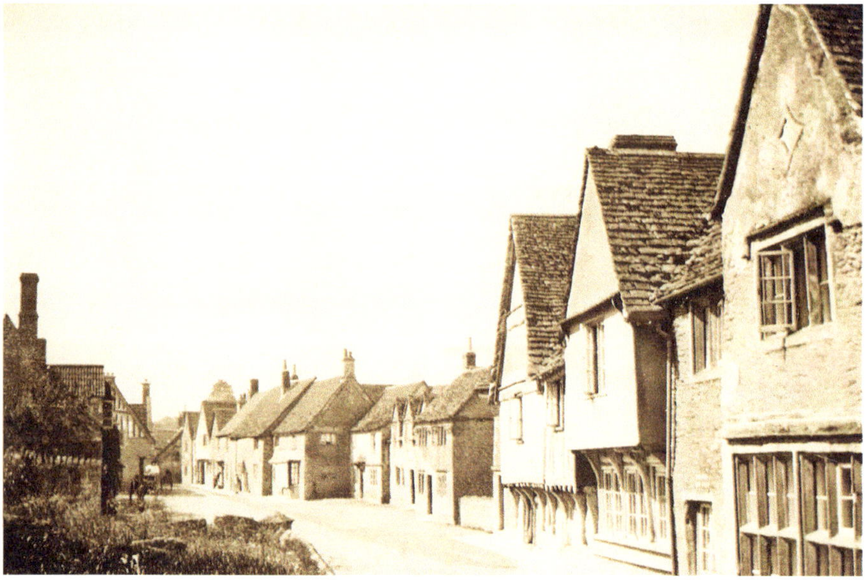

Storey to Tell

Interestingly, this photographic postcard looking west from St Cyriac's Church was either personally taken to New Zealand or sent in an envelope, on the long sea voyage. Typically, this would have lasted over one month. It was then sent internally from Palmerston North to Ashurst in 1905. The writer has identified the view by writing on the front side 'Lacock, Wilts, England'. This unusual and rarely produced scene is not the most recognisable.

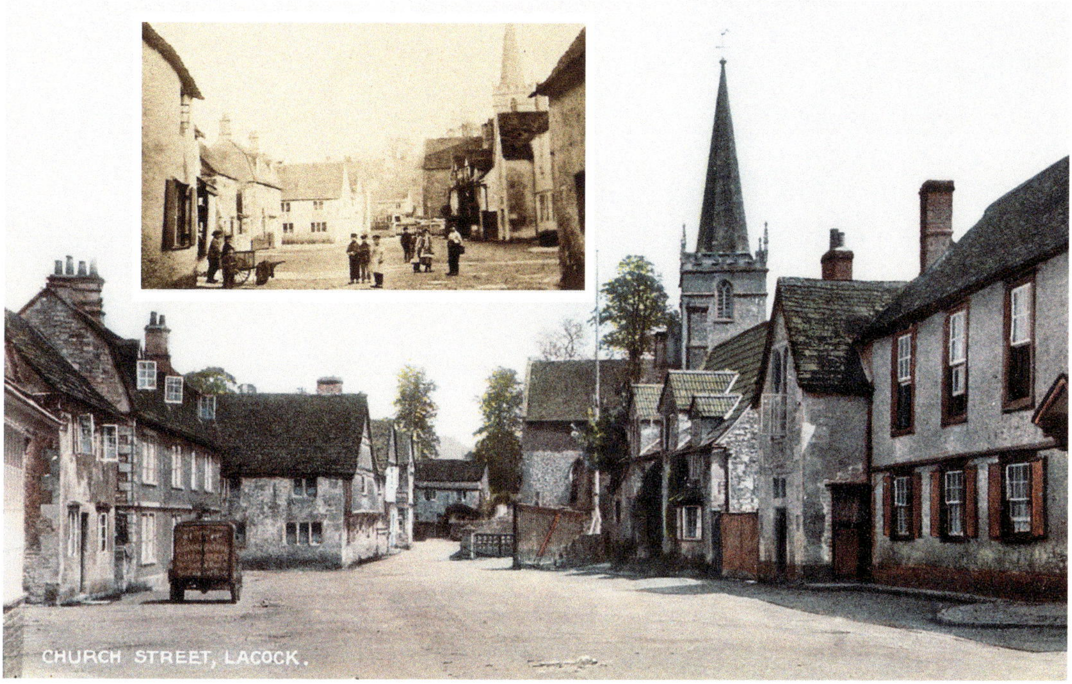

Church Square

Another view showing a former workhouse on the corner. In the past there were several of these institutions in the village. From the sixteenth century, a property at the west side of the churchyard was used by the parish as a workhouse. It was to provide poor people with a reasonable household in return for a day's work. The building with three gables, on the right side before the church, is King John's Hunting Lodge. It is one of the oldest properties in the village with parts of the structure surviving from the thirteenth century. *Inset*: Children with handcart, *c*. 1900. (© National Trust/Rachel Topham)

Cobbler, *c*. 1940s

People passing down this Lacock street could look in through an open window and see boots and shoes being repaired, using the traditional 'last' and hammer. The cobbler would replace soles, heels and make good damaged waterproofing. He was also classified in the 1939 Kelly's Directory as a boot and shoe dealer. Known locally as a radio and television repairman, his skills included replacement of valves, tubes and other components. It is interesting to note that the number of combined television and radio licences when introduced in 1947 amounted to only around 14,500 being issued. Now virtually all the population have a radio and television. (WSA2664/2/3F/10/63BW)

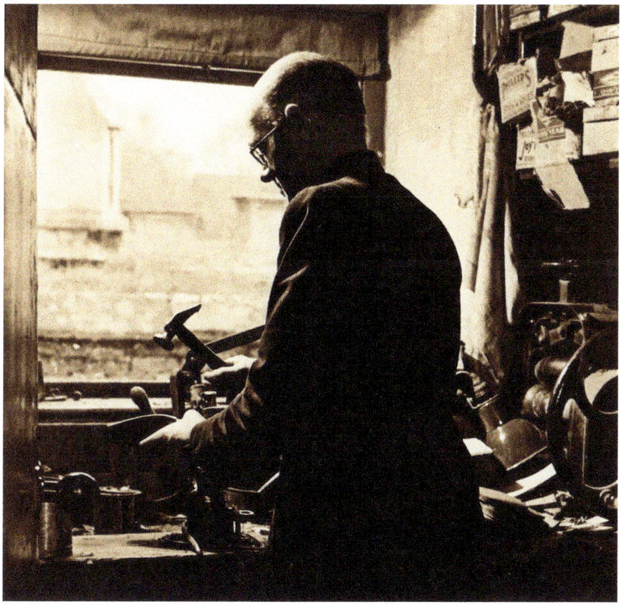

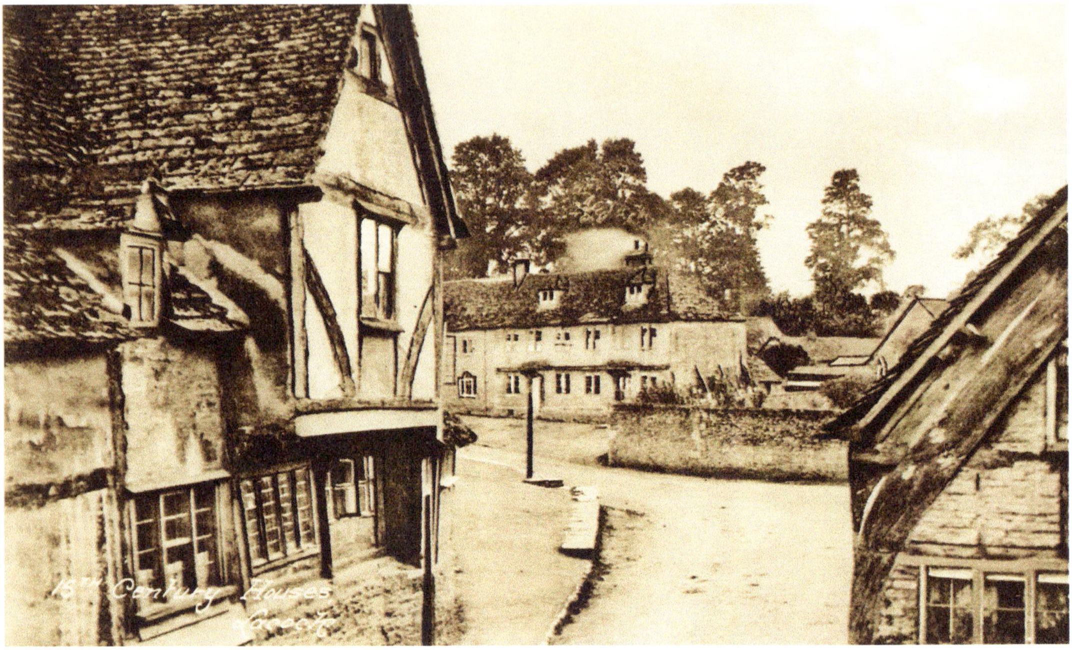

Fifteenth-century Houses

The view from a higher level illustrates historic timbering and a view into West Street and beyond. Timber frame was a popular and relatively easy form of early construction in the development of the village. The oak timbers would normally be worked when newly cut and still 'green', being easier to use. Oak is sturdy and durable with resilient qualities, as is proven by the buildings still here today.

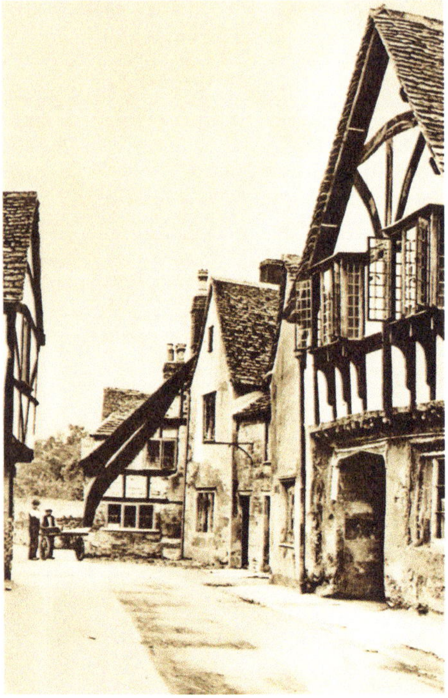

Timber Construction

As Lacock was once on the edge of a vast forest – timber and the supply of oak as a building material plentiful – 'cruck' construction was introduced. An impressive example of this is the small roadside cottage illustrated here, with two villagers and handcart outside. This postcard is only one of a few produced at the time that refers to W. H. Fox Talbot who was, in fact, born in Dorset and in 1826 moved into Lacock Abbey. Known as 'Father of Photography', he helped to make Lacock an important place to visit.

Grocery Store, *c.* 1940s

A more leisurely time in Lacock with customer seated at the counter, probably catching up on local news. Attractive period shop fittings include display shelving, small drawers and a variety of goods on sale. The shop is now the Lacock Bakery and personal service continues. From once being a bustling working village with many shops providing a wide range of goods, these have mostly disappeared. Unlike many villages, it is, however, pleasing that several still remain today. (WSA2664/2/3F/10/51BW)

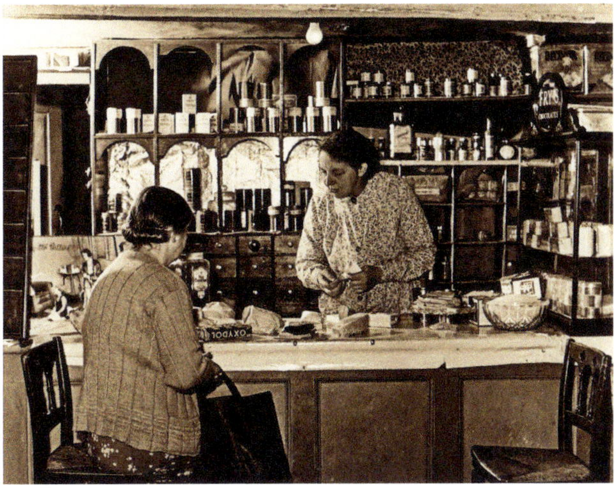

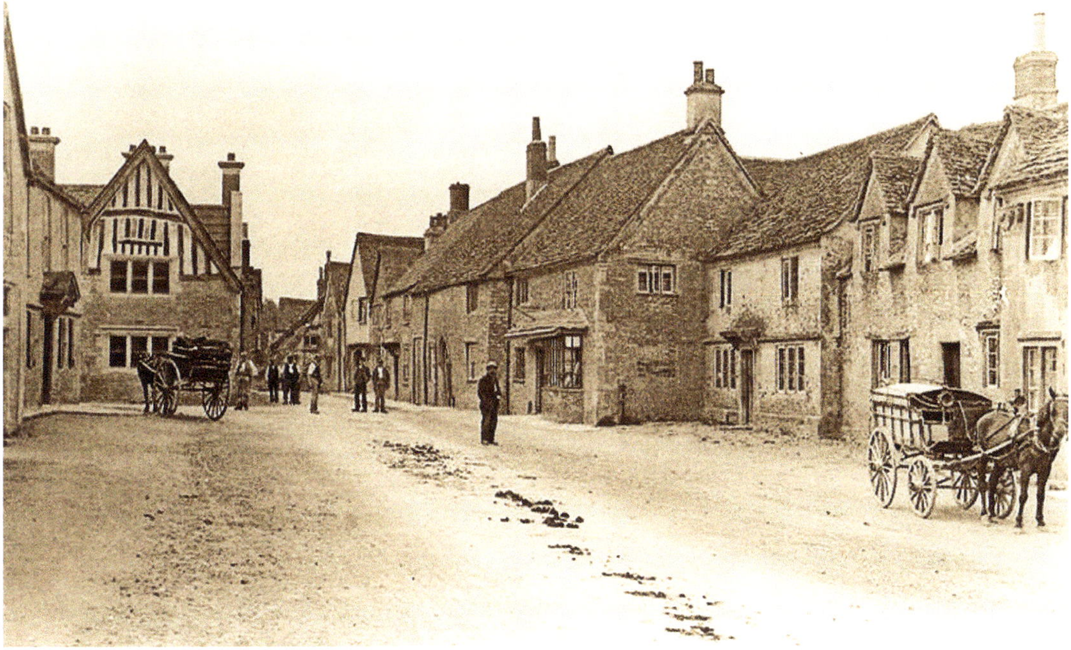

Church Square looking West

This animated photograph shows horse transport of the period and a group of men standing for the photographer. This wide area close to the church provided the space needed for the markets originally held here. The building on the immediate left-hand side with porch canopy is the Carpenters' Arms public house. A large corner-sited premises that was once a coach house, it has records dating back to 1780. The render, at one time applied to the front elevation, has now been removed from the front to reveal an attractive natural stone façade. The front right of this card shows one of the few properties in the village with a bow window. It was once the grocer's shop and is now Lacock Bakery. (Courtesy of Wiltshire and Swindon History Centre).

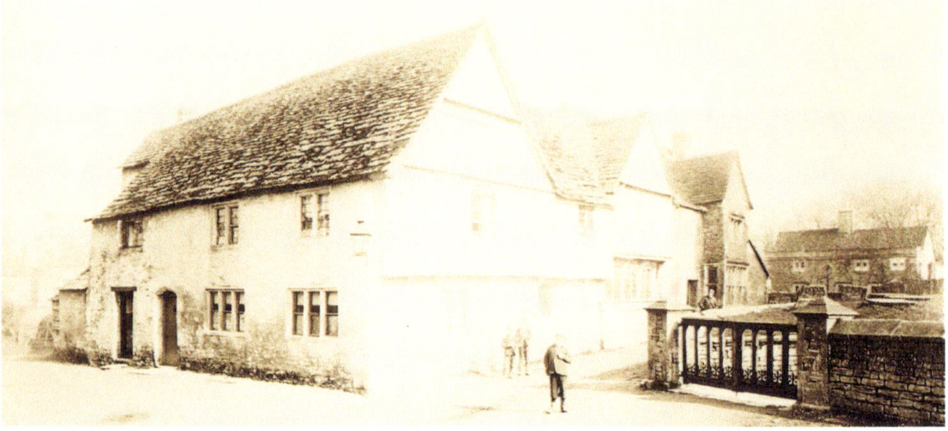

Former Workhouse

A photograph taken *c.* 1900 of this significant property. It was converted into a workhouse around 1766, as growing numbers required accommodation. Children, including orphans, were given a home and taught spinning and carding. Following the decline of the wool trade an increasing number of people were unemployed and became poor. It became necessary in 1833 to build a new workhouse in the Tanyard. Shortly after this, 136 unemployed men found work building Brunel's railway line close by. The workhouse was closed around 1860 and the poor were then sent to another in Chippenham. It is now Lacock Pottery and Guest House.

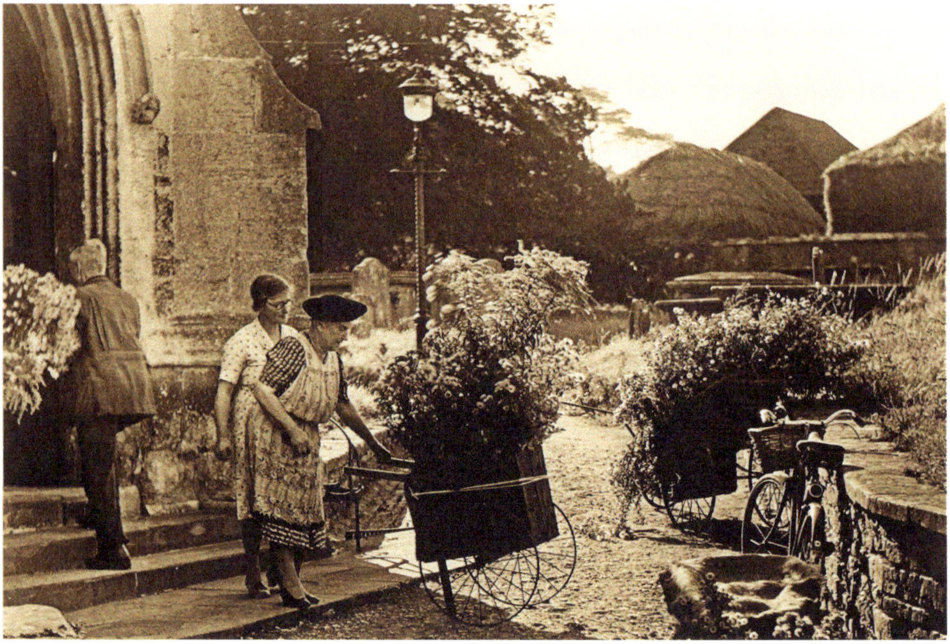

Moving Flowers, 1945

A scene full of activity outside St Cyriac's Church, probably before a special occasion or Harvest Festival. Well-loaded flower carts and a large floral decoration are being taken into the church. The photographer captures these hard-working villagers on this animated photograph. St Cyriac's continues to be known and appreciated for its flower festivals and floral displays. Within its walls it provides a wealth of interest with numerous historic features. (WSA2664/2/3F/10/65BW)

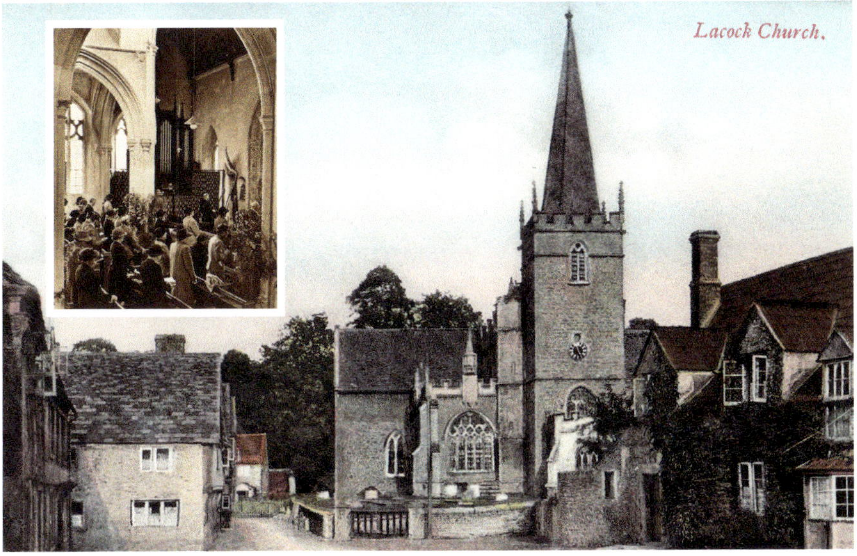

Church of St Cyriac

Originally, there may have been a small Saxon church on the site of this Grade I listed building. It has some fourteenth-century remains but is principally fifteenth century and dedicated to the Norman saint St Cyriac. During the fifteenth century, due to the prosperity from the wool trade in Lacock, a major rebuilding of the church was undertaken. It is full of interest with an impressive octagonal spire, probably built in 1604. Noteworthy features include the chapel, arched chancel window, battlements and amusing gargoyles. *Inset*: Church service. (WSA2664/2/3F/10/2BW)

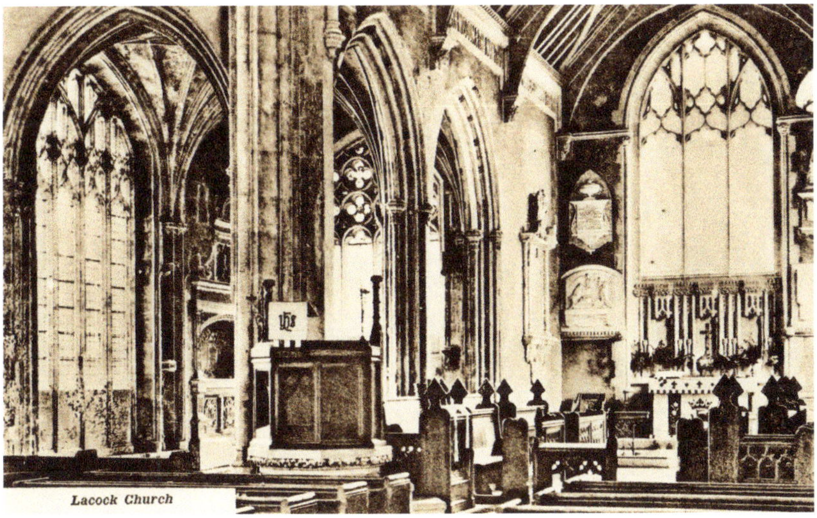

Church of St Cyriac Interior

There have been many alterations to this fine church since it was first built in local stone by skilled craftsmen. Restoration works in 1861 dramatically altered the interior, including the replacement of high pews. Further alterations were carried out in the twentieth century, incorporating sympathetic remodelling of the chancel. This part was done as a memorial to William Henry Fox Talbot. Much history is contained within the church walls and prominent landowners from the past including the Baynards, Sharingtons and Talbots are remembered.

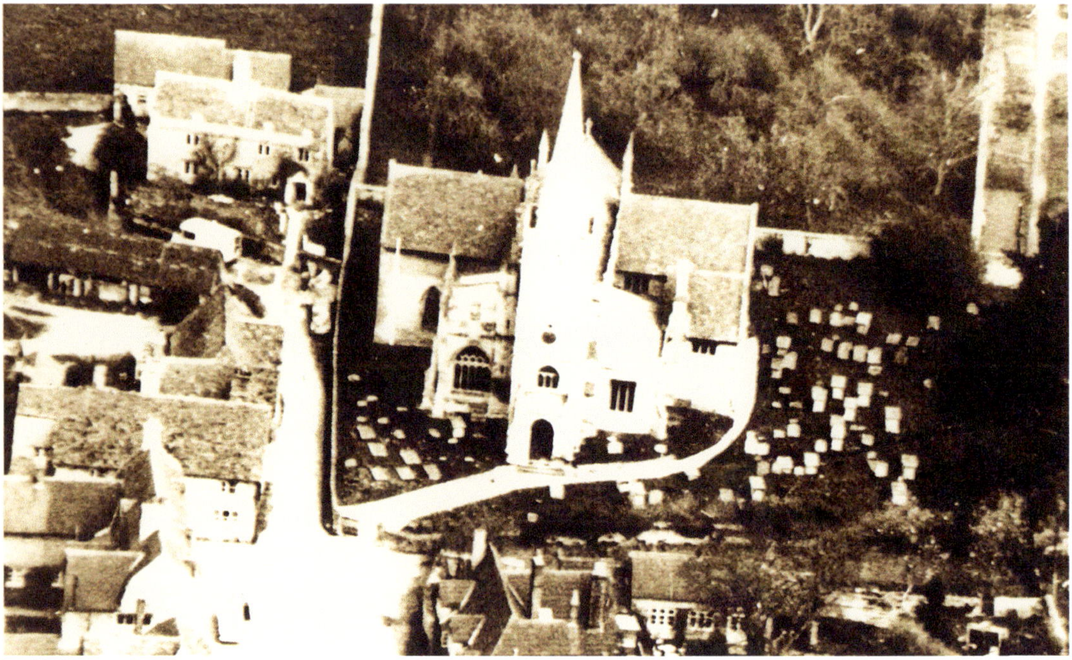

Aerial View

A scene that provides an opportunity to view several important Lacock properties from a different perspective. In the front right foreground is King John's Hunting Lodge with dormers. Behind this is the church of St Cyriac with its graveyard. The wide area is the old Market Place and the house on the left corner, the former workhouse. A lane along the side of the churchyard gives access to the Tanyard, where a van is parked. The house on the far left of the photograph with projecting covered front porch has become well known. It was used as Harry Potter's parents' house in the 2001 film production of *Harry Potter and the Philosopher's Stone*. (WSA3476/1/191)

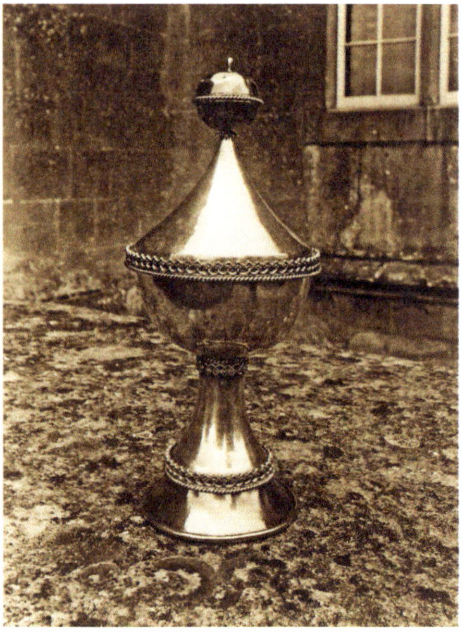

The Lacock Cup

This medieval chalice was given to the church of St Cyriac after the reformation in the fifteenth century. It is one of the most important and unique pieces of secular English silver which is partially gilded. The drinking or feasting cup was used by the congregation for over 400 years. Since 1963 it had been put on loan to the British Museum. It was returned to its home at Lacock until the 1980s for special religious occasions. In 2013, the church decided to offer it for sale and it was jointly acquired by the British Museum (where it is now on display) and the Wiltshire Museum. (WSA2664/2/2F/3BW)

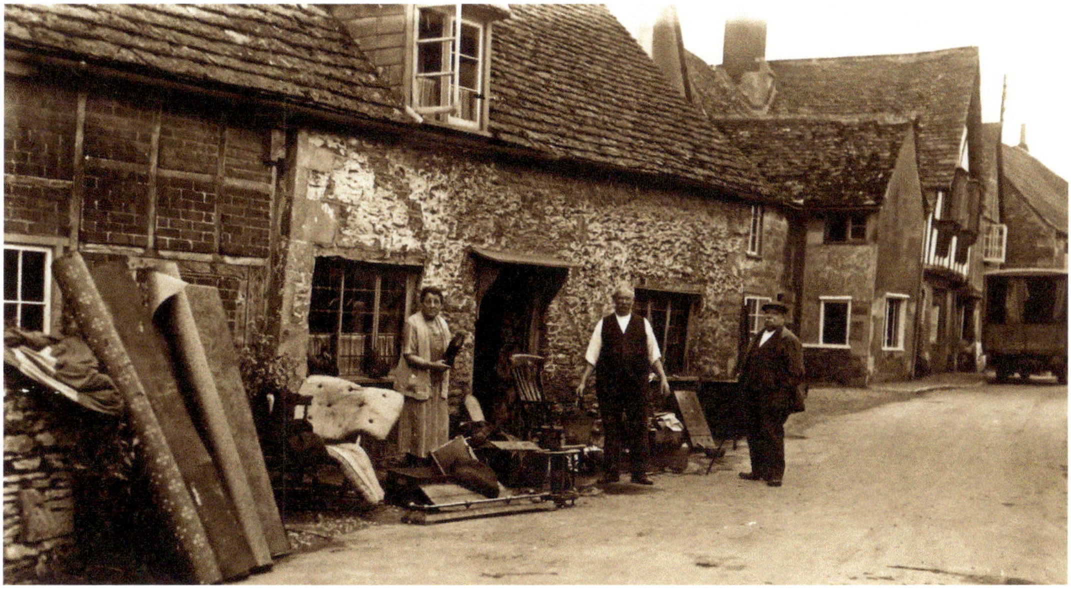

Flood Damage, Church Street, 1935

Byde Brook, sometimes spelt Bide Brook, meanders its way eastwards from Corsham into the River Avon, which runs alongside the Lacock Abbey grounds. On entering the village the brook flows behind the properties in Church Street. There was a disaster in 1935 when it flooded badly, causing considerable damage to many of the houses and their contents. This is a sad scene outside a flood-damaged cottage, with the furniture removed to the roadside. (WSA/F4/840/13)

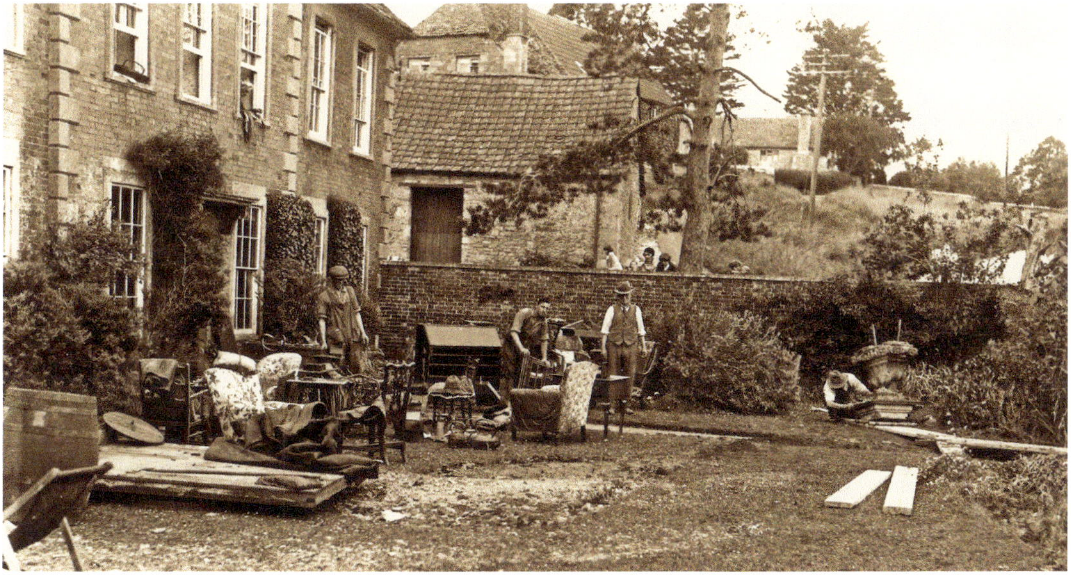

Lacock Floods

It is reported that the River Avon rose around 12 feet in some two hours during the 1935 disaster. The Byde Brook, also referred to as Corsham Brook, dramatically broke its banks flooding Church Street, West Street and part of Cantax Hill. Bridges were also seriously damaged and vehicles left stranded in deep water. The furniture from this property has been taken into the back garden and four men assist. (WSA/F4/840/13)

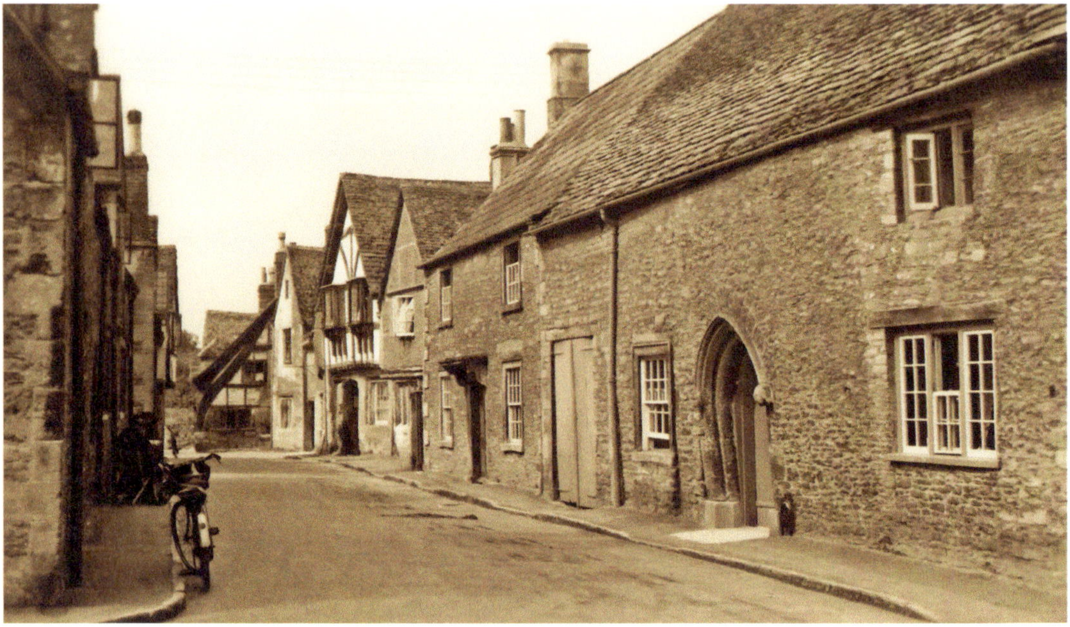

Long Frontage, Hall House

The property, with its neighbour, is clearly shown in the foreground in this Edwardian photograph. Located on the north side of a narrow section of the street and with stone elevation, they are Grade II listed. Together they represent a fine example of an early fourteenth-century 'hall house' with alterations over later centuries. Important external features include the historic arched doorway and a pair of unusual roadside doors. At one time part of the property was occupied by the parish clerk and the other section by a grocer and draper. Two metal tie bars have been inserted over the arched door in more recent years, probably to arrest a bulge.

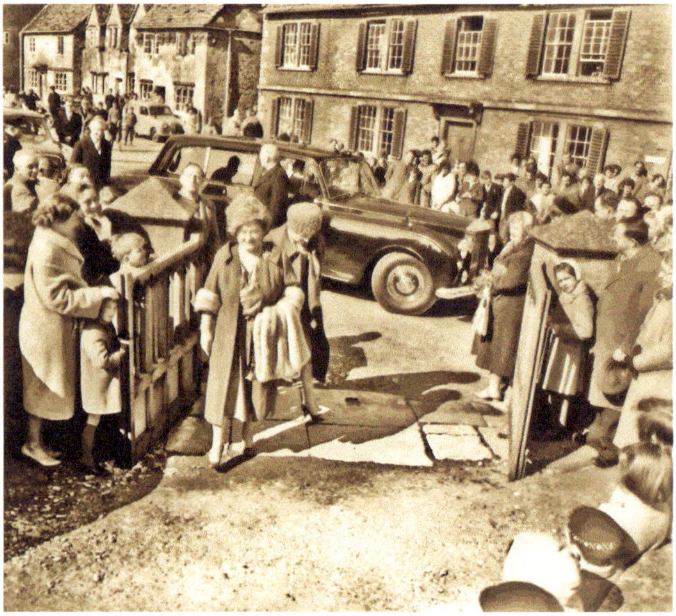

Royal Visit

In the 1950s, Her Majesty Queen Elizabeth the Queen Mother was a regular visitor to Spye Park Estate near Lacock. She was a friend of the owners and whilst visiting would also like to see the crocuses at Lacock Abbey. When in the area she sometimes attended a service at St Cyriac's Church, where she always received a warm welcome. She died in 2002 at the age of 101. The year 2006 also saw another royal visit when HRH Prince Charles, the Duchess of Cornwall, and Princes William and Harry were at the church for the wedding of the daughter of the Duchess of Cornwall. (WSA1772/1/2764)

5
West Street

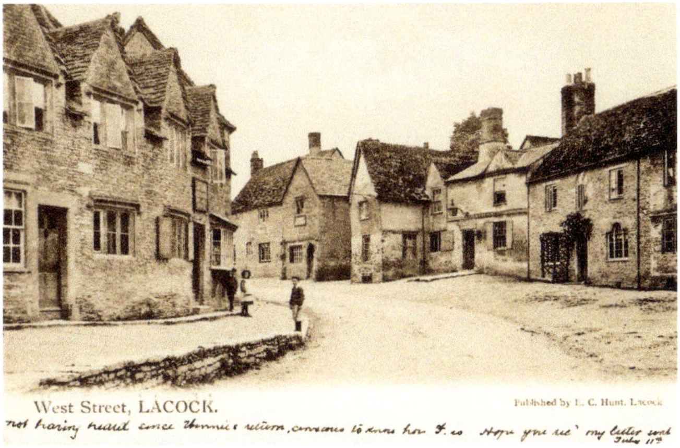

The Brash

We are provided with an interesting wide-angle view by a local photographer. It includes young children outside the shop, George Inn and blacksmiths next door. The postcard, sent in 1908 to The Bronx, New York, reads: 'I am on a cycle tour over Bank Holiday on Salisbury Plain.' Looking at this empty street scene the roads would have been much safer then. On the left is the high-raised pavement known locally as 'the brash', which refers to the ground below. There was a water pump located here for villagers without wells, before piped mains were available.

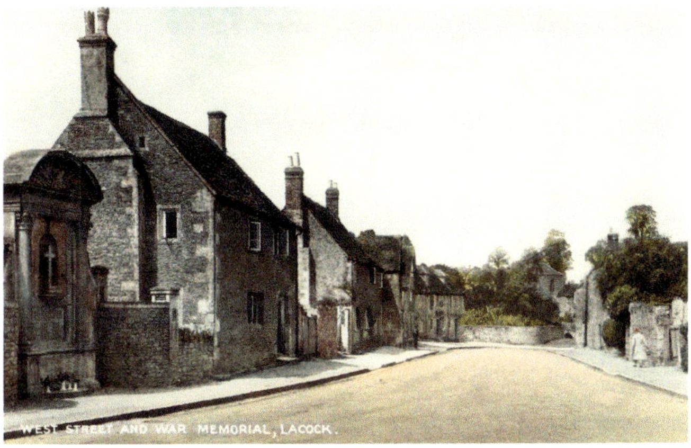

War Memorial

There are thirty names of those who lost their lives in the First World War and a plaque to fourteen in the Second World War. The memorial dates from 1920 and has this inscription: 'For God and the Right. These all gave their lives in the Great War to defend their King and Country. Their memory is enshrined in the hearts of the people of the Parish who erected this monument as a mark of their gratitude and affection.' It is Grade II listed and incorporates a former eighteenth-century memorial. This was in the parish church and dedicated to Sir John Talbot.

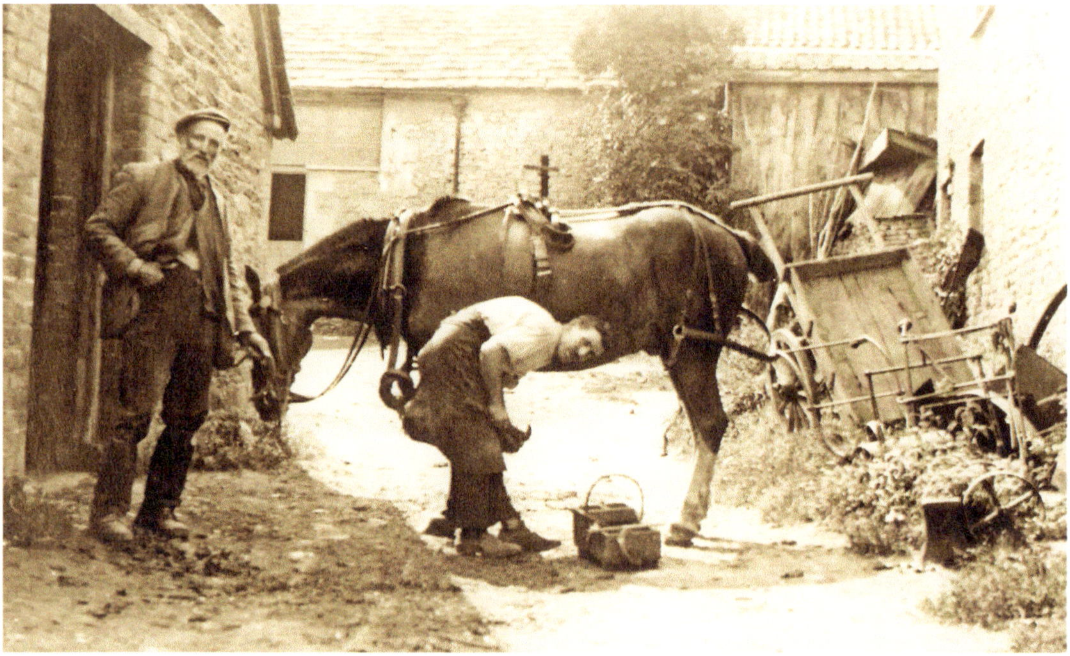

Rural Life

A scarce early Edwardian postcard showing a skilled farrier outside his premises, shoeing a workhorse. The animal stands patiently while old shoes are being removed and new ones applied. Farriers' tools have changed little over many centuries and still include the forge, anvil, tongs, hammer, clincher and those specially made for work on the hoof. This superb animated close-up photograph was taken in the yard, at the side of the George Inn. The building and others are now converted into interesting shops. A bus shelter at the other side of the entrance was also part of the former blacksmith and farrier's property.

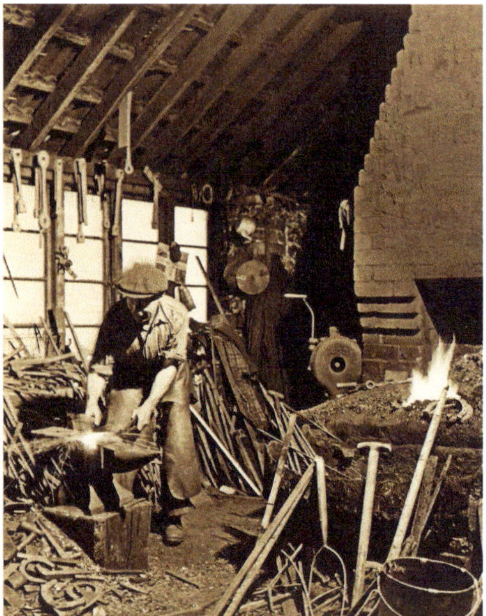

Blacksmith at Work, *c.* 1945

An important part of village life and a hub of activity was the Lacock smithy. The blacksmith is hard at work surrounded by tools, equipment and miscellany. He is seen here hammering hot iron on an anvil to change its shape. The experienced metalworker could repair tools and implements so necessary for a rural community such as this. He would also shoe horses and make metal gates together with railings. In the past, for a nominal sum, the blacksmith provided metal rims on the play hoops of village children. (WSA2664/2/3F/10/50BW)

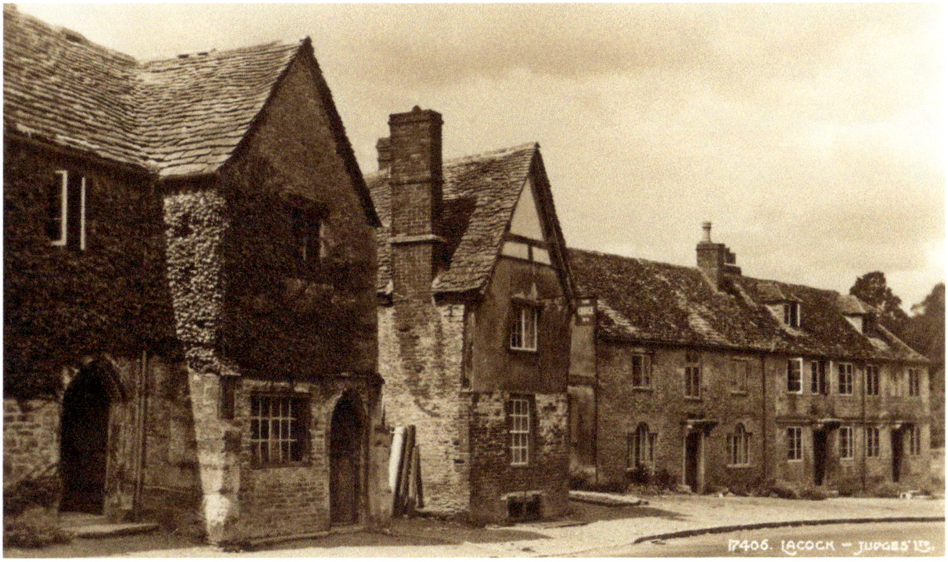

The Forge

In the foreground next to the George Inn is this most attractive and interesting Grade II listed building. The elevations, partly clad in creeper growth, are in rubble stone beneath a gabled stone slate roof. The house was built in the fifteenth century with later alterations and has a nineteenth-century forge wing at the north end. The substantial buttresses could indicate that this section of the property was converted from an earlier building. The business of a blacksmith, farrier and metalworker was conducted from the forge, into the twentieth century. The front part was subsequently converted into a bus shelter, one of the most unusual in the country.

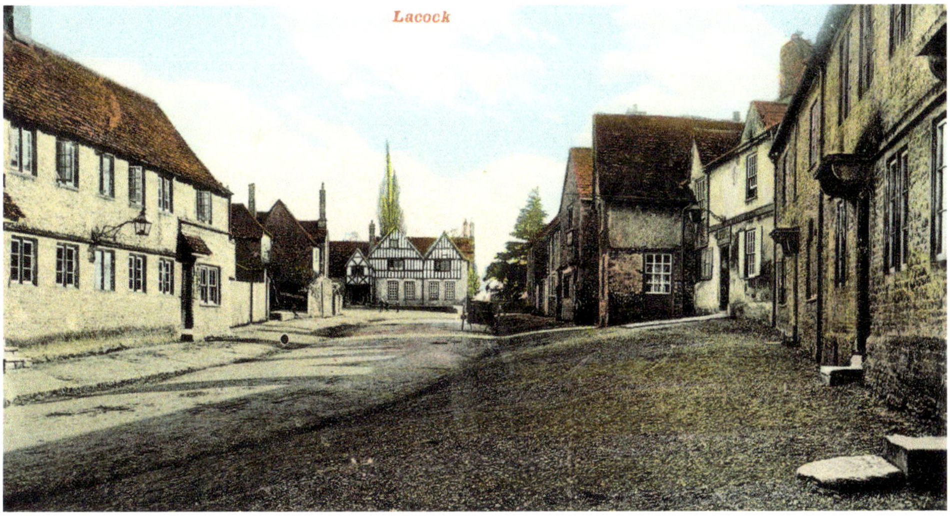

Wide Pavement

Posted from Lacock in 1909 to a local address, the writer refers to 'trap and pony' transport. It is interesting to see on this locally published postcard that a trap is in fact parked outside the blacksmiths. The horse is probably in the yard at the side receiving new shoes. The road here is seen with a fairly deep gutter and wide footpath up to the George Inn. This photograph provides a distant view of the impressive black and white, timbered Porch House at the end of the High Street.

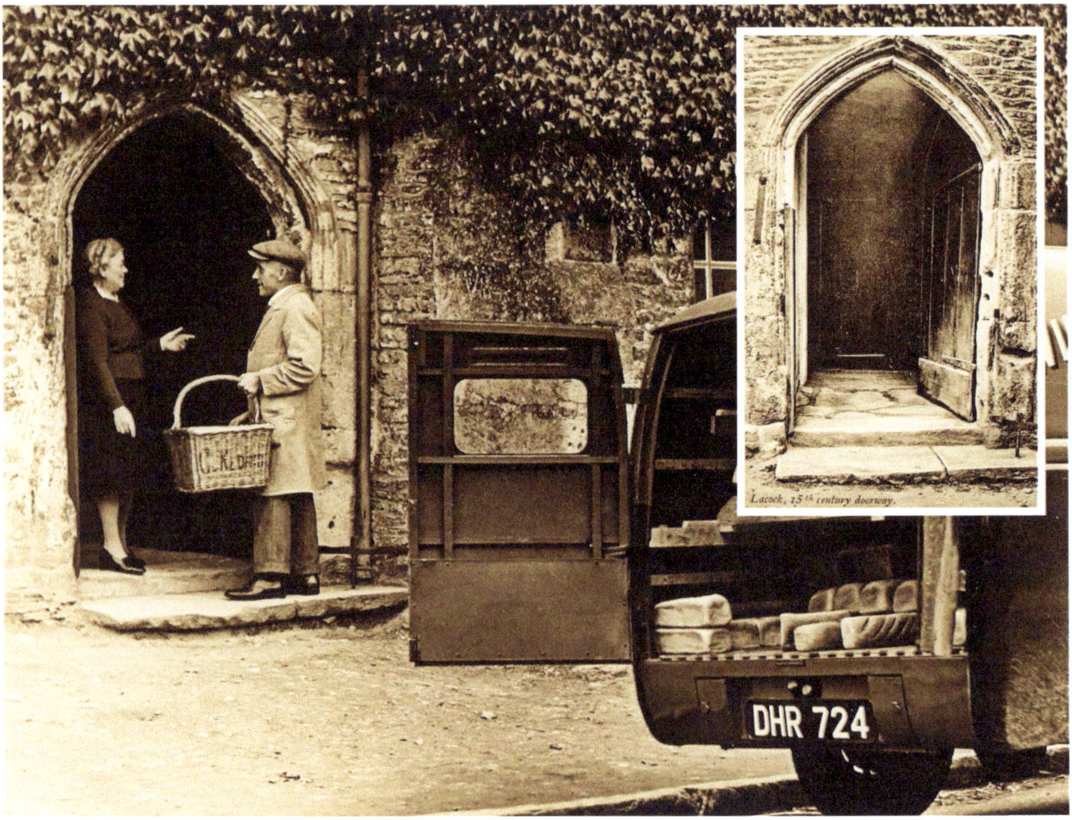

Delivering Bread, *c.* 1945

When Lacock was virtually self-sufficient and before supermarkets, there was a choice of several bakers. Grain from local farmers would be supplied to the mill where the flour would be produced for bread making. In more leisurely times, a door-to-door service was provided by the baker, using a large wicker bread basket. Before motor vehicles were common, a horse-drawn delivery van was used in the village. It is likely the horse knew the delivery round as well as the baker, knowing exactly when and where to stop. (WSA2664/2/3F10/23BW) *Inset*: Close-up of fifteenth-century doorway.

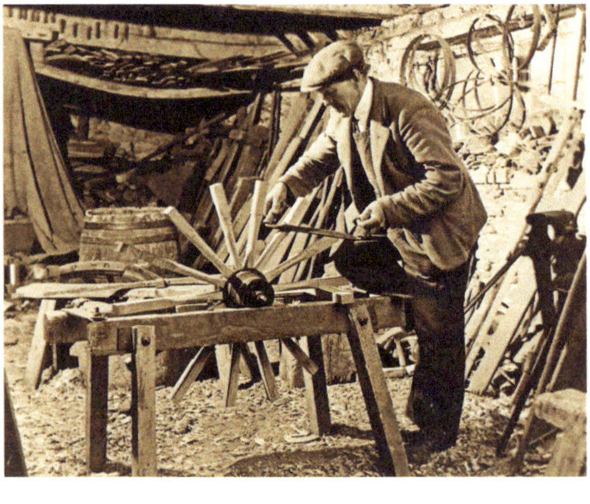

Wheelwright at Work, *c.* 1945

Behind the cottages in West Street was the busy, long-established carpenters' and wheelwrights' workshop. This photograph shows a spoked wooden wheel being made for a horse-drawn vehicle. These were needed for agricultural carts, wagons, traps and coaches. Maintenance, repairs and bonding of these wheels was regularly required. Several sawpits were located in the village, each around 10 feet deep. A man stood in the pit and the other on top, each holding the end of a cross-cut saw to cut logs up lengthwise into planks. This workshop was also known for making and polishing coffins. (WSA2664/2/3F/10/57BW)

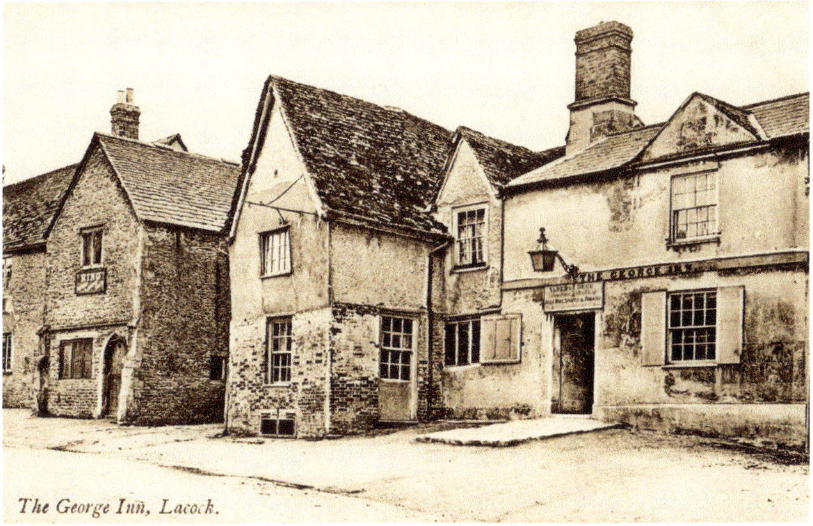

The George Inn, Fourteenth Century

The George Inn is reputed to have been first licensed in 1361 and as such has one of the longest continuously running licences for the sale of alcohol in the country. Originally it may have been on a different site and has been known in the past as the Black Boy and the Inn. At one stage in its history the landlord was Albert Beer, a most appropriate name. Construction of this Grade II listed building includes timber frame, brick, plaster, rubble and dressed stone. Gables, tall chimneys, stone and slated roof add to the attractive elevations. The window shutters have since been removed and there is now a hanging pub sign.

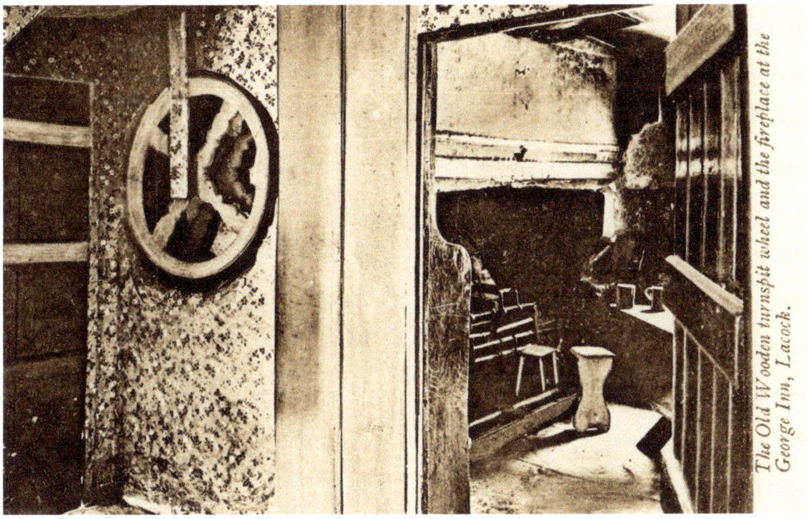

The George Inn, Wooden Turnspit Wheel

An early 1900 postcard shows the basic interior of the inn at that time. More importantly, a rare surviving feature is the seventeenth-century wooden turnspit wheel. This is set into a rough render side wall, with sufficient distance from the open fireplace, to prevent the dog overheating. A terrier-type mongrel, specially bred to run on a wheel, was known as a 'turnspit dog'. It had short legs and a long body being able to turn the spit so that the meat was cooked evenly. Dogs were kept in groups of two and changed at regular intervals while roasting was in progress. The breed is now extinct.

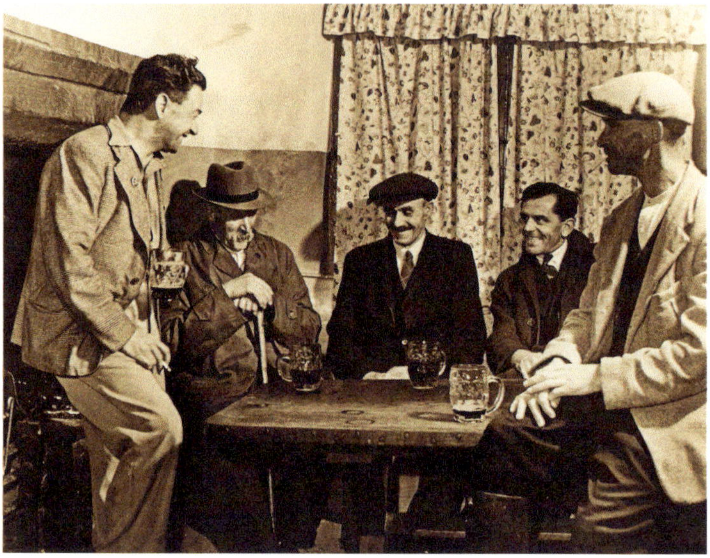

Drinking in the George Inn, *c.* 1940s

A group of five locals enjoying an evening pint, from dimpled glasses, in front of the ancient fireplace. As a hub of village life and always a popular meeting place, it has been continuously serving the community and visitors for well over 600 years. The inn is an important venue in which to relax and socialise. In the past, patrons have enjoyed traditional pub games, including darts, dominoes, cards such as cribbage, bar skittles and shove ha'penny. (WSA2664/2/3F/10/38BW)

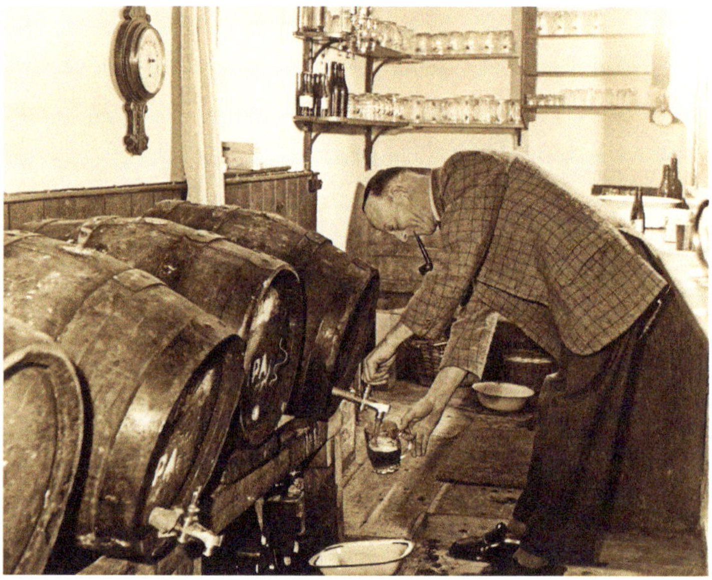

Drawing a Pint, George Inn

A past tradition when beer was kept in racked wooden barrels and delivered through brass taps. The barrels were made by brewery coopers, usually of convex shape, bulge at centre and strengthened with metal hoops. They have been mainly replaced by pressurised metal kegs and counter delivery fonts. Beer glasses are stored on wall shelves and a barometer for weather conditions in view. The photograph was taken around seventy years ago. (WSA2664/2/3F/10/21BW)

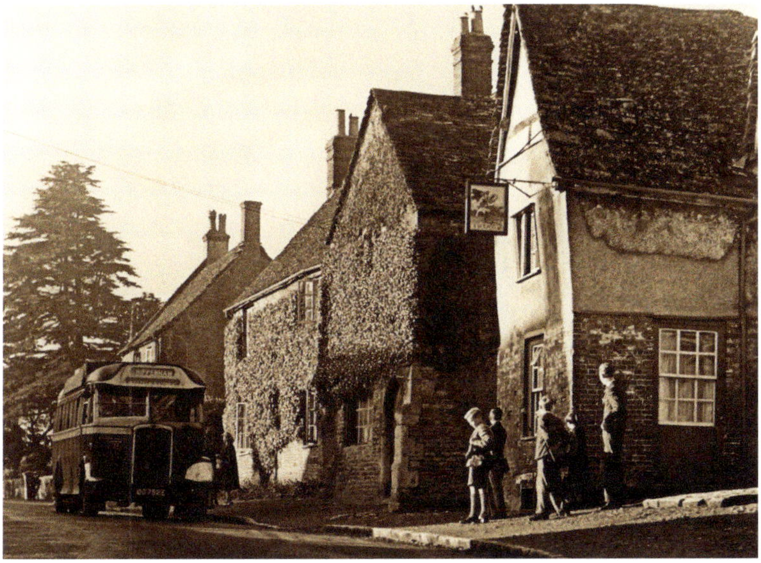

Bus Service, *c.* 1945
This image shows local children waiting to be taken by the Chippenham bus to school in the nearby town. In the early 1900s a service to Lacock was operated by the Bath Electric Tramway Company which stopped outside the Red Lion. This motor bus was a double decker with rear external staircase. Both the driver and conductor were provided with uniforms, including caps. Some of the first motor cars to be seen in the village were owned by Mr H. Harris and Sir John Gladstone, both from Bowden Hill. At the turn of the twentieth century the Wilts & Berks Canal on the village outskirts was still operational and a small bridge was in use at Reybridge. (WSA2664/2/3F/10/15BW)

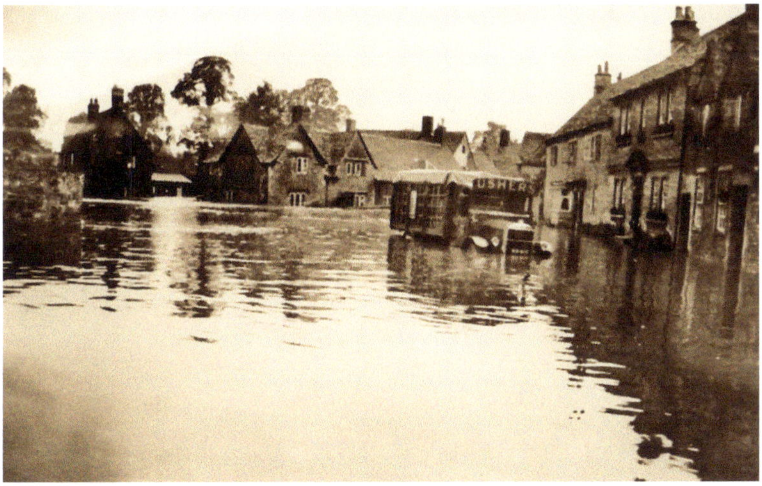

Flood Disaster, 1935
A photograph captures a local brewery delivery lorry stranded in deep floodwater near the junction with Church Street. Serious flooding took place following very inclement weather conditions. This resulted in much damage being caused to many village properties, as can be seen here. Fields and roads in the vicinity are still prone to flooding. It is sometimes necessary to close roads and divert traffic. Pedestrians are provided with raised footpaths to the side of the main river bridges in the village and at Reybridge. (© National Trust/Rachel Nordstrom)

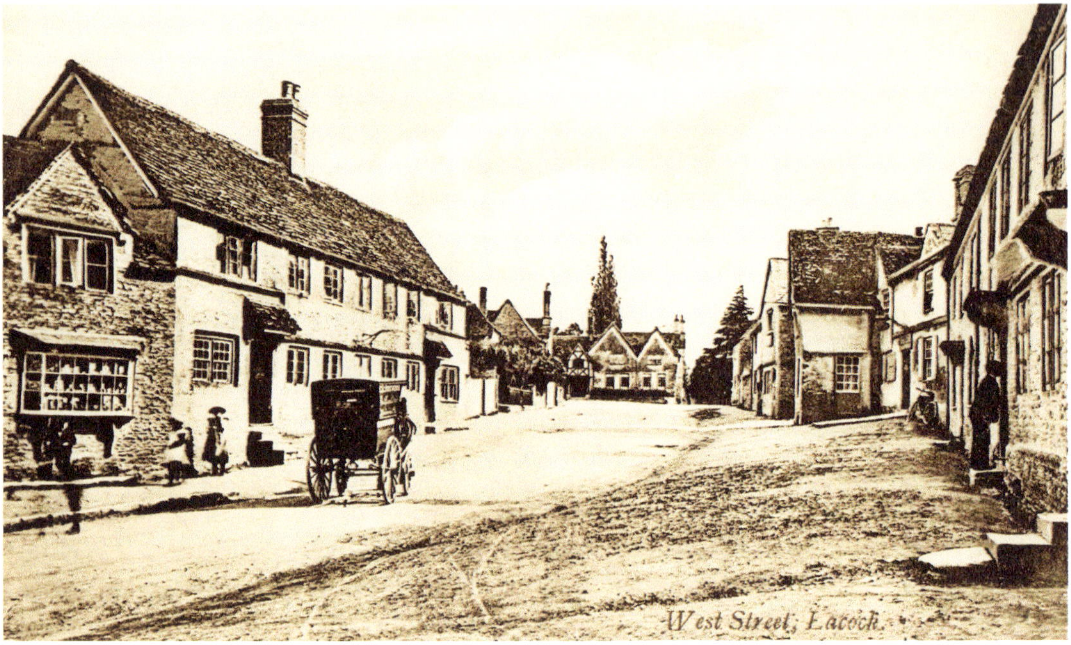

Horse-drawn Baker's Cart, *c.* 1905

A quiet road being the main access route from Chippenham to Melksham, via Notton and Beanacre. At a time when the village was virtually self-sufficient, we see a horse-drawn baker's van stationary in a wide part of the street. It is interesting to note that during the Lacock Pageant, the ancient style of bread making, using similar ingredients, was recreated. As this type of bread proved popular, the baker continued production after the event. The George Inn, smithy and Porch House can also be seen on this postcard.

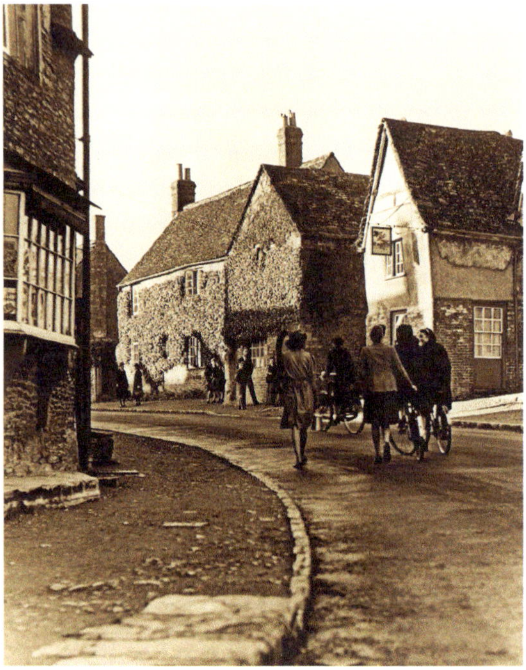

Unusual View, *c.* 1940s

The animated photograph provides an interesting village scene on the bend, with ladies and their cycles. Schoolchildren wait for the bus outside the Old Smithy; the George Inn is in view, as is the shop on the 'brash'. Motor vehicles in this rural area do not seem to present a significant problem as some ladies walk in the road. However, it is likely the Chippenham bus is due shortly. (WSA2664/2/3F/10/7BW)

6

Cantax Hill, Packhorse Bridge, Nethercote Hill

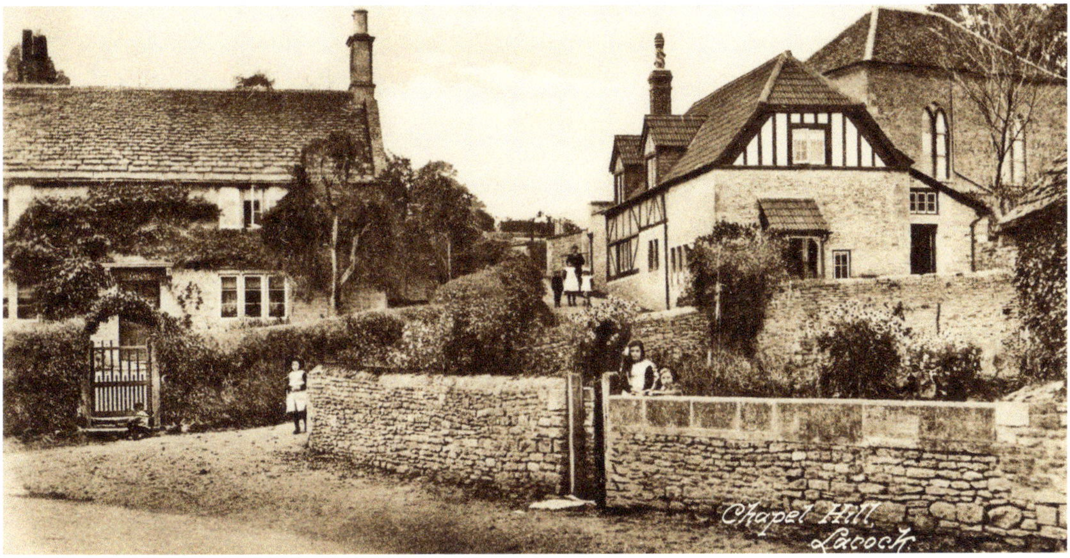

Chapel Hill, off Cantax Hill

This narrow lane on an incline provided access to the chapel and working men's club. In the top right-hand corner on this early Edwardian postcard, the Methodist Chapel can clearly be seen. Before it was built in 1812, local congregationalists met in each other's houses. In the early 1970s the chapel became the United Reform Church of St Stephen. Sadly, it eventually became redundant and was then converted into a private house. Small children in a garden and the lane pose for the local photographer's camera.

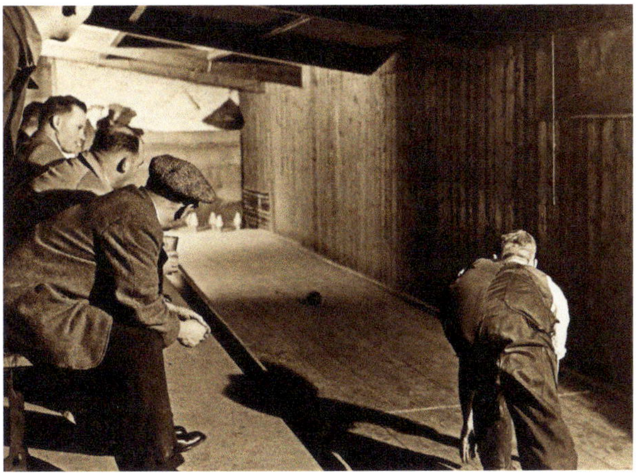

Skittle Alley, *c.* 1940s

Amongst the many activities available at Lacock Working Men's Club were the whist nights, bingo, flower shows, darts and skittle teams. Long before people could move freely outside the village for entertainment the Club was a busy and valuable meeting place. The former rifle range proved ideal for conversion into a skittle alley. It is shown with a game in progress on this animated photograph taken around seventy years ago. In 1928 Lacock Club and Institute were winners of the Skittles Club League. (WSA2664/2/3F/10/66BW)

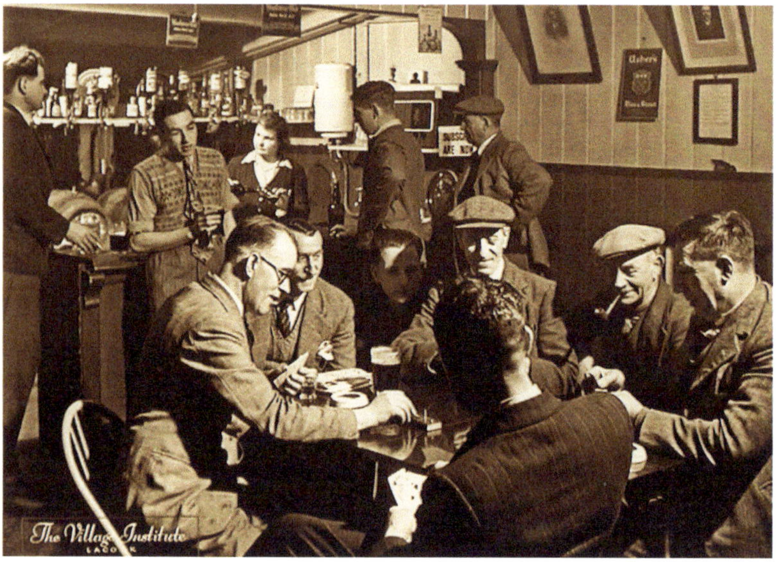

Working Men's Club, Village Institute

The premises on Chapel Hill, off Cantax Hill, served Lacock well until sold by auction in 2008. Built in 1898, the original single-storey clubhouse was first used as a rifle range. It was passed to the village a few years later and became a Working Men's Club in 1900. Also known as an 'Institute', to provide reading rooms for the betterment of local people. The club was a venue for many family parties and arranged charabanc outings to such places as Cheddar Gorge. The evocative photograph from the 1940s shows a card game in progress. (WSA/X3/164/4)

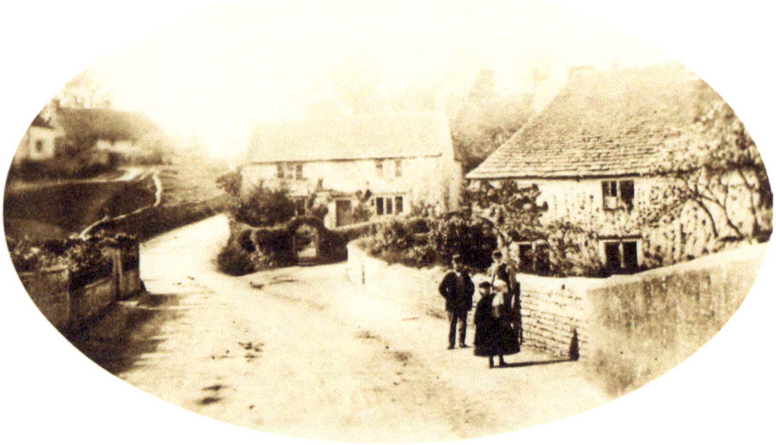

Unusual Image

The narrow road from the village runs north over an early nineteenth-century bridge, just beyond Church Street. It is here, close to the watercourse, that the original settlement may have been founded. There are some fine buildings on the left as we leave Lacock, but these are out of view. One was the old Cantax Surgery which may have been used for textile manufacture at one stage of its life. Photographers from a bygone era have captured this and other scenes from the past, for us all to appreciate today. We thank them and are grateful for their work. (© National Trust/Rachel Nordstrom)

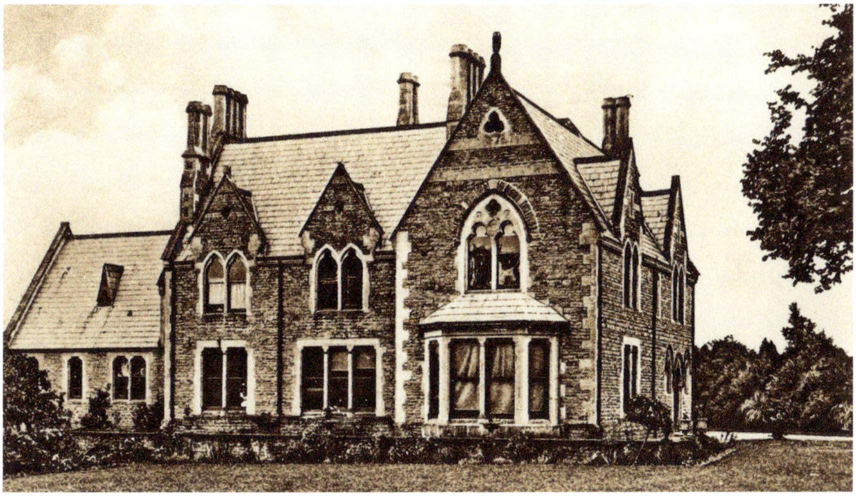

The Former Vicarage, Cantax Hill
This image shows a large Victorian house, built as the vicarage *c.* 1865 for the vicar of Lacock Church. On entering the village on the north side from the Chippenham to Melksham road, it is the first prominent residence to come into view. It is built of stone with steeply pitched slated roof with dormers and tall chimney stacks. This 1906 postcard shows its Victorian Gothic style of architecture which also incorporates several ecclesiastical features. The distinctive property is set within its own large grounds and is now known as 'The Rectory'. (WSA3476/1/191)

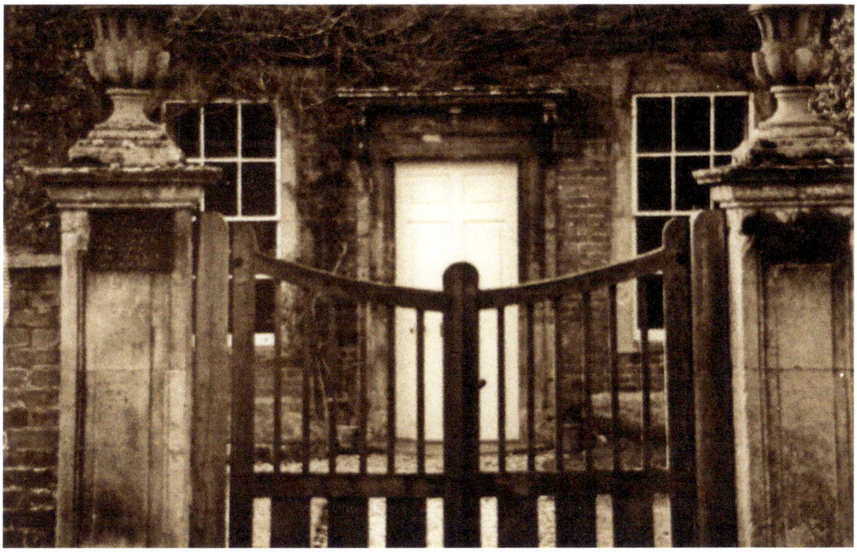

Cantax House, Cantax Hill
This is an unusual old photograph of part of this fine period property, showing the elegant stone gateposts and panelled front door. It is a spacious residence built *c.* 1700 with brick elevations and stone dressings. It is set beneath a hipped stone slate roof and is Grade II listed. Probably built for a wealthy wool merchant, it is one of the best formal homes ever built in Lacock. At one period of its life and until 1866 it was used as the vicarage. Then it was later occupied by a doctor and his family. The impressive façade has featured in several film and television productions including Harry Potter and BBC's *Emma*. (WSA3476/1/191)

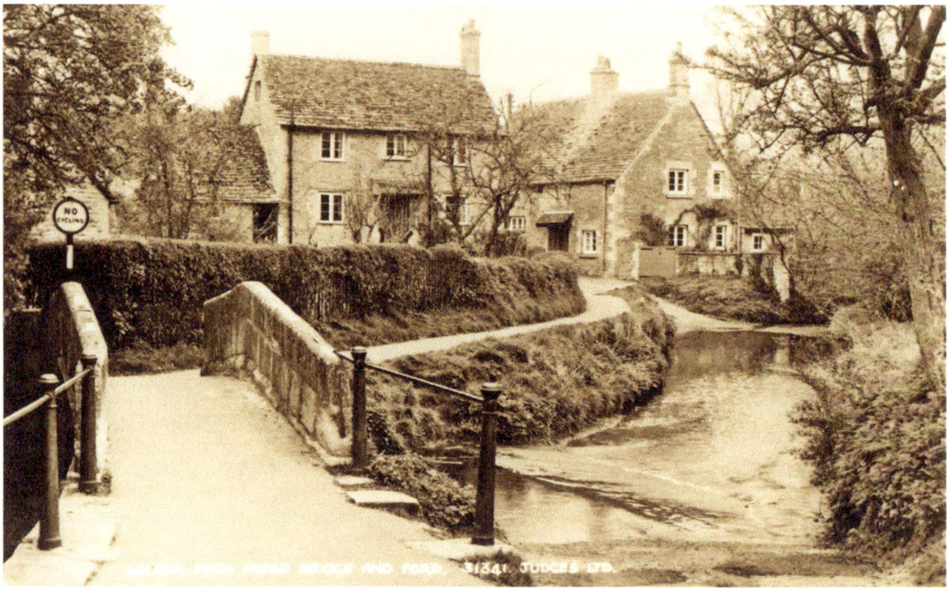

Packhorse Bridge

The packhorse bridge was probably originally built to enable goods to be transported by packhorses from the village when the brook was in flood. The humpbacked stone bridge with two arches has low side walls to prevent loads being carried by the horses from obstruction. It is a Grade II listed building, eighteenth century and marked as 'Dummer's Bridge' on the Lacock Tithe map. It is a most attractive and interesting part of the village with considerable historical background.

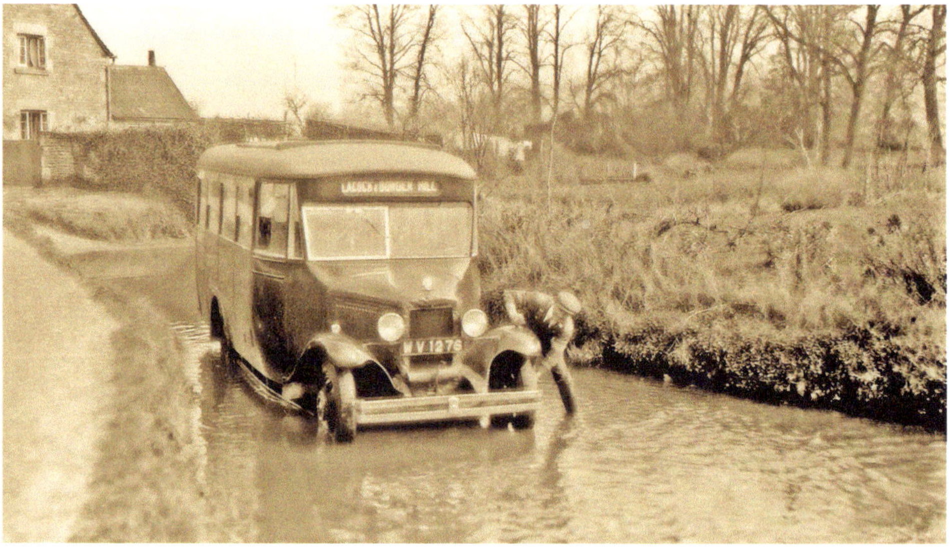

Lacock Ford

Around this small stream, the Saxons were thought to have settled during the Anglo-Saxon period of our history. Until the Lacock bridges and causeway were constructed around the seventeenth century, the Packhorse Ford and Reybridge were the only crossing points of the River Avon. It now provides access to Nethercote Hill and this old photograph shows the ford being used to wash wheels of the Lacock and Bowden Hill motorbus. (WSA1772/1/69/3)

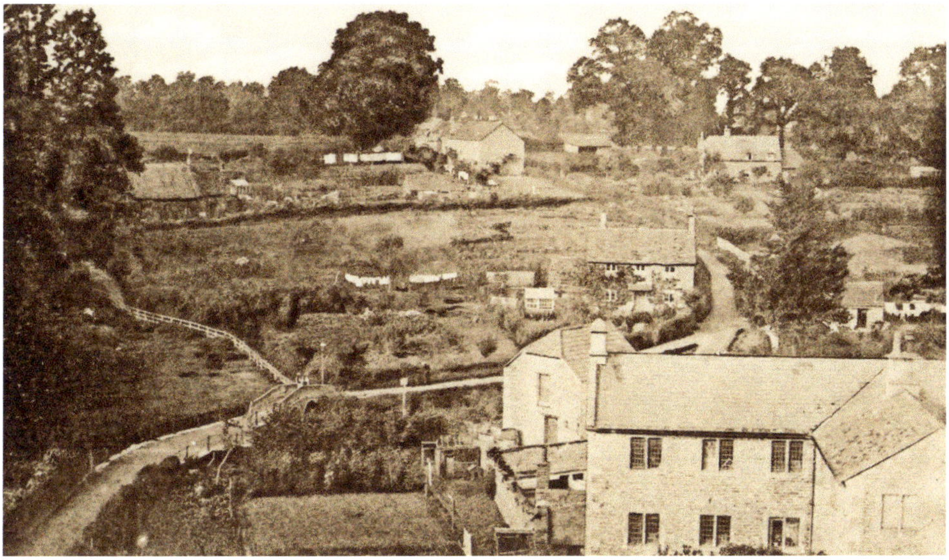

Former Workhouse

An unusual and rare view of this part of the village outskirts. In the foreground is the old workhouse, which is now a pottery. Access to this Grade II listed building is from the Tanyard, close to the church. It had a rectangular addition to provide accommodation for the governor. This was probably added around twenty years before it closed in 1859. This scene, full of detail, also reveals the Packhorse Bridge, Nethercote Hill and village allotments. The pathway on the left with post and rail fencing is Lovers' Walk. There are a pair of historic thatch cottages from this footpath.

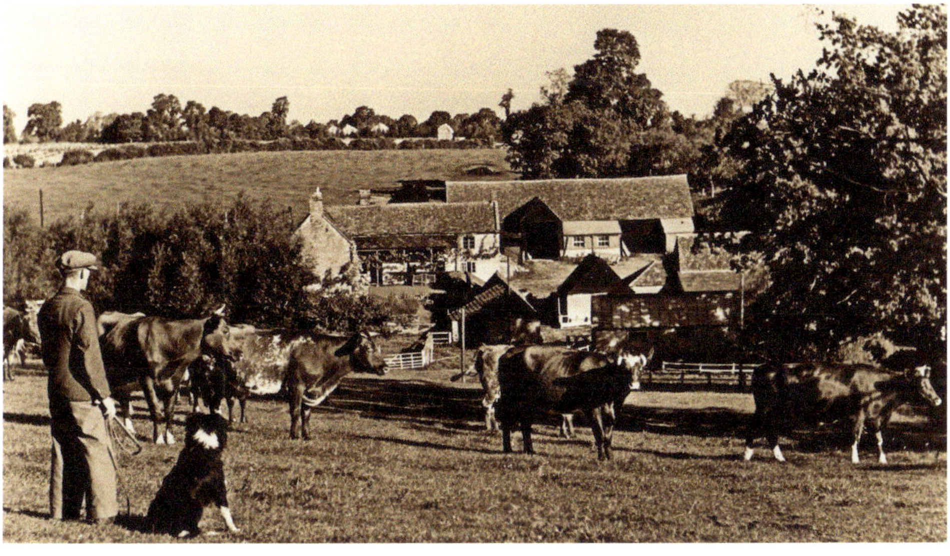

Rural Scene, *c.* 1945

Farming has always played a necessary part in the everyday life of Lacock. As the most important and oldest industry, it was labour intensive before the age of mechanisation. Many craftsmen were needed including carters, hedgers, hand milkers, stack builders and people to care for livestock. At the time of this photograph a technological revolution had started and the number of full-time farmworkers was in decline. (WSA2664/2/3F/10/70BW)

7
Bewley Common, Bowden Hill

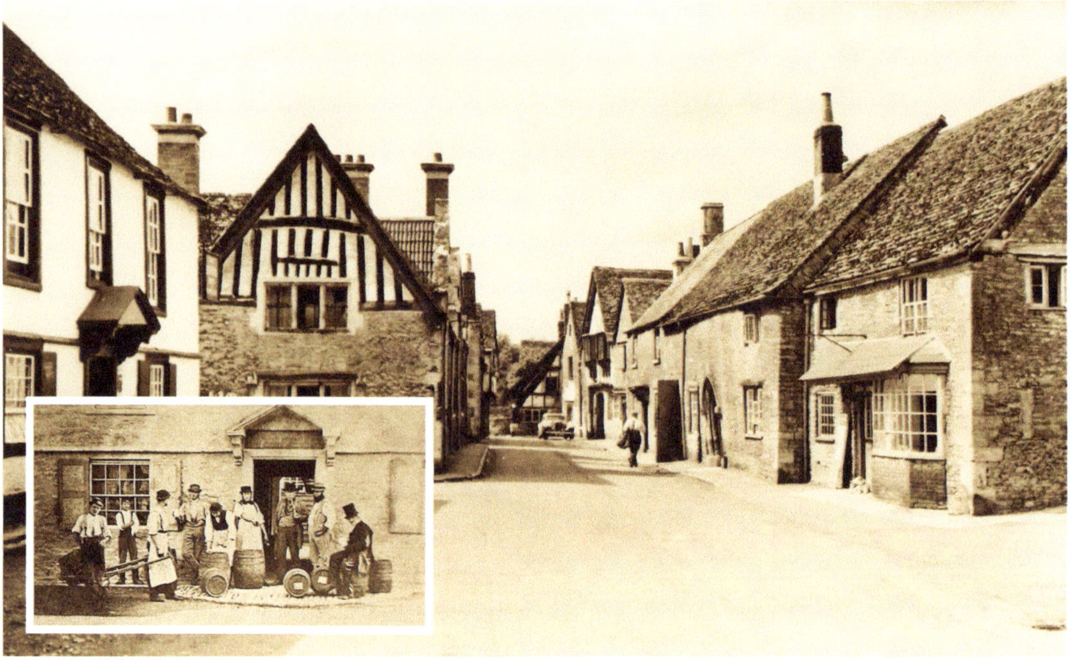

Lacock Brewery

Records indicate that the Lackcock Brewery started around 1841 as an establishment in Bewley Lane, near Lacock Wharf. The premises was subsequently extended and for a short period before 1900 owned by Mr F. Kingsford. He sold beer and ales to the Red Lion in the village, evidenced by previous signage. In 1897 he put the brewery with twenty-one tied houses for sale by public auction, which realised £26,000. The new owner carried on the business until brewing ceased in the 1920s. This postcard shows the Carpenters' Arms with distinctive porch. *Inset*: Brewery workers outside the front door, *c*. 1900. (© National Trust/Rachel Topham)

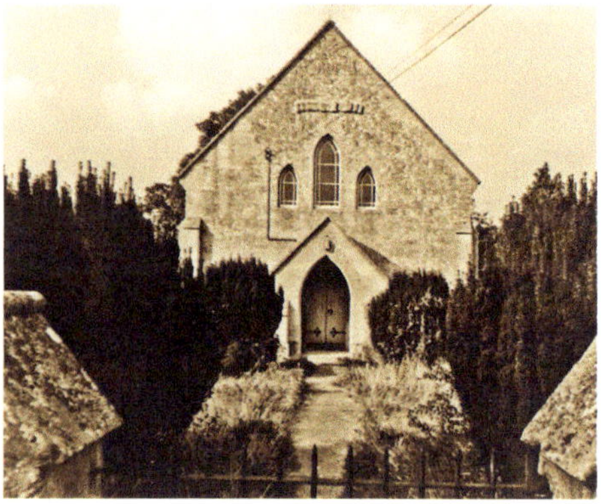

Wesleyan Methodist Chapel

Although there was a relatively sparse population in the immediate neighbourhood to the chapel, this was once a busy location. The Wilts & Berks Canal, which closed in 1914, was close by at the bottom of Bowden Hill. It was served by a wharf, coal merchant and other businesses. The chapel was opened in 1863 with a large crowd of around 700 people attending the ceremony, followed by refreshments. During the twentieth century the congregation was in decline. In the 1970s the Methodists held their services at the United Reform Church in the village. The Bowden Hill chapel closed and it is now an attractive residence. (P9636HPPC c/o WSHC)

Bewley Court, Bewley Lane
Bewley Court is a fine medieval manor house in a rural hamlet location on the outskirts of the village, probably built in the fourteenth to early fifteenth century of rubble stone with ashlar dressings beneath stone slate roofs. In the sixteenth century, it was owned by the Sharington family of Lacock Abbey. Restoration and extension works were carried out in the 1920s and the house is now a Grade I listed building. This rare photograph and the one below was taken around 1900.

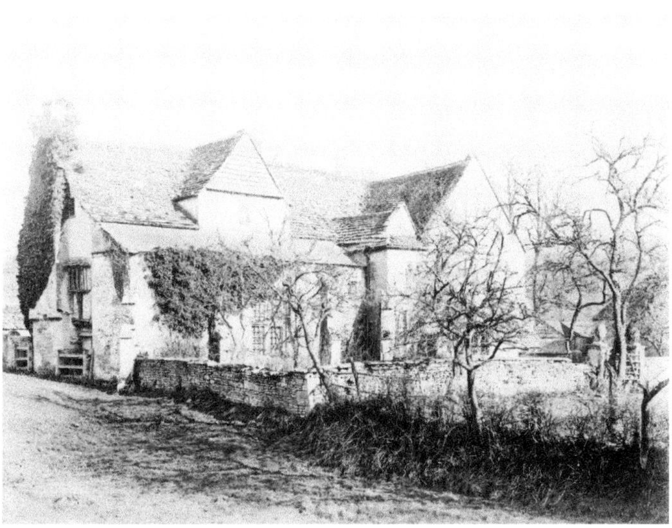

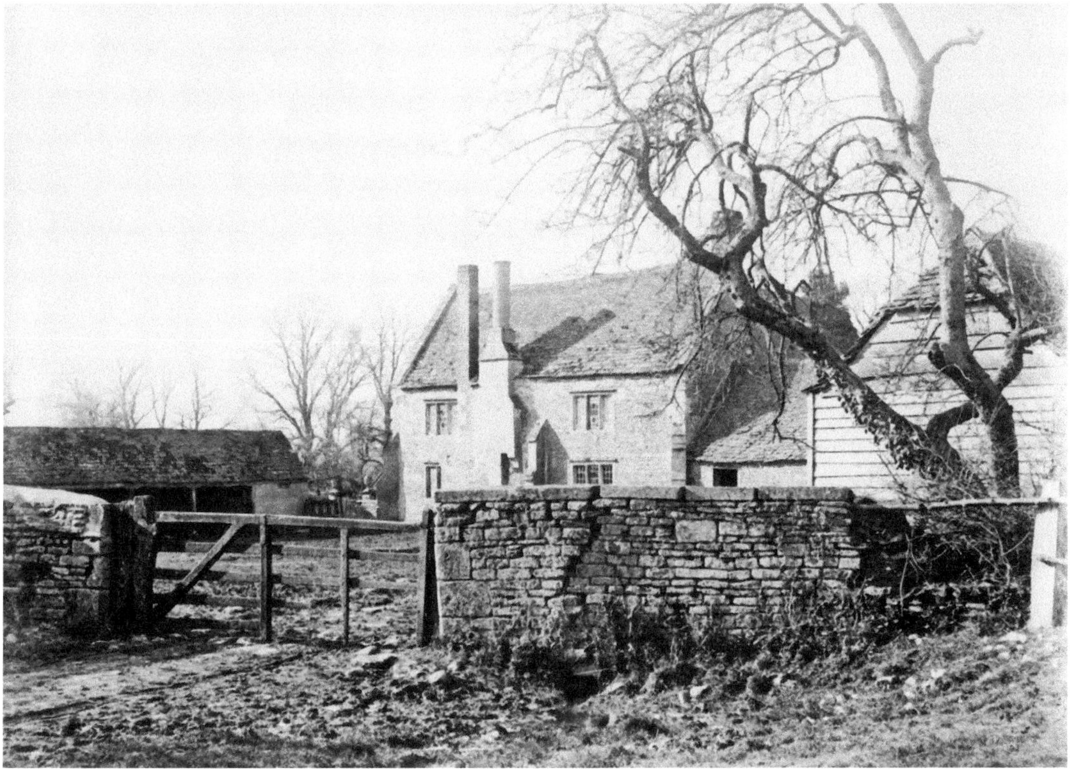

Bewley Court
Another view of the imposing house but appearing rather neglected from the state of the stone wall by the gate. In more recent times, it was owned by a famous interior designer until his death in 1992. Bewley Court had its own chapel and the designer owner undertook renovations to the property and created many individual gardens in the grounds. It is remembered that somewhere along the lane to Bewley Common was the site of the Pest House. This was where smallpox victims were once kept, at the expense of the parish and fed on a generous diet which included beer.

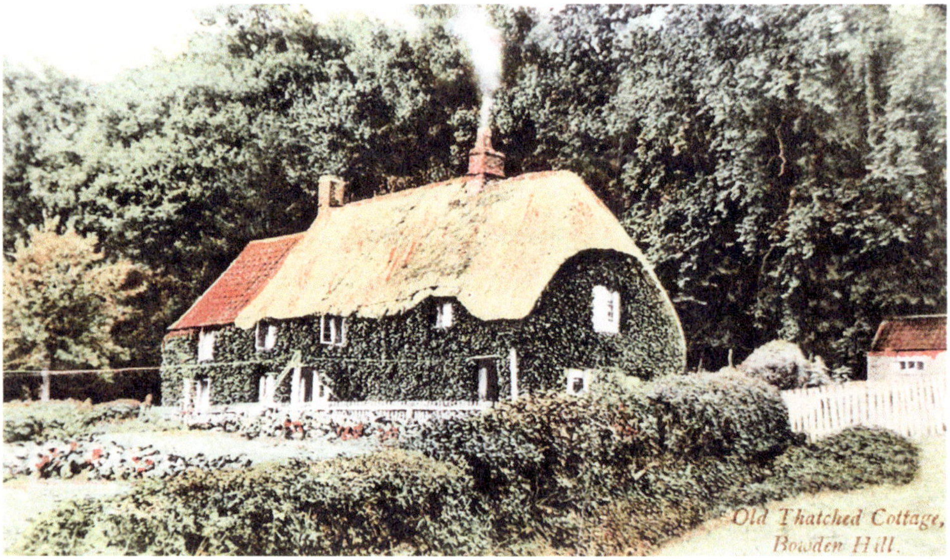

Old Thatched Cottage, Bowden Hill

A locally published card sent from Lacock in 1906 to Trowbridge in Wiltshire. The writer tells her friend Lil: 'We are getting on very well at this place and are in the church.' There are only a few thatch roof properties in Lacock, Bowden Hill and Reybridge, although there are many in Sandy Lane, a short distance away. According to early maps, Bowden was originally Bowdon. A reason for this may have been that the name comes from 'bow' meaning bow shaped and 'dun' meaning hill. Another suggestion is that the name means winding hill, which it certainly is.

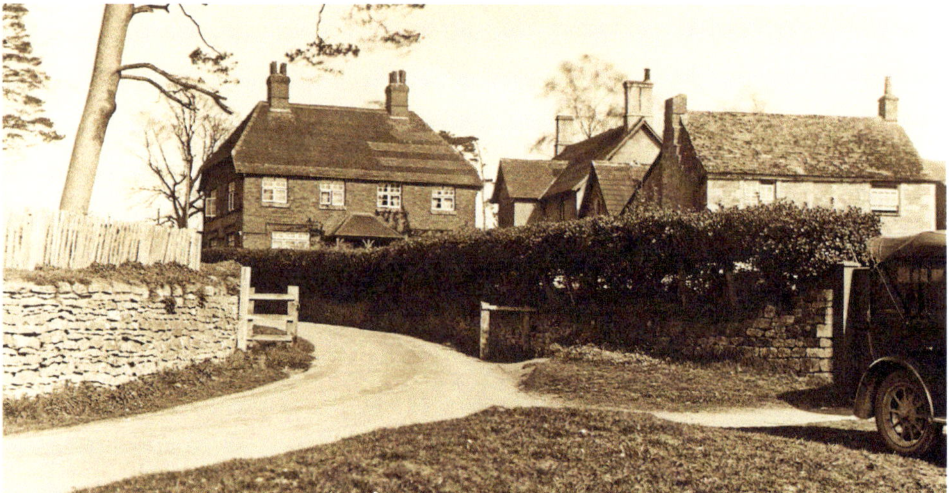

Bend on Narrow Road

A rare postcard showing a group of cottages that will be familiar to people using this narrow road. Parked on the right-hand side is a convertible motor vehicle with spoked wheels. This part of the parish comprises some fifty houses, public house with far-reaching views and it now includes a small industrial estate. At the lower part of Bowden Hill, dwellings were built along Wharf Road, where a special coal wharf was constructed. Stone could also be imported via the Wilts & Berks Canal before the convenience of the railway.

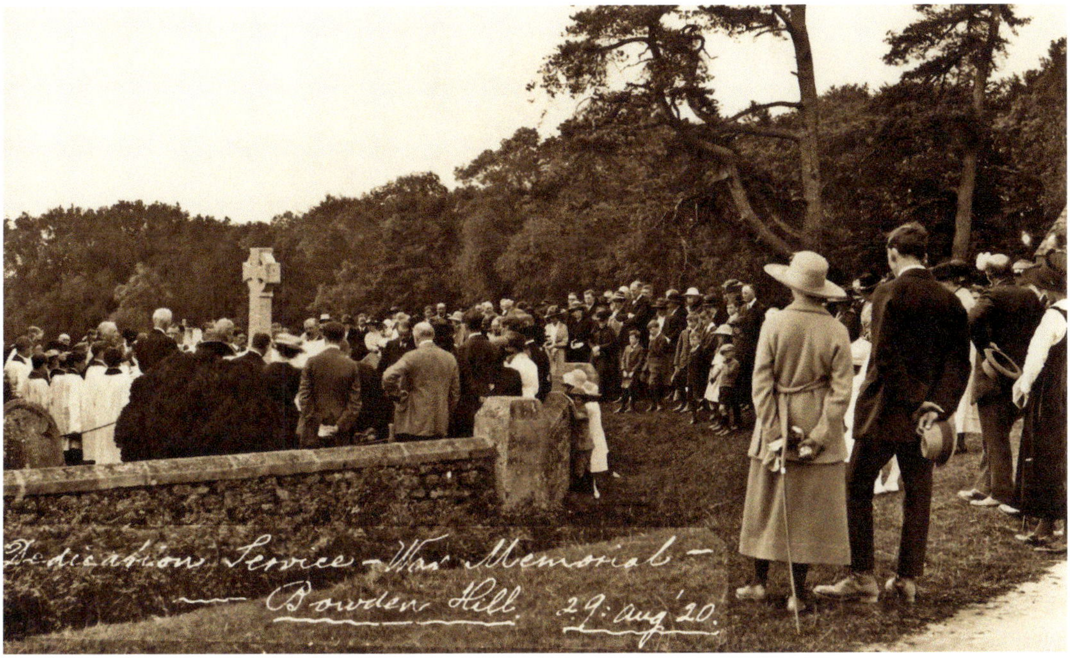

War Memorial, Dedication Service

This postcard records an important, well-attended ceremony on 29 August 1920 at the church of St Anne, Bowden Hill. A commemorative First World War memorial was unveiled by Mr Gladstone, the churchwarden, and dedicated by Revd W. A. S. Merewether. Many parishioners had served during this war and the memorial is a permanent testament to the sacrifice of the ten members of the local community who lost their lives. The hewn stone cross is in Cornish granite, in the Celtic style and set on a square plinth. It is Grade II listed and prominently situated in the north-east corner of the churchyard.

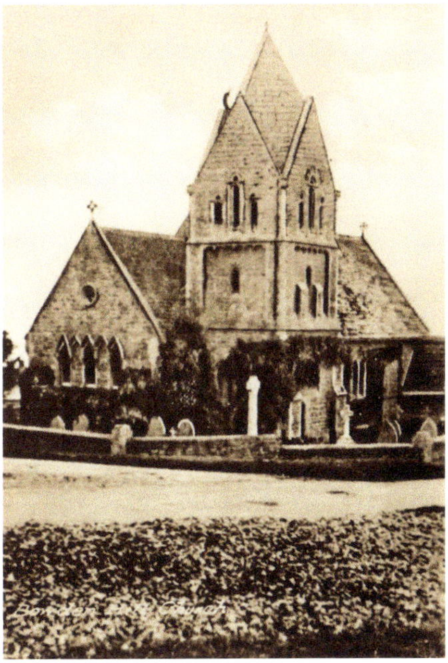

St Anne's Church

The church enjoys an outstanding setting on the hillside with common land around. It is about 1.5 miles to the east of Lacock. In 1849 Captain J. N. Gladstone, elder brother of the Liberal Prime Minister William Ewart Gladstone, purchased Bowden Park. He built the church in 1856–57 to celebrate the birth of a son into the Gladstone family. It is Church of England and relatively modern. The architect, S. B. Gabriel of Bristol, designed it in the Early English Gothic style but gave the north-east tower Norman details and a Romanesque roof.

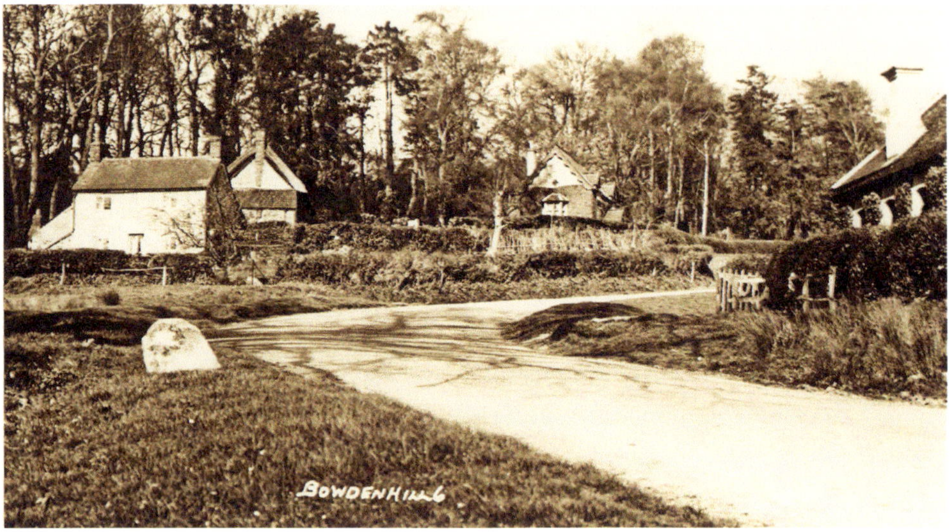

Turnpike Road

On the right-hand side is the single-storey reading/clubroom. It was probably the earliest in the county and established by the vicar of Lacock in 1854. It was originally supported by several prosperous local people. No smoking or intoxicating liquor was permitted. A supply of newspapers, periodicals and books was provided until its closure in 1939. This was one of the first Wiltshire roads to be 'turnpiked' at Bowden Hill on the route from Sandy Lane to Corsham, Kingsdown then Bath. Rates for use in the 1730s were one shilling for a coach or wagon and one penny for a horse. A London newspaper advertised a stagecoach service to Bath in 1657.

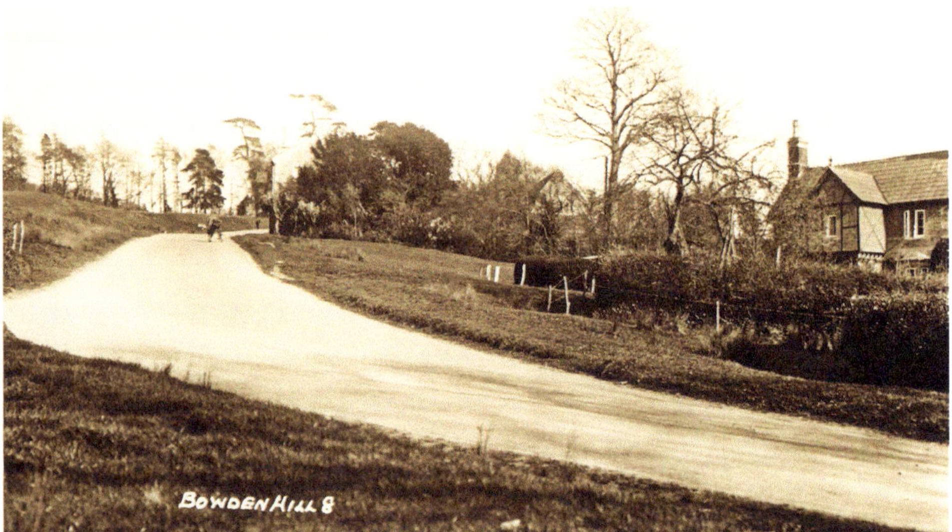

Tranquil Scene

The parish of Bowden Hill was created to serve people in the immediate area. Lacock parish was separate until 1958 when both were reunited. In the distance, on the right-hand side, can be seen the Rising Sun public house and its hanging sign. A cycle is being pushed up this steep incline. The Edwardian view was taken by an Oxfordshire photographer, but sales of the card would have been limited. Since this time, the Rising Sun has been altered and enlarged, still enjoying the splendid views.

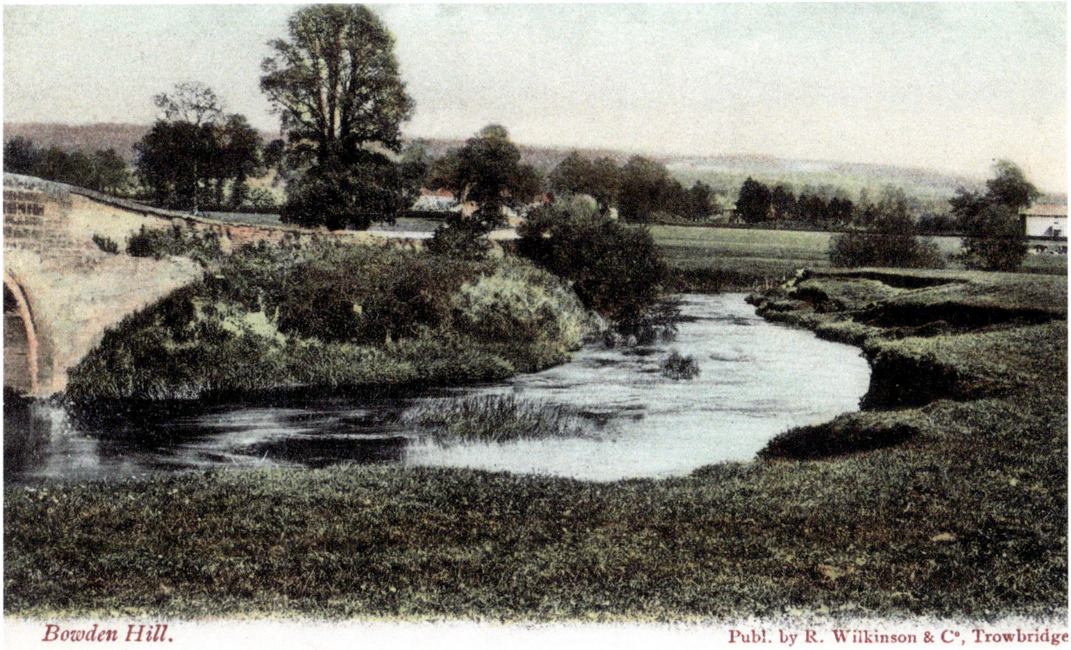

Lacock Bridge

At the bottom of Bowden Hill there are a pair of historic bridges that are linked by a pedestrian causeway. The principal one is over the main flow of the River Avon and they are both stone built. The bridges are Grade II listed and around 14 feet between the parapets. They date from between the late medieval period, the seventeenth century and with nineteenth-century additions. It is likely that part of the fabric is a replacement of the original which fell into disrepair. The river, as seen here, provides a significant feature in the surroundings of the abbey and its grounds.

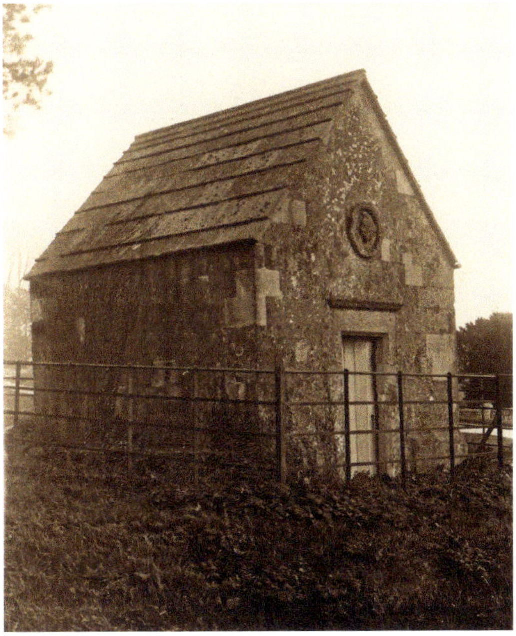

Conduit House near St Anne's Church

The first Conduit House was medieval and probably built after 1280. The owner of Bewley Court granted Beatrice, Abbess of Lacock Abbey, permission to construct and maintain a building and watercourse on his land to serve the nunnery below. Hillside water was collected at this point, as a clean supply to monastic establishments was essential. The Counduit House was subsequently replaced over this water source in the sixteenth century by Sir William Sharington, who had purchased Lacock Abbey. Construction of this small listed building is of stone with steep gabled roof, enclosed by a gated metal rail fence. (WSA2664/3/4H/5)

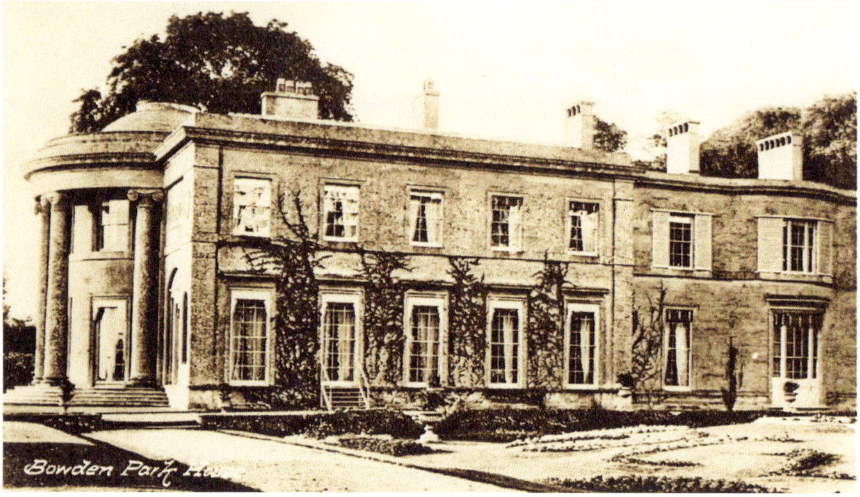

Bowden Park

A splendid landmark house on the slopes of Bowden Hill enjoying far-reaching views and a secluded location, this classical mansion is Grade I listed. It is built of stone with low pitch slate roof and a principal feature is the semicircular bow front with Ionic columns. The house was constructed in 1796 and later purchased by Captain John Gladstone in 1849. He was the brother of Prime Minister William Gladstone. A message on this Edwardian postcard, probably sent by an employee, reads: 'my room is third window from front'. The fine view from here is over the pleasure gardens and surrounding woodland.

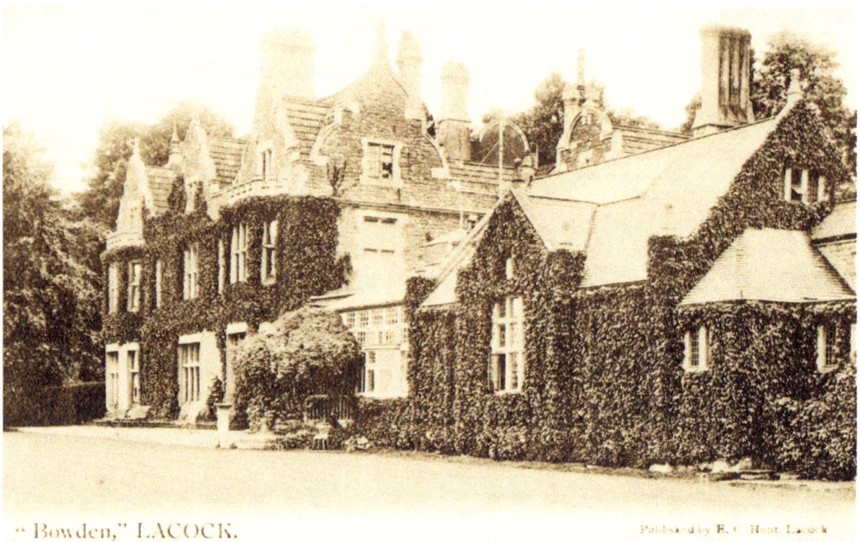

'Bowden', Lacock

Bowden Hill House was built for H. A. Merewether QC in the mid-nineteenth century. Stone construction under tiled roofs, it has two storeys with attic and in the Jacobean style. Herbert James Harris, part of a large bacon and pork products business, purchased the estate in 1882. The census of 1891 lists H. J. Harris as a retired bacon factor and JP of Lacock, and prior to this as a bacon curer of Calne but, sadly, the business no longer exists. The postcard was sent in 1906 by a member of the Harris family to Lady Willis of Holt to arrange a visit by motor vehicle the next day.

Spye Arch

Spye Arch is a unique landmark steeped in history with battlement parapet, at the top of Bowden Hill. It has had several past locations as the entrance to important properties, the first being Stanley Abbey. It was, subsequently, acquired, demolished and re-erected by Sir Edward Bayntun as the entrance to his new home Bromham House. The arch was then rebuilt as a gift from Catherine of Aragon, a wife of Henry VIII. It bears the arms of the king below the oriel window. Bromham House was destroyed during the Civil War in 1645 but the gatehouse survived. Sir Edward Bayntun built a replacement house at Spye Park. Once again, the gatehouse was dismantled and re-erected as its entrance, where it still proudly stands today.

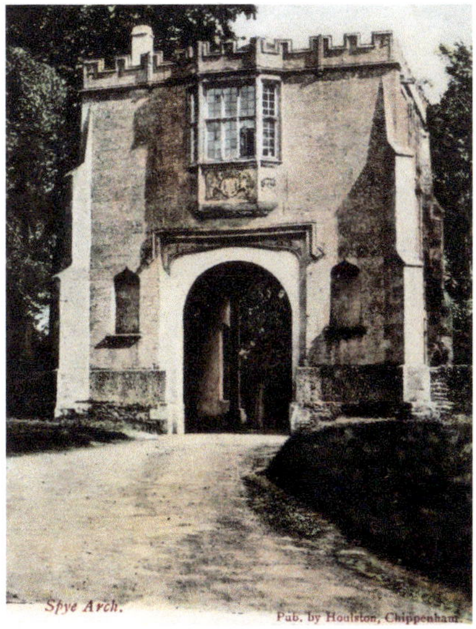

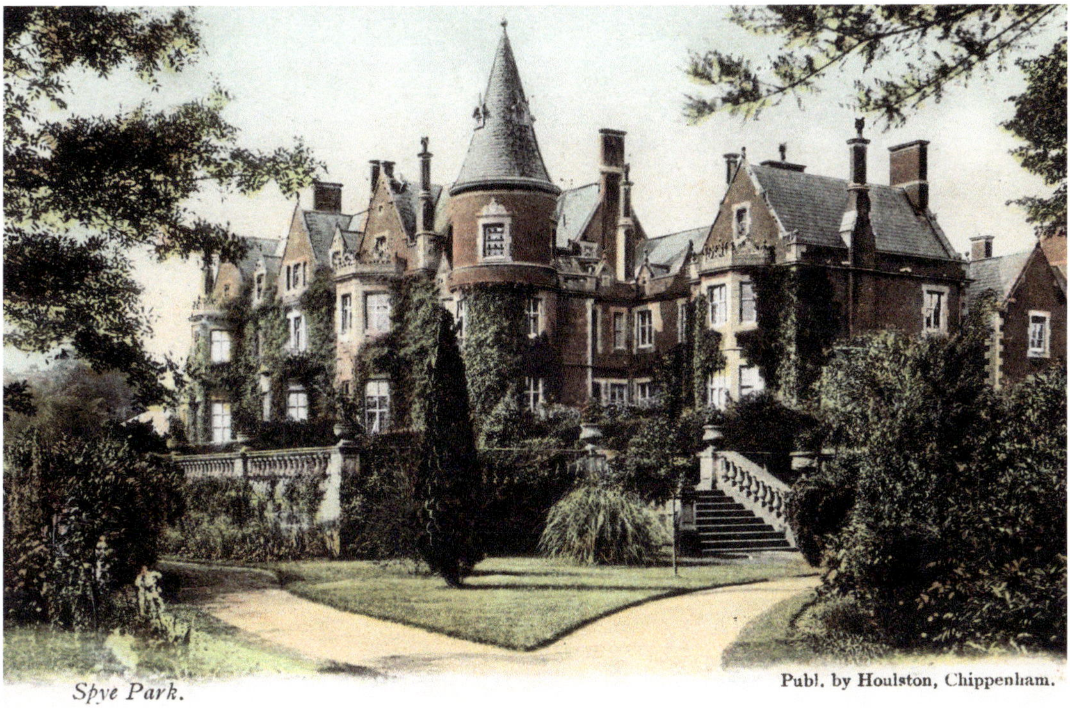

Spye Park

The name 'Spye' was probably due to the commanding location of the property having views over the village of Lacock. The original Palladian house built by the Bayntun family in the seventeenth century was demolished following the sale of the estate in the mid-nineteenth century. It was replaced by this three-storey Victorian mansion with brick elevations, slated roofs and impressive tower. The noteworthy landscaped park and pleasure grounds include a cricket club. This was founded in 1882 for the benefit and recreation of the estate workers and the club still exists. Unfortunately, Spye House was destroyed by fire in 1974 and the owners subsequently demolished the ruins.

8

Notton, Reybridge, Lackham, Railway

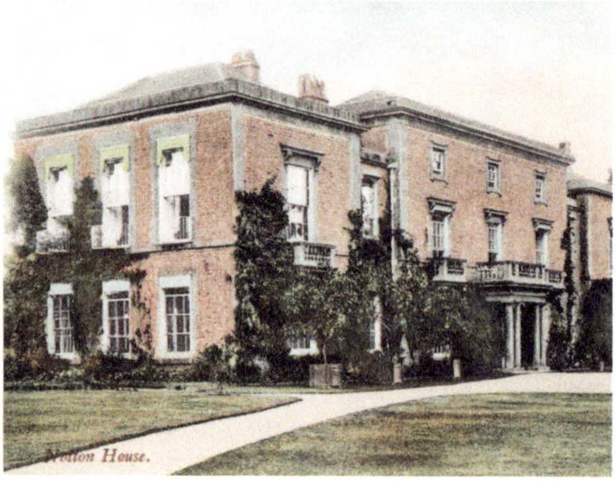

Notton House

This postcard was sent by an employee in 1905. The house was built *c.* 1750 and is Grade II listed, refronted and extended, probably around 100 years later. When sold in 1972 it was stated that it had fourteen bedrooms. Features of the older part of the house are the leaded bell tower, original one-handed clock and private chapel. The residence had been in the ownership of the Awdry family since it was purchased from Edward Montague in 1766. It is recorded that in 1839, Sir John Awdry took office as Chief Justice of the Supreme Court of Bombay. The house is now a special residential school.

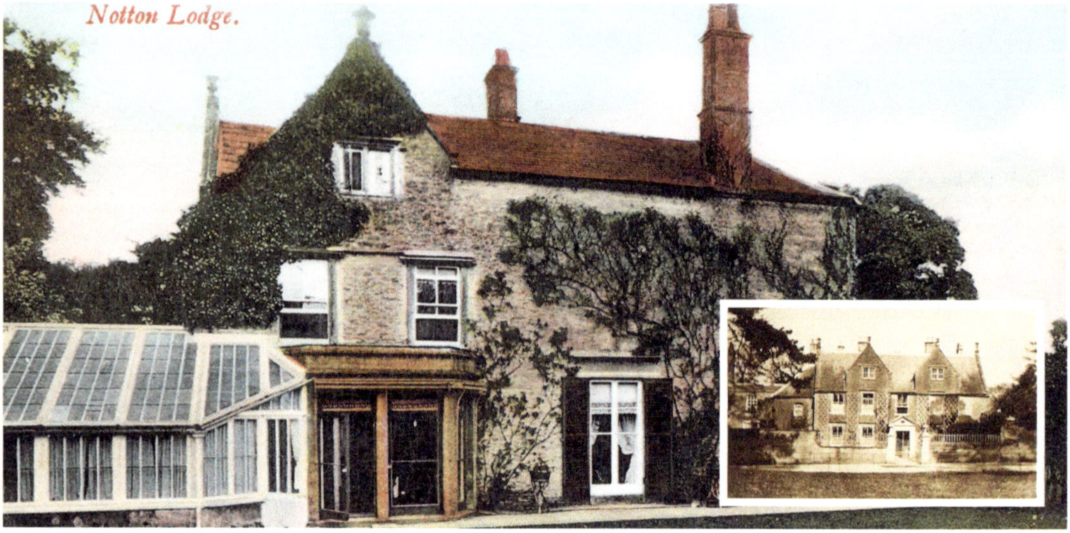

Notton Lodge, *c.* 1900

This is an unusual view from the garden of this distinctive country residence. It adjoins a narrow road that was once the main traffic route from Chippenham to Melksham, passing through the village of Lacock. The house was probably built around the mid-eighteenth century and incorporates parts of an earlier building. It has been extended and altered in more recent years. This fine property is of rubble stone, rendered to the front elevation, beneath slated roofs, and is Grade II listed. The front façade is particularly noteworthy, having two large gables, both with urn finials. A low stone wall to forecourt with handsome stone gateposts is also interesting. *Inset*: Front elevation. (© National Trust/Rachel Topham)

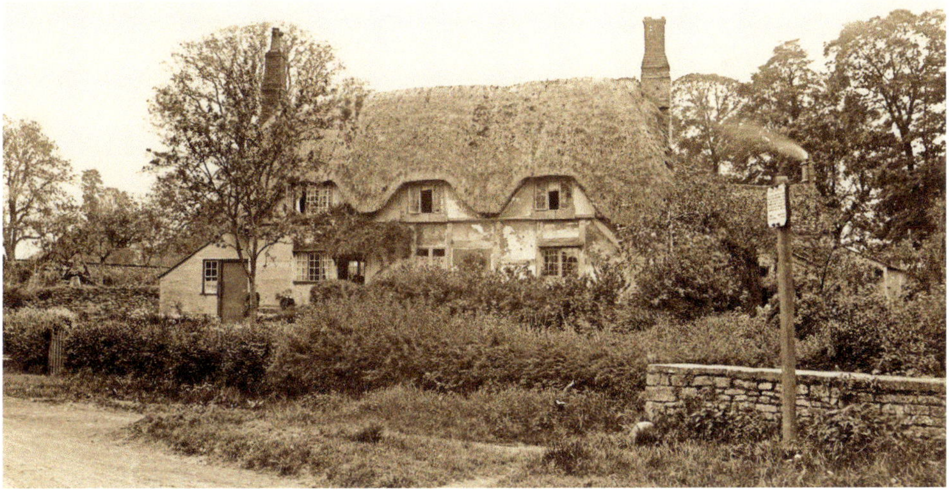

Pair of Thatched Cottages, Notton

The property, one of only a few thatched cottages in the parish of Lacock, is constructed of timber frame, some angle bracing with render and brick in-fill panels on a stone plynth. It was built around the seventeenth century as two dwellings for estate workers, each with a large garden for vegetable crops. There was a shared well at front for domestic water. This early Edwardian photograph was taken before the roof was tiled and dormer windows provided. Over thirty years ago a conversion and enlargement scheme was carried out to provide a single property, which is now Grade II listed.

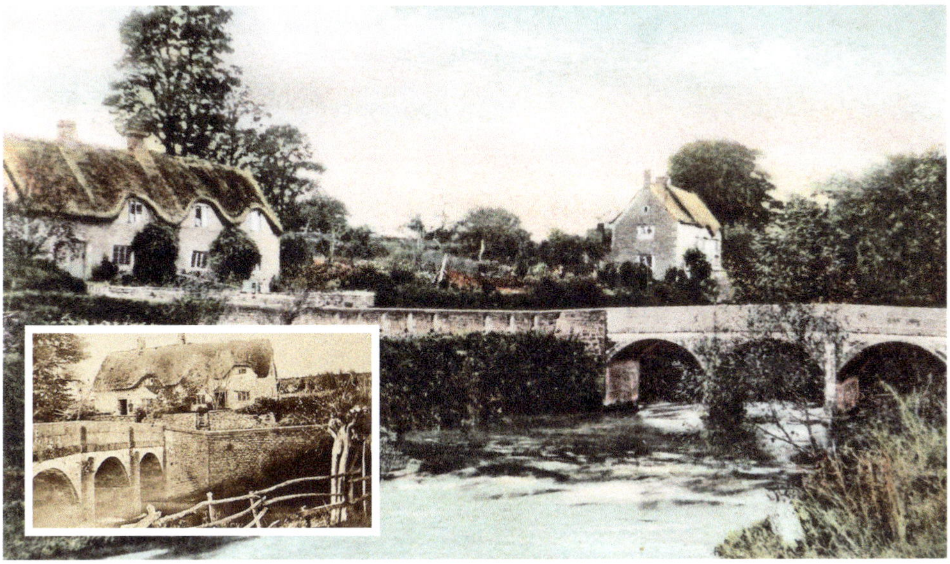

River Scene, Reybridge, 1905

Another scarce view on a postcard is presented by a respected Lacock photographer. The card, with its social history content, was sent from the village on 16 December 1905 to an address in Chippenham. It records the result of a local football match at the time: 'Derry Hill 5, Lacock 0'. This is a particularly picturesque riverside location and the pair of thatched cottages complete the scene. Inclement weather conditions are the cause of the River Avon to flood here at Reybridge. A raised footpath is provided by the bridge for the convenience of pedestrians. *Inset*: Another view. (© National Trust/Rachel Topham)

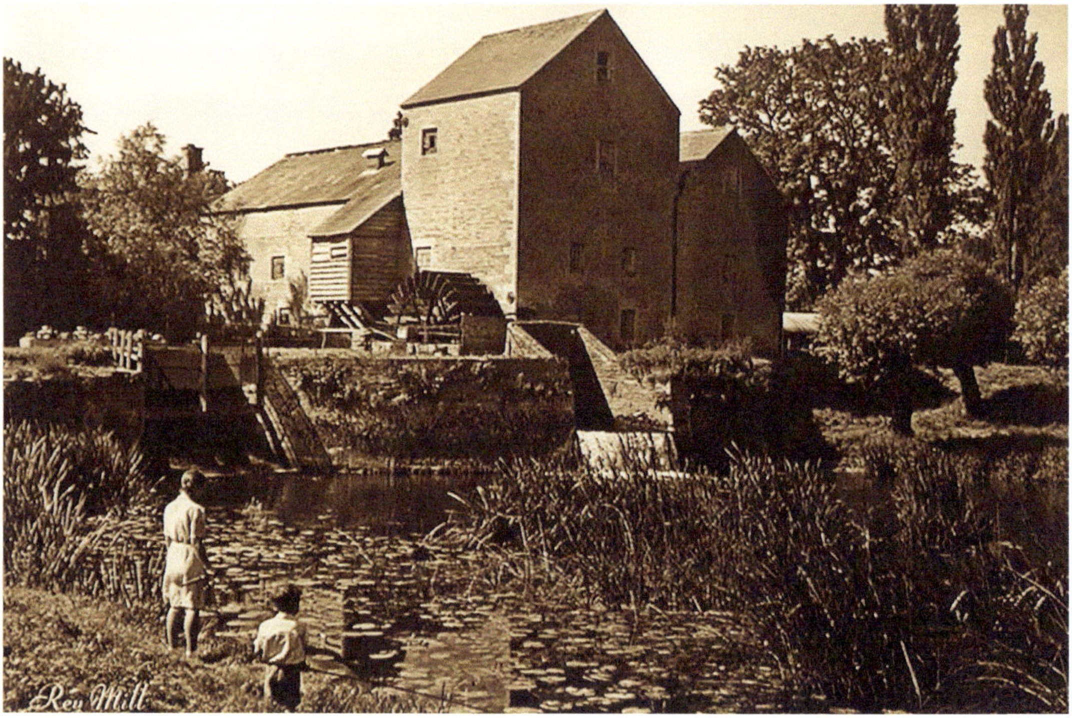

Rey Mill, *c.* 1940s

In the hamlet of Reybridge, on the north side of Lacock, is this water-powered mill, in an idyllic rural setting. It was located here to harness the available natural energy source from the River Avon and it has its own sluice gates. The mill is clearly shown on a map of 1773. It is likely that a fulling mill used by the Lacock weavers was sited here. Recent particulars indicate that there are now low headwater turbines and presumably it no longer grinds cereal crops. (WSA/X3/173/15)

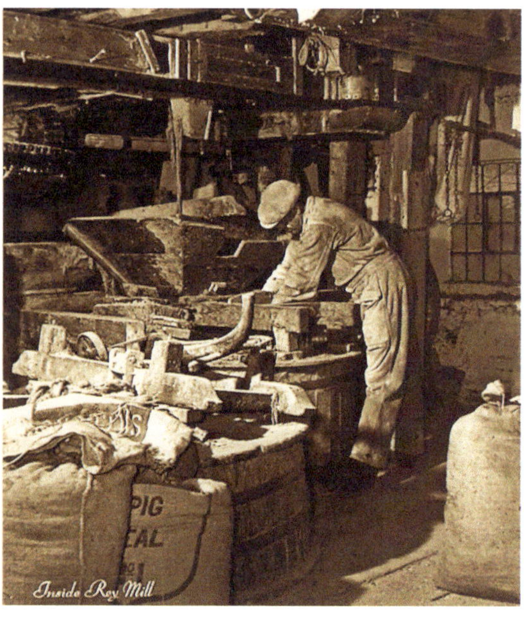

Inside Rey Mill, *c.* 1940s

This image shows the miller at work, carrying out one of the oldest occupations. Not only was flour being produced but also animal feed, as evidenced by a sack of pig meal in the front of this photograph. Turning the corn into flour involved the use of a large fixed stone as a base (quern-stone) and another upper mobile stone (handstone), driven by power from the watermill to do the grinding. (WSA/X3/164/18)

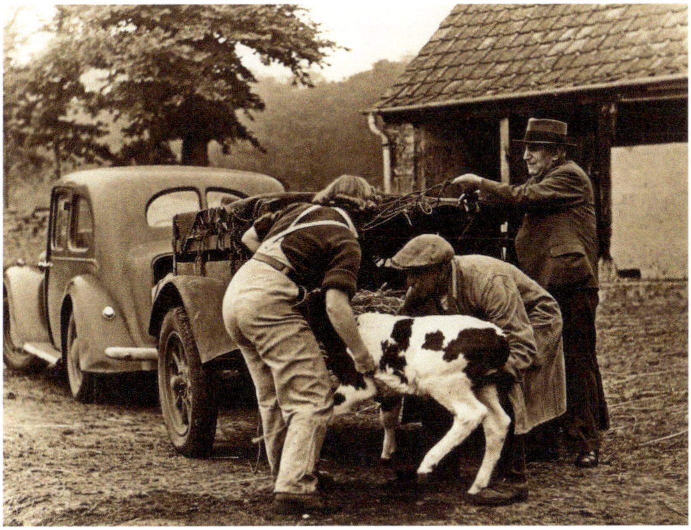

Farming
Another splendid animated photograph taken by Harold White, a professional photographer. A calf is being loaded into a car trailer in this busy country scene. Reybridge and the surrounding area provided fertile land for productive farming and dairying and has played an important part. This photograph, and others recording the social history of Lacock, were commissioned by the British Council in the 1940s for propaganda purposes. They were included in a booklet entitled 'English Villagers – The British people and how they live and work'. Its purpose was to show that life was continuing as normal during the war. (WSA2664/2/3F/10/42BW)

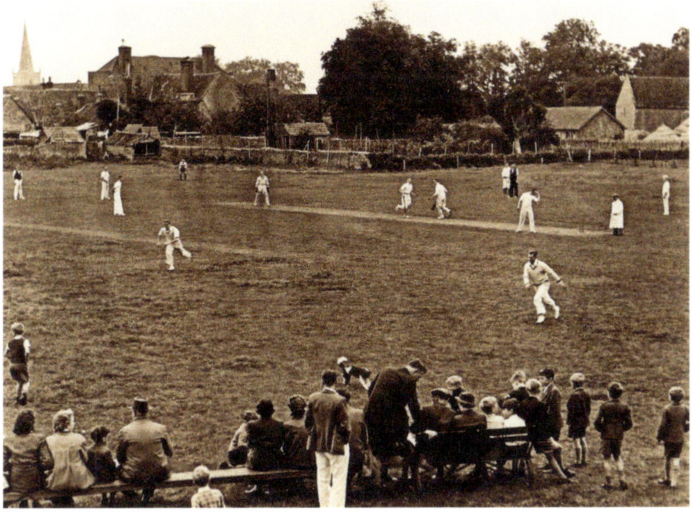

Sporting Activity, *c.* 1940s
At the beginning of the twentieth century the village had two cricket teams. Before this it had not always been easy to attract players, but the situation improved and there is still an active cricket club. Lacock also had football teams that played in the Lion and Turnpike fields. At one stage, the cricket field was rented from The Red Lion and flower shows were held here. Before the First World War, the Band of Hope and Temperance Society had a local branch to discourage drinking alcohol and drunkeness. Sporting and other recreational interests were encouraged. (WSA2664/2/3F/10/67BW)

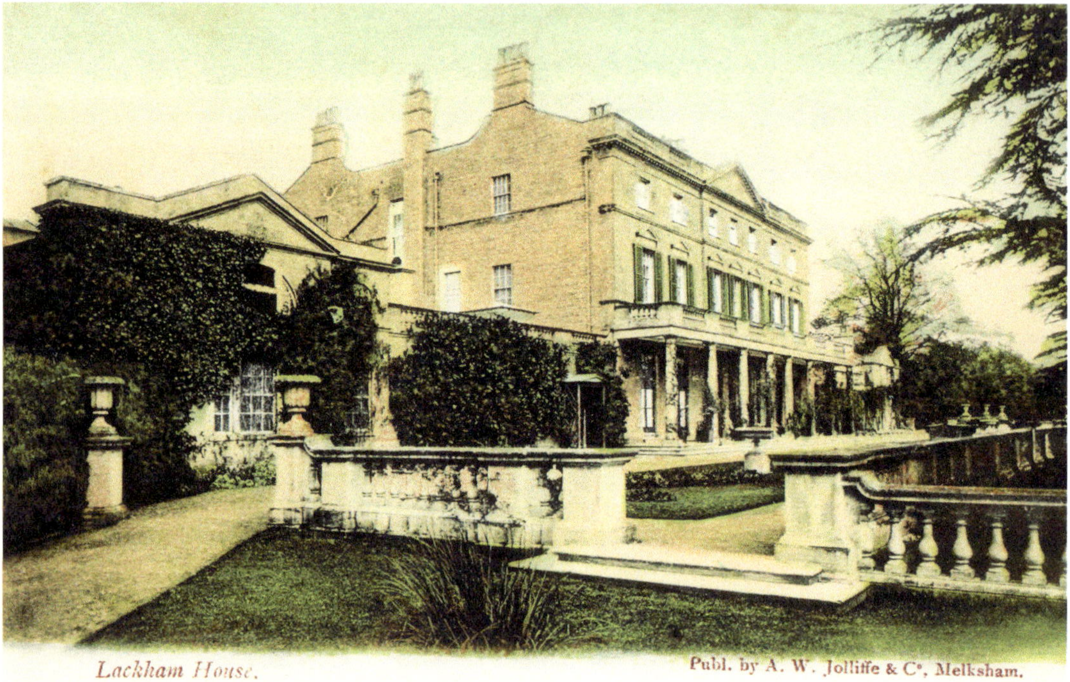

Lackham House, 1904

A superb Grade II listed three-storey Palladian-style mansion built of stone and having low pitch slate valley roofs. Since the Saxon period, there has been a manor at Lackham but under different family ownership. The Baynards occupied the property from around the fourteenth century to 1636 when it then passed to the Montagu family. The medieval house was subsequently demolished by James Montagu V in 1791. Just before the eighteenth century began, the old house was replaced by that which we see today. It is reported that the manor was visited by Henry VIII in 1535 whilst he was in the area to see Lady Jane Seymour.

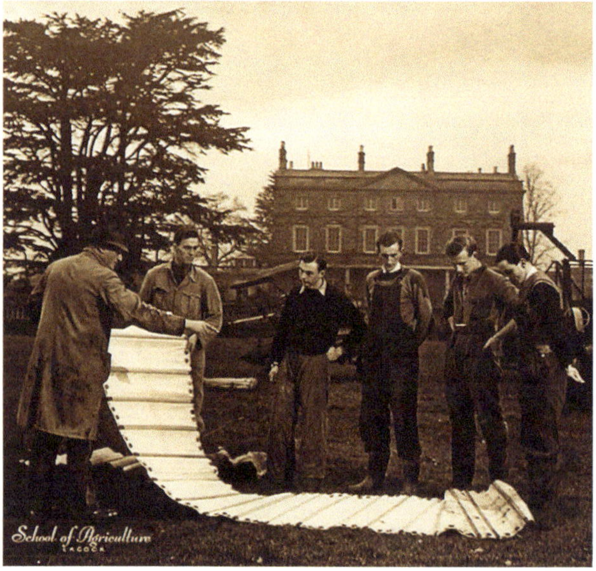

School of Agriculture, Lacock, *c.* 1945

Wiltshire County Council purchased Lackham as a farm institute in 1945. The large estate acquired included Lackham Home Farm, together with farms at Naish Hill, Cuckoo Bush, Great Notton and Biddestone Lane. Many houses, farm buildings and woodland were also included. The school was originally opened in 1946 to just twenty-five pupils with limited subjects only being taught. Now called Wiltshire College, it is able to provide a wide range of full- and part-time courses. Over the years it has grown to some 1,700 acres and gives tuition on arable, beef and dairy farming. Other areas include pigs, sheep, poultry, horticulture, engineering and equine programmes. WSA/X3/164/13)

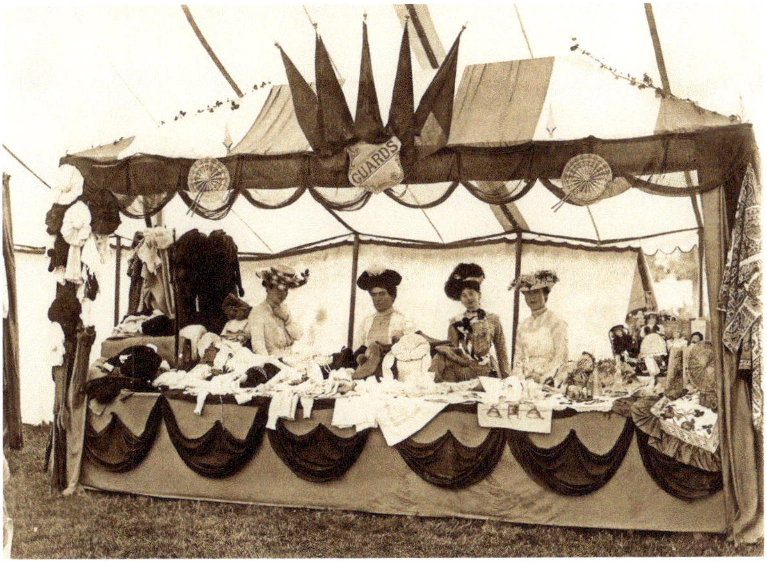

Lackham, Decorated Display
Four elegant ladies with an impressive range of clothes, toys and haberdashery, probably for sale. Proceeds are likely to be for the benefit of military funds as there is a Guards shield and flags over the front of the stall. Lackham House has strong military connections as it was purchased by Brigadier General George Llewellyn Palmer CBTD in 1893 for £17,652 and later sold by the family in 1919. Lackham took part in the local celebrations after the relief of Mafeking in 1900. During 1943–44, it was the headquarters of a United States Army armoured infantry battalion, under the command of General George Patten. (WSA3839/11/2BW)

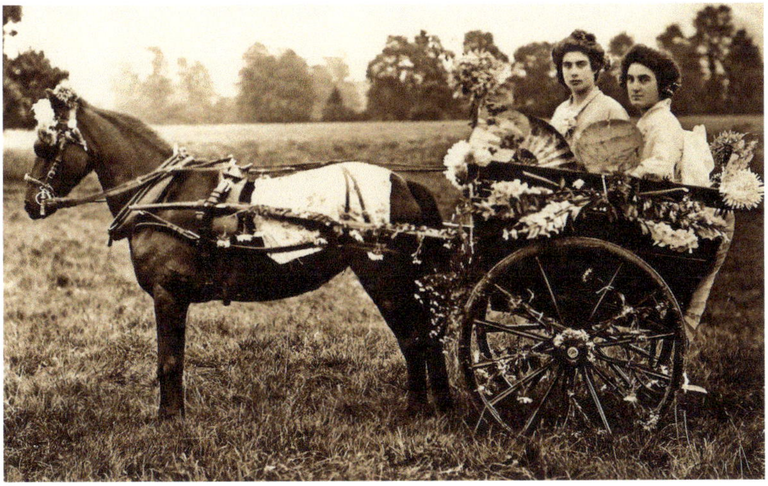

Lackham, Decorated Pony and Trap
An early Edwardian photograph of two ladies enjoying a ride in the countryside, probably the grounds at Lackham. They have come to a standstill and take time to pose for this picture. George Palmer, the owner of Lackham, was a great sporting man who enjoyed his horses. He built a new stable block for the mansion in 1902. Sadly, one of the grooms who had worked for him before the First World War was killed on active service. This was in France in 1918, just two months before the armistice. (WSA3839/11/2BW)

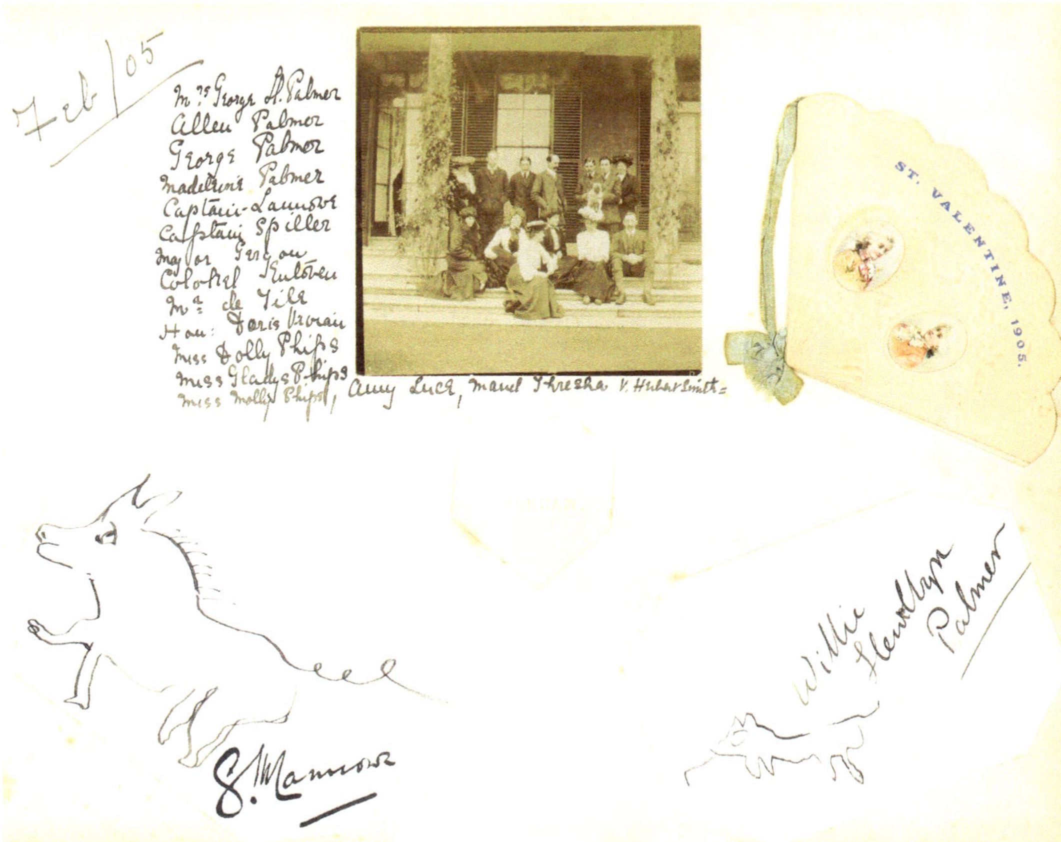

Lackham House, 1905

A scrapbook page provides a unique opportunity to look at a photograph taken on the front steps of this historic mansion. It was purchased in 1893 by G. L. Palmer, who came from an influential mill owning and weaving background. It was later sold by him in 1919. Handwritten notes on the page probably identify members of his family in this group. Displayed there is an embossed Lackham motif, 1905 St Valentine miniature fan and animal drawing by Willie Llewellyn Palmer. (WSA3839/11/2BW)

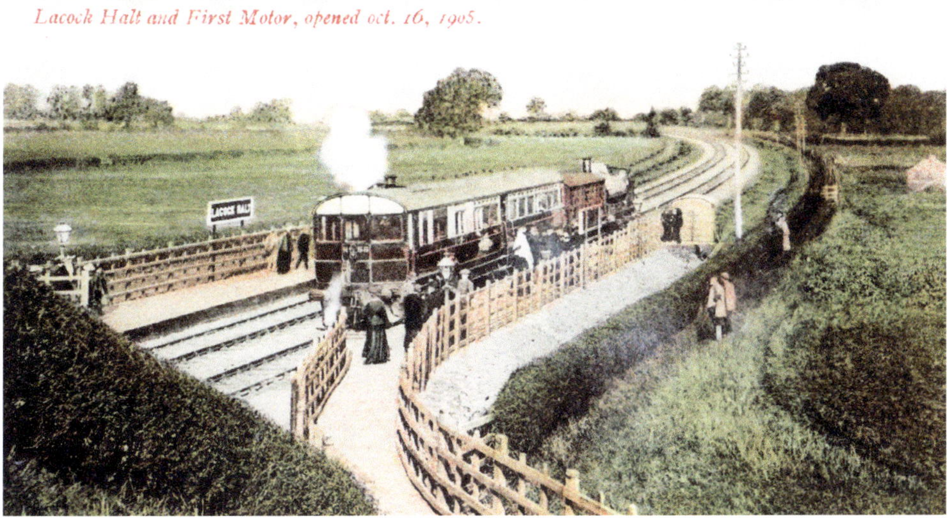

Lacock Halt

Lacock Halt was opened on 16 October 1905, just two weeks after the start of a new steam rail motor service. Situated about 1 mile from the village, on the west side. In 1845 the Wilts, Somerset & Weymouth Railway obtained parliamentary powers to construct a railway from near Chippenham to Salisbury, terminating at the popular coastal resort of Weymouth. Although completing the first part, it had insufficient funds to continue and sold the line to Great Western Railway in 1850. Car No. 56, although in steam, is accompanied by an additional truck and small steam engine, captured on this postcard recording the event. The halt closed in 1966.

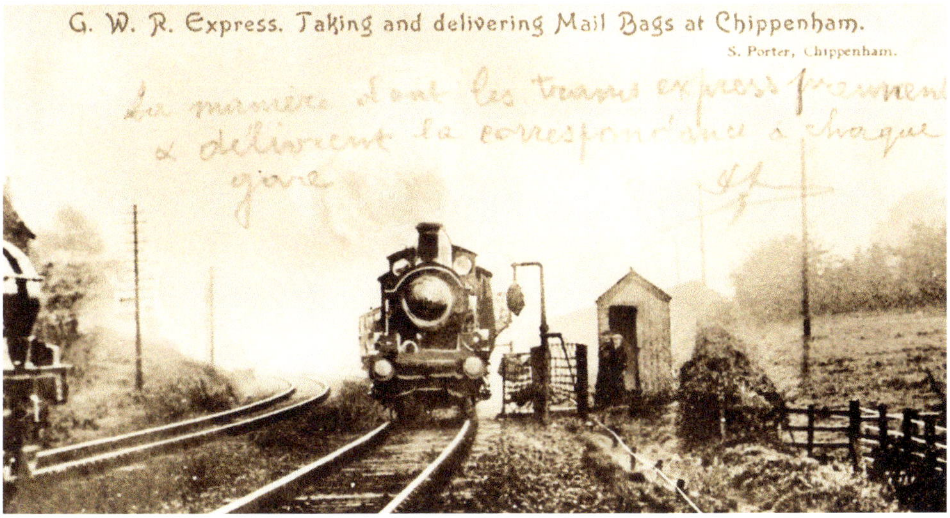

Lacock Mail via Chippenham

This image shows ingenious hanging exchange apparatus at the side of Brunel's Great Western Railway track. It was used for collection and delivery of mailbags from the Post Office sorting carriage, without the necessity for the express train to stop. Mail could then be taken to the new sorting office, virtually adjoining the station. From here it was distributed to Lacock Post Office and other centres, for hand delivery. This postcard was sent to Belgium in 1905 with a one penny stamp and it arrived the next day.

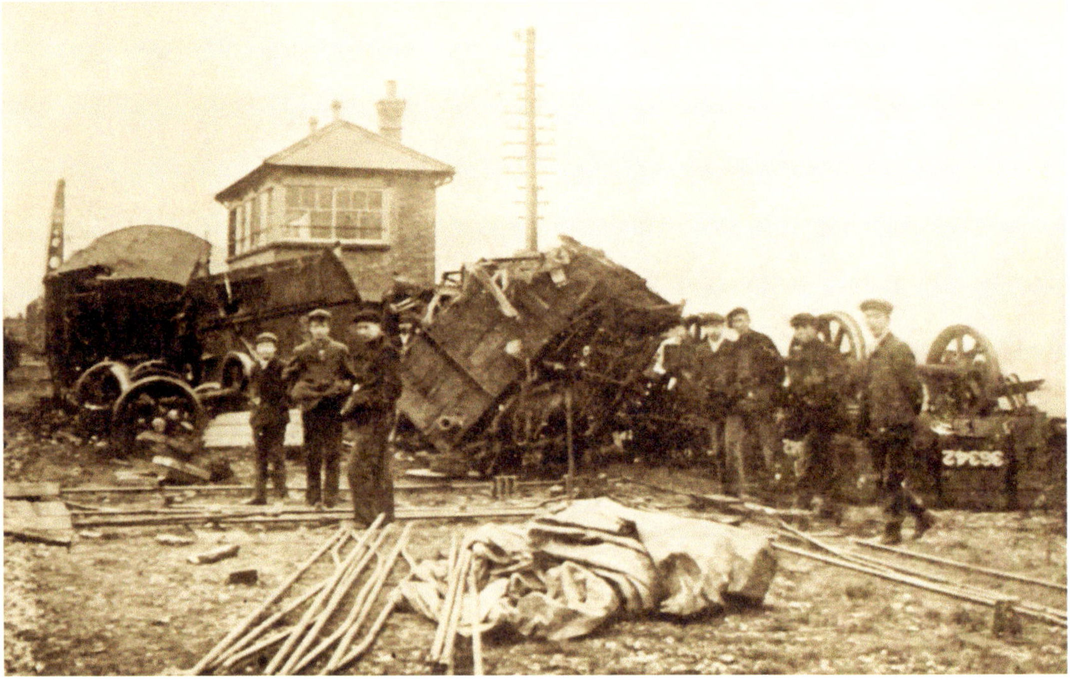

Rail Accident, Thingley Junction

This occurred on the evening of 16 January 1907 at six-thirty on the line near Chippenham and Lacock. The passenger train from Westbury to Paddington, on the Great Western Railway, failed to stop at a signal and passed at danger. This caused the train to collide with the five o'clock goods train from Swindon to Plymouth, which was passing the junction on the down line.

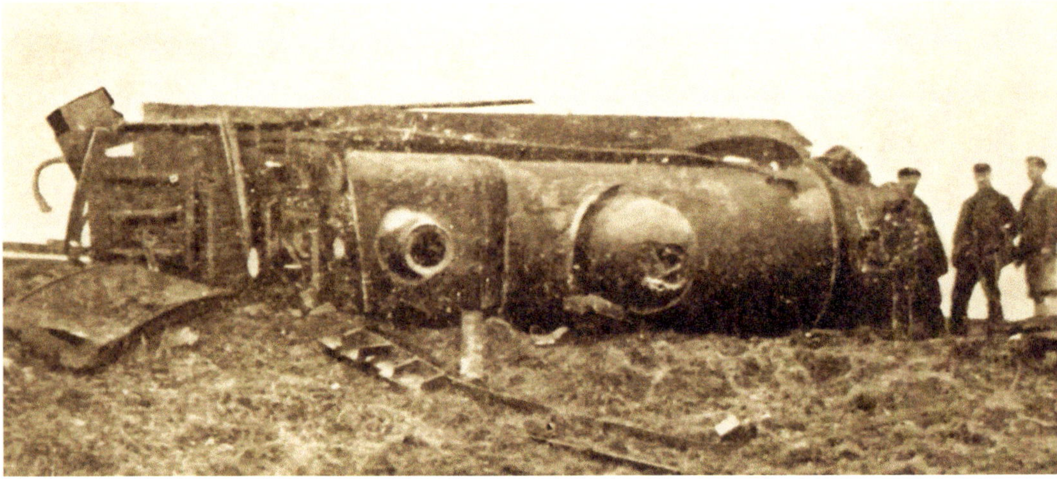

Rail Accident, Thingley Junction

The head-on collision resulted in a derailment following this crash in 1907. The goods engine, as can be seen on this postcard, overturned and fired off. It is reported that five passengers were injured but fortunately there were no fatalities. The drivers and firemen of both trains sustained bruises and burns, though the driver of the goods train and his fireman were the most seriously injured. The incident was subject to a Board of Trade enquiry.

9

Lacock Abbey Pageant

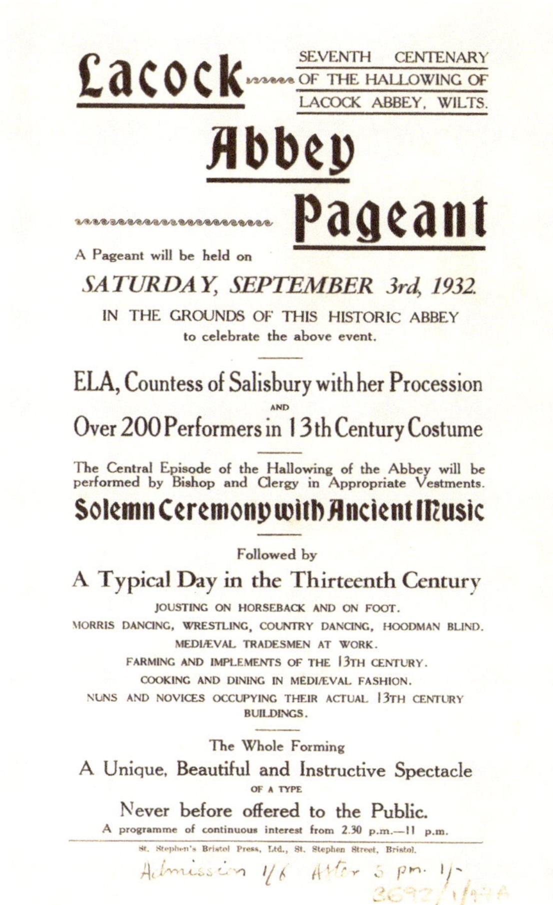
Lacock SEVENTH CENTENARY OF THE HALLOWING OF LACOCK ABBEY, WILTS.

Abbey

Pageant

A Pageant will be held on

SATURDAY, SEPTEMBER 3rd, 1932.

IN THE GROUNDS OF THIS HISTORIC ABBEY
to celebrate the above event.

ELA, Countess of Salisbury with her Procession
AND
Over 200 Performers in 13th Century Costume

The Central Episode of the Hallowing of the Abbey will be performed by Bishop and Clergy in Appropriate Vestments.

Solemn Ceremony with Ancient Music

Followed by
A Typical Day in the Thirteenth Century

JOUSTING ON HORSEBACK AND ON FOOT.
MORRIS DANCING, WRESTLING, COUNTRY DANCING, HOODMAN BLIND.
MEDIÆVAL TRADESMEN AT WORK.
FARMING AND IMPLEMENTS OF THE 13TH CENTURY.
COOKING AND DINING IN MEDIÆVAL FASHION.
NUNS AND NOVICES OCCUPYING THEIR ACTUAL 13TH CENTURY BUILDINGS.

The Whole Forming
A Unique, Beautiful and Instructive Spectacle
OF A TYPE
Never before offered to the Public.
A programme of continuous interest from 2.30 p.m.—11 p.m.

St. Stephen's Bristol Press, Ltd., St. Stephen Street, Bristol.

Admission 1/6 After 5 pm. 1/-

Pageant Handbill, 1932

This handbill advertised Lacock Abbey Pageant, a return to the thirteenth century, held on the 700-year anniversary of the founding of the abbey as an Augustinian nunnery in 1232. It was to be held in the grounds of the historic abbey with over 200 performers to represent a typical day in the life of the abbey in 1232, at a time of consecration by the Bishop of Salisbury. It was an instructive spectacle, took months to prepare and research involving many villagers, friends and residents of Bowden Hill, as players. There were no professional participants in the event and thousands attended. A leading role as Ela, Countess of Salisbury, was played by Matilda Talbot from the abbey who, in full costume, rode a horse. Admission was one shilling and sixpence, reduced after five o'clock in the afternoon. It is reported that visitors were able to obtain a drink of mead from the nuns' cauldron, normally kept in the abbey cloisters and drunk from horns, as they would have done at the time. Photographers and the local press recorded the proceedings and a fine selection of postcards was produced. (WSA3692/1/118)

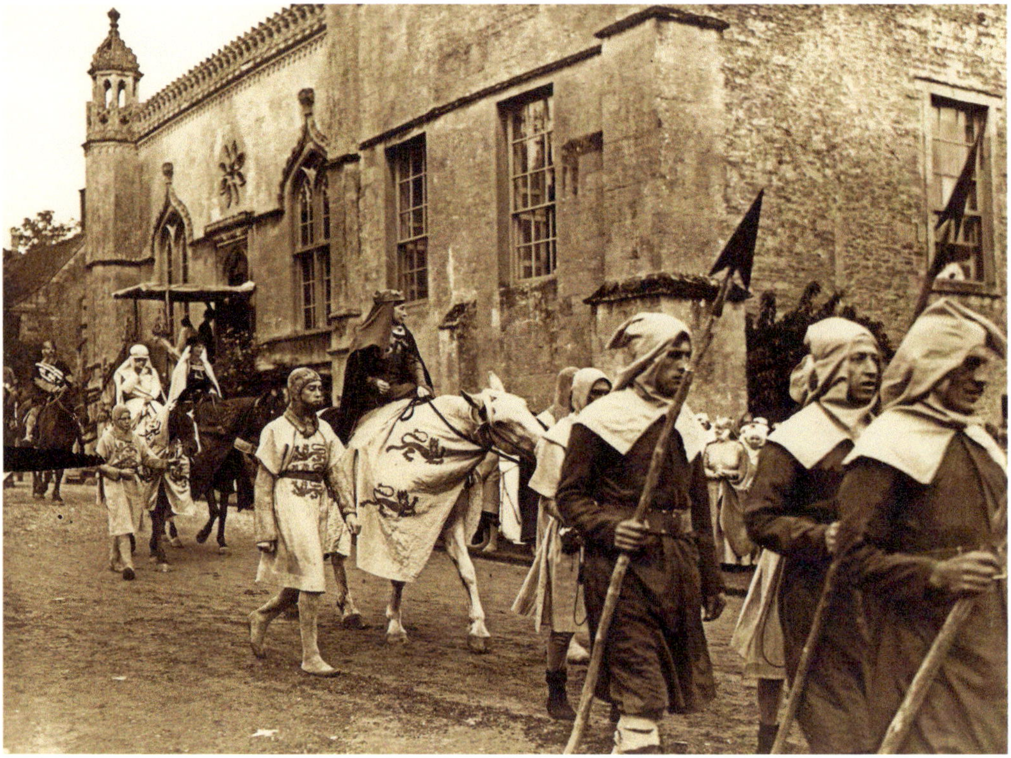

Matilda Talbot as Ela

A scene in the thirteenth-century re-enactment religious ceremony of the hallowing of the abbey by the Lord Bishop of Salisbury. Matilda Talbot takes the part of Ela, the Countess of Salisbury, and she is seen here on horseback. In her capacity as High Sheriff of Wiltshire she wears a coronet. Preceeding her in the procession are pikemen with two ladies in waiting riding behind. The colourful proceedings also included knights in chain armour, jousting, dancing, wrestling and hoodmans' blind (blindmans' buff). Itinerant minstrels known as janglers performed the story of *St George and the Dragon*, and even a witch turned up. (WSA3692/1/118)

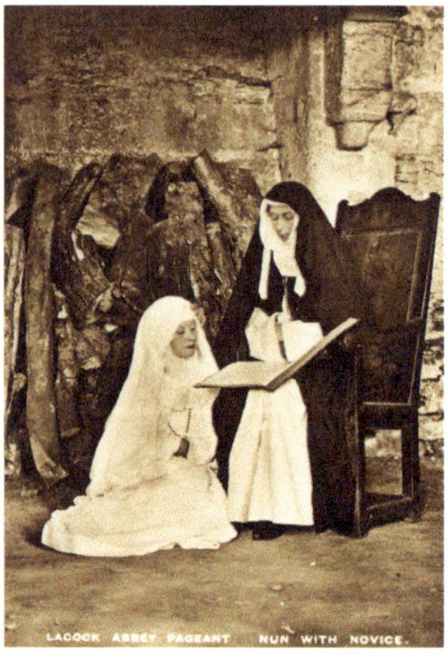

Nun with Novice

The novice was a prospective member of the order being trained to be a nun. She would, typically, live under the vows of poverty, chastity and obedience. This novice, dressed in a white habit and veil, is receiving tuition from a large book. When the monastery was founded, the number of nuns was unknown but there may have been more than twenty-two residents in 1395. The number dropped to just fourteen in 1473 and there were the same number present at the dissolution in 1539, with a further three novices.

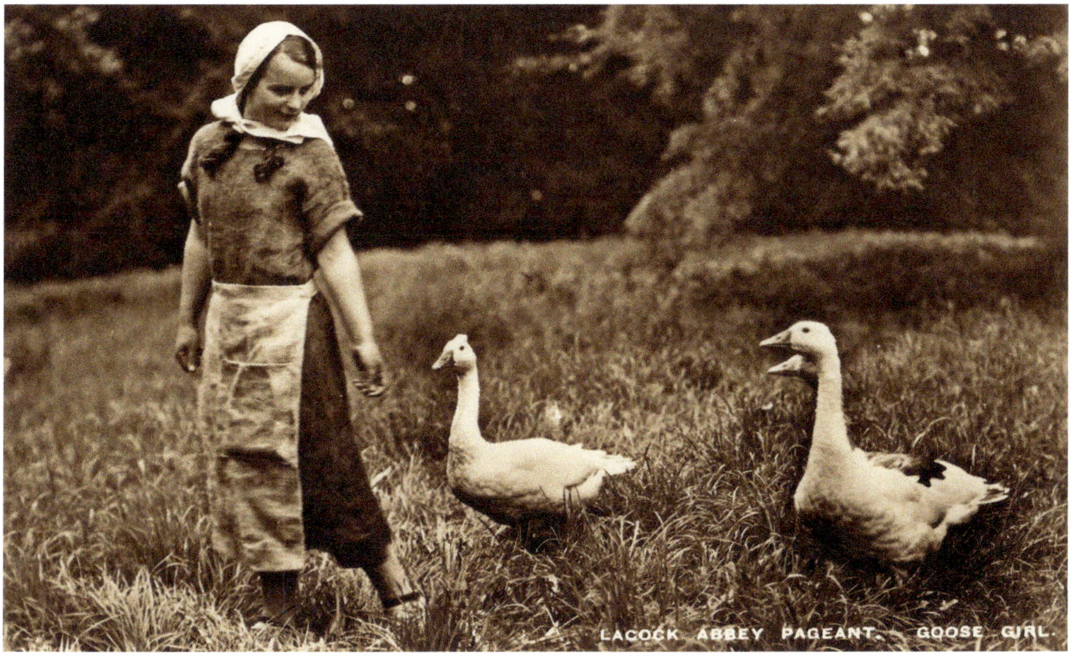

Goose Girl

During medieval times the keeping, raising, breeding and profiting from geese production was an important household activity. Usually, with a labour reserve of children to care for them and a need for ready money, keeping geese was important to a family. It was a labour-intensive occupation as they fed on greenery and required careful herding and protecting. Many essential products were provided by the goose. These included quills for writing, down for pillows and blankets, fletching arrows, wings for sweeping, eggs, fat and flavoursome meat.

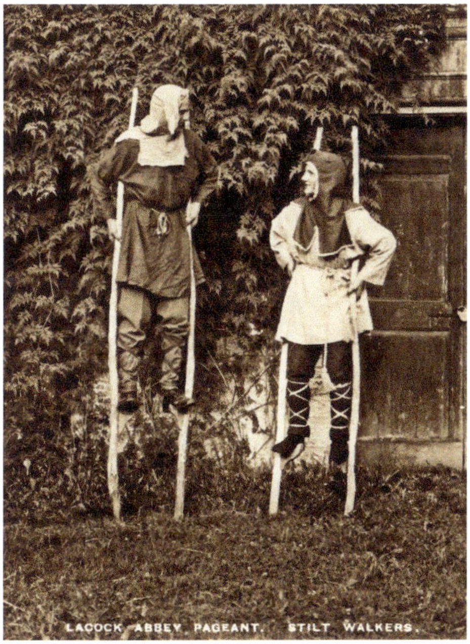

Stilt Walkers

The River Avon and other watercourses around Lacock are known to burst their banks following inclement weather. Consequently, lands around the village have been prone to flooding. In the past, villagers of low-lying ground, marshy or flooded areas have used stilts for practical purposes. Whilst standing high, medieval stilt walkers were able to extend the field of vision and keep their livestock in view. Stilts are still used today in many countries, for entertainment purposes and walking record attempts.

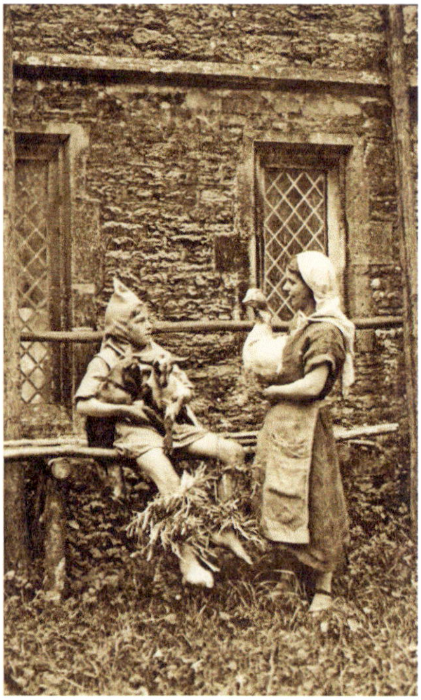

Goose Girl, Gosling and Goatherd

The photographer has created an unusual photograph of two village children re-enacting a medieval scene. The young boy without shoes is carefully holding two kids and the goose girl has a large gosling under her arm. There was a large number of workers at the abbey who were also involved in agriculture. The goatherd looked after the goats in a similar capacity to that of a shepherd. As the pageant was so successful in September 1932, it was decided to repeat the event the following year, but in June.

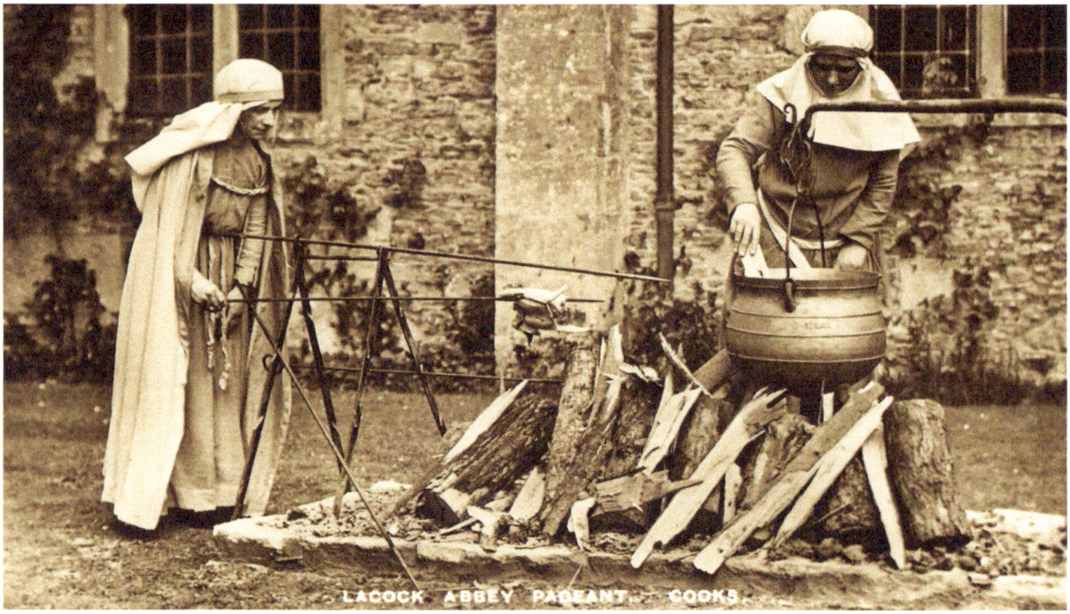

Cooks

In medieval times most cooking was carried out over an open fire, using an iron pot known as a cauldron. Spits, skillets, ladles and a pestle and mortar for spices were also to be found. Cooking methods included baking, smoking, boiling, spit roasting and salting. Cooks for the nobility and wealthy had a coveted position as they were able to eat more and better-quality food. A wider variety for them probably included a selection of fish, poultry and fresh meat. Uniforms were often worn, as was head attire, as seen on this postcard. It was not until the eighteenth century that ovens were introduced.

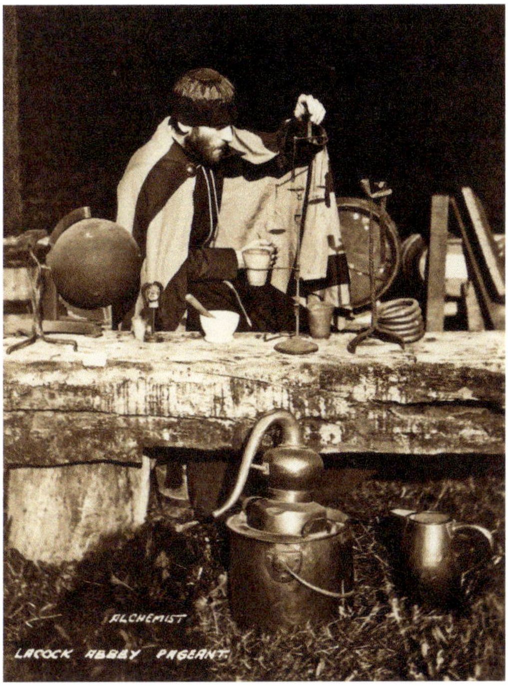

Alchemist

Medieval alchemy supposed that all matter was composed of just four main ingredients. These were earth, water, air and fire. With the correct combination of these elements, it was thought that any substance on the planet earth may be formed. Alchemists believed that the 'transmutation' of one substance into another was possible and strived to turn lead into gold. They produced hydrochloric and other acids and provided the foundation stones for chemistry as a science.

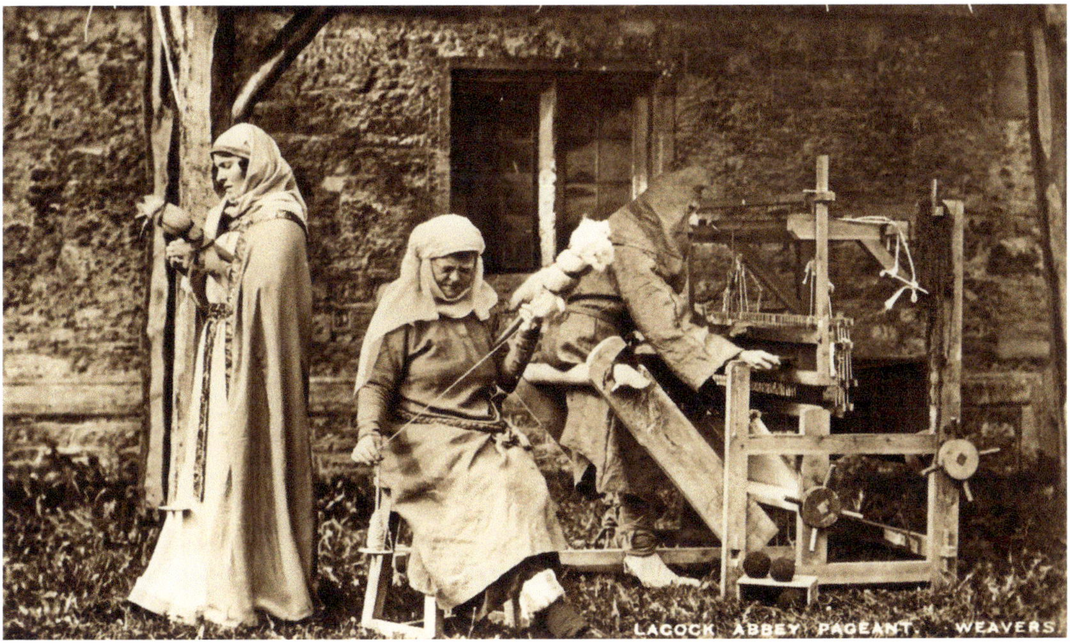

Weavers, Thirteenth Century

Lacock has played an important part in the cloth industry over many centuries. The craft was passed on through the generations. This busy scene illustrates the preparation of the yarn for the weavers working at the upright loom. The process to produce fabric or cloth involved two separate threads interlaced at right angles. Many of the tools used during this period have changed little, such as needles, pins, scissors and shears.

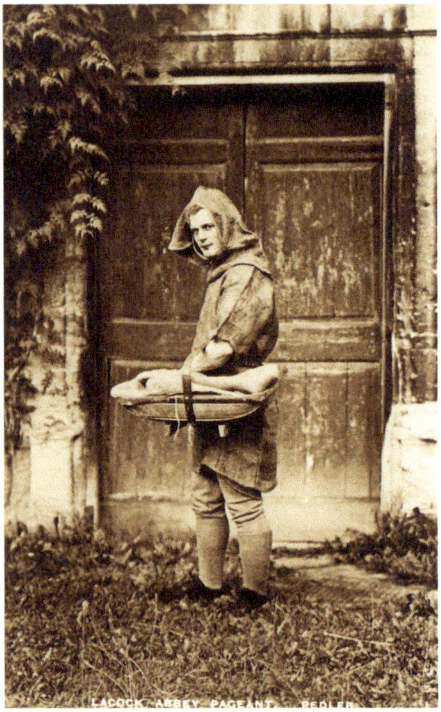

Peddler

Another photographic postcard from a captivating collection. These many images have recorded this historic event held at Lacock Abbey in 1932 and again in 1933. The peddler was a common trader who travelled from place to place. In the medieval period goods available to be sold included candles, small novelty items and sometimes souvenir products. Although enterprising, the peddler would only make a small income as any profit was subject to taxation. The lords and nobles required part of any money made in their area, so there were few rich peddlers.

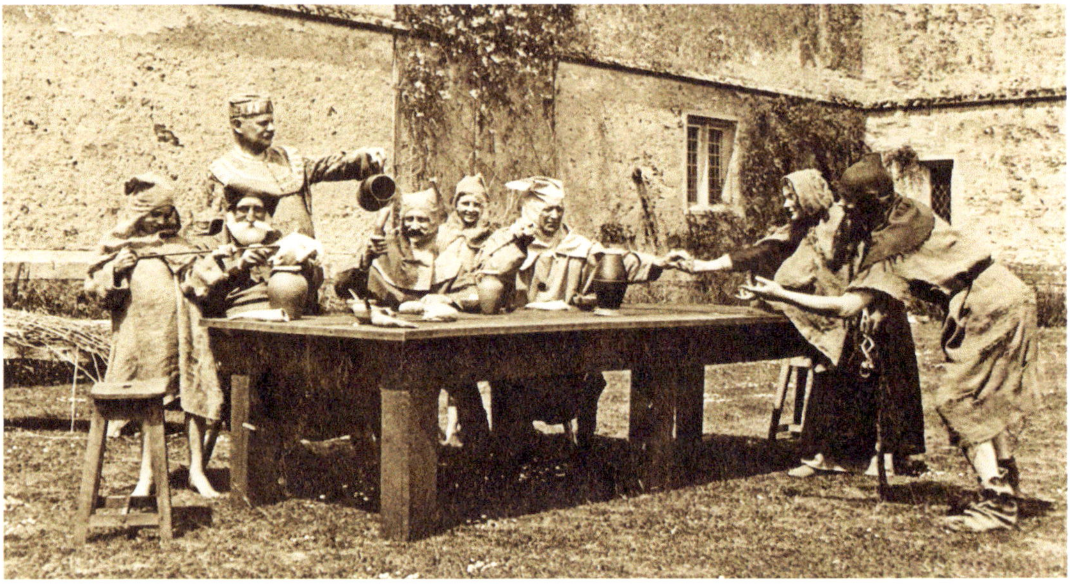

Dining Party

A fascinating insight into medieval life with beggars (local villagers playing the part) receiving food from the end of a long table. The menu may have included broth, a selection of fish and meat together with exotic presentations with unusual fayre such as peacocks. It is likely the meal would also have included a variety of cheese, sweet or savoury pastries and candied fruit. Often, as part of the occasion, interludes for entertainment were provided between the three or four courses. The proceedings would have been accompanied by alcohol, sometimes drunk from drinking horns, as shown on this postcard.

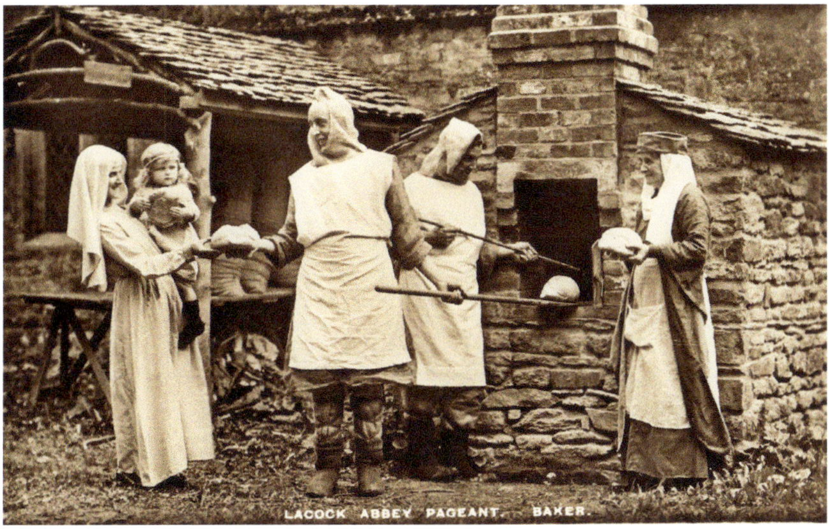

Baker

Bread, generally unleavened, was an important part of the daily diet in medieval life, so the baker and miller were common occupations. There was a time when the bakers began to cheat their customers. This news reached the ears of several kings. Laws were passed to make bakers honest and lower their prices. The term 'a baker's dozen' (meaning thirteen instead of twelve) arose from this. If a baker was caught selling less than an even dozen there would be harsh punishment. This resulted in the baker adding an additional loaf to be sure of an accurate count, to be on the safe side.

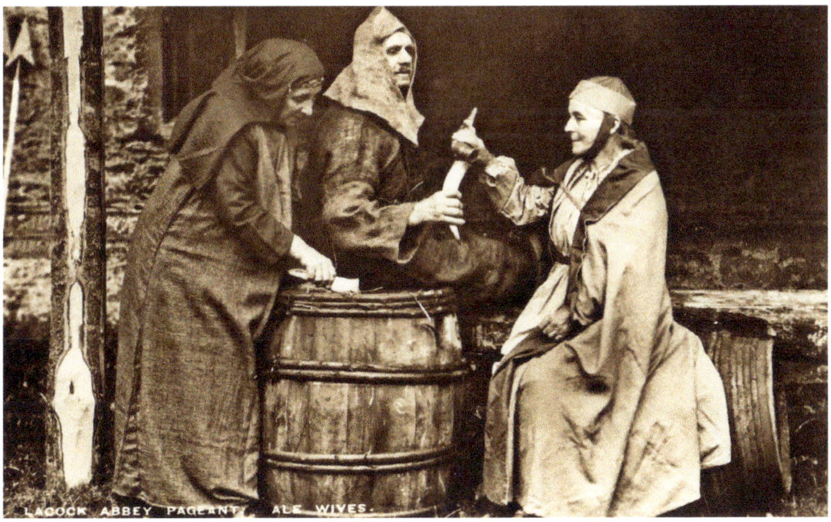

Alewives

Alewife was medieval term for a woman who brewed ale for both domestic and commercial use. Most of their brewing was carried out before the Black Death (1347–51) but some women continued to make ale into the seventeenth century. At one stage, prior to the Black Death, records indicate that regulation legislation existed. This treated the brewing of ale as a solely female occupation. The ingredients for the ale were water, added grain and fermented yeast. It was an important part of the medieval diet as the quality of the water was poor. Large quantities were consumed as it was a preferred, inexpensive and clean daily drink.

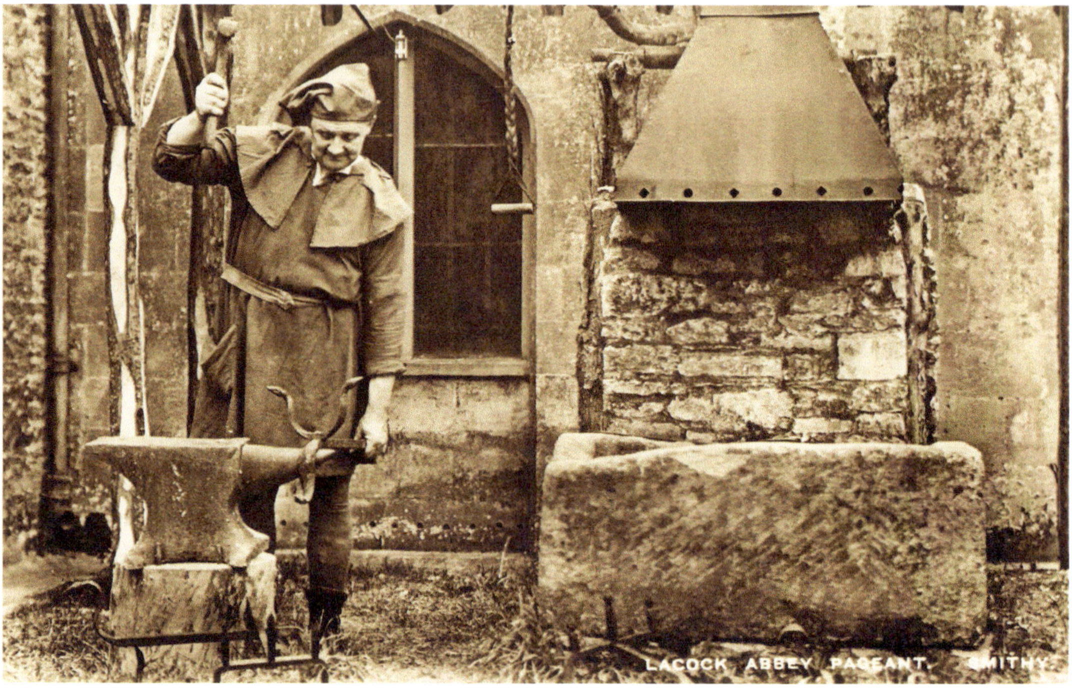

Smithy

This interesting scene was built and worked by the farrier and smith, from the forge in the village. He was a versatile craftsman, also able to produce ornamental and antique ironwork made to any design. The type of equipment being used here was similar to that shown on a thirteenth-century drawing. The stone trough and anvil seen on the photograph are both of considerable age and belonged to his family. Since the Middle Ages, the craft of the country blacksmith has changed little.

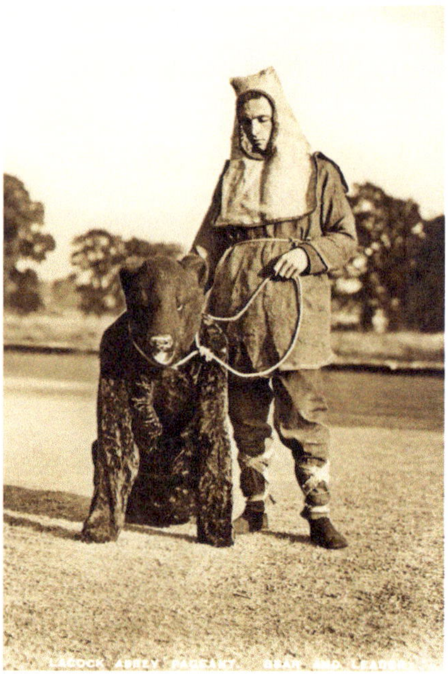

Bear and Leader

Two local men dressed in costume to take the part, one as the tame or dancing bear as it was often called, and the other as the handler. The bears were either bred in captivity or captured in the wild when young. They were then used to perform and entertain people in the streets and taverns. Fairly commonplace from the Middle Ages to the nineteenth century, they would periodically visit Lacock with other entertainers. It is rumoured that when the handlers got drunk, they would be thrown into the lock-up on East Street together with the bear.